RHETORIUS THE EGYPTIAN

ASTROLOGICAL COMPENDIUM

CONTAINING HIS

EXPLANATION AND NARRATION

OF

THE WHOLE ART OF ASTROLOGY

Translated from the Greek
By
JAMES HERSCHEL HOLDEN, M.A.
Fellow of the American Federation of Astrologers

The first edition of this translation was circulated privately in 1985, the second edition was circulated privately in 2000, and the third edition was also circulated privately in 2005. The present volume contains the fourth edition of the translation as the first published edition.

Copyright 2009 by James Herschel Holden

No part of this book may be reproduced or transcribed in any form or by any means, electronic or mechanical, including photocopying or recording, or by any information storage and retrieval system without written permission from the author and publisher, except in the case of brief quotations embodied in critical reviews and articles. Requests and inquiries may be mailed to the American Federation of Astrologers at 6535 S. Rural Road, Tempe, AZ 85283, U.S.A.

First Printing 2009

ISBN-10: 0-86690-590-1
ISBN-13: 978-0-86690-590-9

Published by:
American Federation of Astrologers, Inc.
6535 S. Rural Road
Tempe, AZ 85283

Printed in the United States of America.

Table of Contents

Translator's Preface to the First Edition ix
Translator's Preface to the Second Edition xv
Translator's Preface to the Third Edition xvii
Translator's Preface to the Fourth Edition xix

Rhetorius the Egyptian: *Astrological Compendium*

Preface 1
1. Masculine and Feminine Signs and Houses, and Stars That Become Masculine and Feminine 3
2. The Sects of the Stars 4
3. The Natures of the Twelve Signs 5
4. Rough-skinned, Leprous, Mangy, and Scurvy Signs 5
5. Licentious Signs 6
6. Signs Harmful to the Eyes 6
7. Exaltations and Falls 6
8. The Oppositions of the Stars 7
9. The Sect of the Rulers of the Triplicities 8
10. The 36 Decans and the Paranatellonta and the Faces 9
11. The Bright Fixed Stars and the Powers of the Paranatellonta 12
12. The Terms According to the Egyptians and Ptolemy And the Bright and Shadowy Degrees. 12
13. The Risings in the Seven Climes 13
14. The Parts of the Body Ruled by the Signs 14

15. Trines and Squares and Oppositions and Those That Are Disjunct with Each Other as with the Oppositions	14
16. Disjunct Signs and Those Having Sympathy with Each Other	16
17. Squares That Are Sympathetic and Those That Are Not	17
18. The Dodecatemories of the Stars	17
19. Hearing and Seeing [Signs]	19
20. Beholding	19
21. Casting a Ray	19
22. Dexter and Sinister Aspects	20
23. The Doryphory of the Stars	20
24. The Out-of-sect Doryphory	21
25. [Doryphories With] Harmony	21
26. Dominance	21
27. Affliction and Ineffective Houses	21
28. Effective Houses	22
29. In Proper Face	22
30. Joint Possession	22
31. Incongruity of Position	22
32. Joint Rulership	22
33. The House-ruler	23
34. Kollesis	23
35. Application	23
36. Intervention	23
37. Separation	23
38. Bonding	24
39. Void of Course	24
40. Juxtaposition	24
41. Besieging	24
42. Fortified Stars	24
43. Chariots	25
44. When the Stars Rejoice	25

45. Stars under the Sun Beams	25
46. Times [Of Life] of the Angles, Succedents, and Cadents	26
47. Signification of the Lots	26
48. Signification of These [Lots]	27
49. The Complete and Least Years [Of the Stars]	29
50. How One Calculates the Increment of the Signs and The Hours of the Climes	30
51. The Greatest Years and the Complete Revolution Of the Seven Stars	31
52. Stars Disjunct with the Lights	31
53. Influences of the Doryphories of the Sun	32
54. Topical Examination [of the Horoscope]	32
55. Childbirth	41
56. [The Kinds Of] Natives [Indicated] by the Day-ruler And the Hour-ruler	42
57. Significations of the Twelve Houses of the Chart	43
58. The Power of the Fixed Stars	100
59. General Configurations of the Moon	109
60. The Dodecatemorion	110
61. General Configurations of Injuries and Sicknesses	112
62. Degrees Injurious to the Eyes	117
63. Those Who Are Bold	118
64. Those With Gout	118
65. Madmen and Epileptics	119
66. Lechers and Drunkards and Homosexuals	121
67. Houses and Degrees Producing Lechers and Homosexuals	122
68. Decans Producing Lechers	122
69. The Sun	124
70. The Moon	124
71. Saturn	124
72. Jupiter	124

73. Mars	124
74. Mercury	124
75. The Ascendant	125
76. Lecherous Signs	125
77. General Configurations of Those Dying Violently	125
78. General Configurations of Those Who Are Exiled	129
79. The Phases of the Moon	130
80. The Ascending Node and the Descending Node	131
81. General Configurations of Those Enjoying Good Fortune	132
82. Action and Pursuits	134
83. The Three Stars Signifying Actions	137
84. Trades	141
85. Orators and Teachers	141
86. Astrologers or Diviners	142
87. Bath-workers	142
88. Removers of Corpses	142
89. Architects and Potters	142
90. Drunkards and Lewd Persons and Sorcerers	143
91. Carpenters and Tanners and Stone-masons And Gem-engravers	143
92. Masters of the Hounds and Falconers and Bird-keepers And Painters	142
93. Sailors and Steersmen	143
94. Tailors	144
95. Mechanics and Jugglers	144
96. Mimes	144
97. Parents	145
98. Parents Who Are Foreigners	147
99. Patricides and Matricides and Enemies of Their Parents And Outcasts	148
100. The Longevity of the Parents	149

101. Parents from New Moons and Full Moons	149
102. Which of the Parents Dies First	150
103. The Number of Children Born Previously	151
104. Brothers, Their Friendship, and How Many There Are	152
105. The Friendship of Brothers	153
106. The Third Sign from the Asc	153
107. Elder and Younger Brothers	154
108. How Many Brothers	154
109. Application and Separation	155
110. An Example	157
111. Bonding	159
112. Void of Course	159
113. The Nativity of a Grammarian	159
114 Why He Was a Grammarian	162
115. Why He Was a Traitor	162
116. His Lechery	163
117. The Rising of His Fortune	163
118. The Nativity of a Child Who Died Early	164

Appendices

1. The Twelve Signs	167
Index of Constellations and Star Names	191
2. The Nature and Force of the Seven Planets	195
3. Judging an Eclipse	207
4. How the Points of the Twelve Houses must Be Found to the Exact Degree	211
5. The Time of Life According to All the Rulers and the Ruler of the Nativity	215
6. Comparison of Chapter Numbers	217
Bibliography	218
Index of Persons	221

Translator's Preface.

Preface to the First Edition

I.

Rhetorius the Egyptian is a shadowy figure. His name means "orator" and could imply an advocate, a politician, or a teacher of rhetoric.[1] Nothing is known of him other than what little can be inferred from his writings. He is assumed to be the author of a long Astrological Compendium in 117 chapters.[2] The fullest form of the title of this work seems to be *Rhetorius the Egyptian's Exposition and Explanation of the Entire Art of Astrology from the* Treasury *of Antiochus*. It is a gold-mine of classical astrology.

As it stands, this *Compendium* contains many chapters that are attributed in certain MSS either to Antiochus of Athens (late 2nd century ?), or to Porphyry the Philosopher (late 3rd century) who wrote an *Introduction to the Tetrabiblos*. It also contains some 5th century horoscopes and some star positions for 504 A.D. (3°40' from Ptolemy's Catalogue). In Chapt. 110 some planetary positions are given to illustrate the preceding chapter on separations and applications. David Pingree has mistakenly assumed that they

---

[1] *Cf.* John Malalas (c.491-578), the Byzantine chronicler, who was a younger contemporary of Rhetorius and whose surname means "orator" in his native Syriac.

[2] In MS Parisinus Gr. 2506 a short unnumbered chapter, "Nativity of a [child that was] not reared" follows immediately after Chapt. 117. Franz Cumont identified it as the nativity of a child of the Byzantine emperor Leo I and considered it to be the last (hence, the 118th) chapter of Rhetorius's compendium. I have added it following Chapter 117.

constitute a horoscope¹ cast or cited by Rhetorius, and has dated the positions unconvincingly to 601 A.D.² Consequently he has stated that Rhetorius wrote at the beginning of the seventh century. But this is wrong! The best inference from the entire text is that Rhetorius wrote at the beginning of the sixth century.

The individual chapters of the *Compendium* cite the Egyptians, Phnaes the Egyptian, Dorotheus (1st century), Ptolemy (2nd century), [Vettius] Valens (2nd century), Antigonus (2nd century), and "the Philosopher," presumably Porphyry (late 3rd century), by name. Some of the material resembles certain parts of the *Mathesis* (c. 352 A.D.) of Julius Firmicus Maternus, and some seems to be related to passages in Paul of Alexandria's *Introduction* (378 A.D.).

Some additional material is attributed to Rhetorius in the MSS, most notably the chapters on the natures of the twelve signs and the seven planets, which are said to be from Teucer of Babylon³ (1st century?). These chapters do not appear to have been part of the main *Compendium*, although they would fit in well because its treatment of the signs and planets is rather skimpy. However, since they are ascribed to Rhetorius and are of prime importance, whatever their source, I have included them in Appendices 1 and 2. Some other chapters ascribed to Rhetorius are included in the later appendices. In particular, Appendix 4 contains a worked out example of House Division by the so-called Alchabitius Method. It is the earliest known example of the use of that method.

---

¹Chapter 110 does not give the position of the ASC, nor does it give any facts about a particular person. In no case is an entire horoscope ever given without the position of the ASC and without some significant facts of the native's life, for lacking that information it would be worthless as an astrological example. Hence, this is not a horoscope! It is merely some arbitrarily postulated positions used to illustrate the topic of the chapter.

²See Pingree's edition and translation of the Arabic Dorotheus, *Dorotheii Sidonii Carmen Astrologicum* (Leipzig: B.G. Teubner, 1976), p. xii.

³According to Wilhelm Gundel, not the famous city on the Euphrates, but the Roman fortress town of the same name, which is now in the southern part of the city of Cairo, Egypt.

It seems to me that Porphyry's *Introduction* presents a problem. It has come down to us in 55 chapters, but internal evidence shows that it is incomplete. Therefore, what we have may well be an abbreviated version assembled by some medieval compiler. Porphyry seems to have created his book by selecting chapters from Antiochus and adding a small amount of material himself.[1] But what are we to make of the fact that some chapters in Rhetorius are virtually identical to chapters in Porphyry? It is possible that Rhetorius had before him Antiochus's *Treasury* and Porphyry's *Introduction* and that he selected chapters from both books. But if Porphyry's book was largely copied from Antiochus, why would Rhetorius have bothered with it at all? It seems more reasonable to suppose that Rhetorius copied directly from Antiochus and that the resemblances between his compilation and that of Porphyry are due to their both being independent copies of Antiochus. If this is true, then where Rhetorius and Porphyry agree, we are certainly reading Antiochus.

Pingree discusses the MSS and their contents in great detail in a paper in *Classical Philology* (1977, vol. 72, pp. 203-223), in which he says he proposes to edit both Antiochus and Rhetorius. Perhaps more facts will emerge from his work on those editions. In the meantime, I am proceeding on the assumption that Rhetorius flourished in the early 6th century and that he produced his compilation mainly from earlier works by Antiochus and others. Thus, the citations of Ptolemy and other authors are sometimes his, sometimes those of his sources, and sometimes marginalia that have been incorporated into his text or deliberate interpolations made by the medieval copyists.

For convenience I have assigned the descriptive title *Astrological Compendium* to the work in general. I hope Rhetorius would not mind. His purpose was evidently the same as mine—to make the works of the older astrologers available to the public. In his

---

[1] Porphyry, *Introductio in Tetrabiblum Ptolemaei.* ed. by Emilie Boer and Stephen Weinstock in CCAG V.4 (1940). Some writers have challenged his authorship of the book and would attribute it to a "pseudo-Porphyry."

case, by excerpting and assembling them; in mine, by translating them into English.

I have generally followed the same plan of translation as that which I set forth in the preface to my translation of Paul of Alexandria's *Introduction*.[1] In brief, the translation is addressed to a 20th century astrologer with some interest in the older literature in his field. Modern astrological terminology is used wherever possible, older terms where necessary, and transliteration or paraphrase where ancient terms have no modern counterpart. I have used a few terms of my own devising where neither the ancients nor the moderns "had a name for it."

The footnotes likewise are addressed to a modern astrologer with no specific classical background. They contain some information that may be useful to classical scholars, to "science historians," or to students of what used to be called "the history of ideas." But that is not their purpose. Modern Western astrology has its roots in Greek astrology. The footnotes are intended to help the modern astrologer understand the techniques and terminology of the classical astrologer.

II.

The reader interested in details of the MSS should consult the *Catalogus Codicum Astrologorum Graecorum* [Catalogue of Greek Astrological MSS] and Pingree's paper. I have not examined any of the MSS myself, but I have used the editions of Franz Boll and Franz Cumont in the CCAG and of David Pingree in the Fragments that he placed at the end of his edition of Dorotheus. The principal MSS are these:

    L   Laurentianus Plut. 28,34 vellum ff.170 XI century contains Rhetorius Chapts. 1-53 on ff. 84-93^v

---

[1] In MS, not yet published.

V   Marcianus graecus 335 ff. 434 XV century
     contains chapters 3, 4, 7 (incomplete), 8 (incomplete),
     17, 21, 23-44, 46, and 47; and Epitome IV

A   Parisinus 2424 ff. 241 end of XIV century
     mostly copied from Parisinus 2506

P   Parisinus Graecus 2425 paper ff.285 XV century
     neatly written in a miserable semi-cursive hand with
     many abbreviations and misspellings, but copied from
     a good source; it contains Rhetorius Chapts. 1-117 on
     ff. 76-141^r and summarizes Antiochus Chapts. 1-90 on
     ff. 229^v-232^r

A   Parisinus Graecus 2506 or. paper ff.216 early XIV
     century contains Rhetorius various chapters on ff. 1-24

B   Berolinensis 173 paper ff.204 XV century
     contains the two chapters from Teucer on ff. 139-145^r

James Herschel Holden
Dallas, Texas
1985

Preface to the Second Edition

Since the initial completion of the translation in 1985, I have made corrections in the translation and in its format. In 1992 I changed word processors from AllWrite to WordPerfect, and in early 1999 I changed again from WordPerfect to Microsoft Word. Each of these changes necessitated a revision of the format of the text. And following each change of word processors, I reviewed the entire translation and made some revisions in the translation itself and the footnotes.

In the summer of 1999, I reviewed the translation of the influences of the planets as given in Chapter 57 for houses 2, 6, 8, and 12 for my paper "Four Evil Houses" that appeared in the American Federation of Astrologers *Journal of Research* (Winter 1999), and I made a few changes there and elsewhere in the translation.

I had expected that the long-awaited editions of Rhetorius and Antiochus by David Pingree would have been published by now, but unfortunately this has not occurred. We may hope that they will eventually become available.

James Herschel Holden
Phoenix, Arizona
July 2000

Preface to the Third Edition.

In the present edition, I have corrected some typographical errors that had previously escaped my notice, and I have made a few minor changes in the previous edition of the translation.

I have also added in Appendix VI a comparison of the chapters in Rhetorius's work with those listed in the Summary of Antiochus's *Treasury*, which is found in the *Parisian Epitome of Astrological Works* published in CCAG VIII.3.

In the two previous editions I had omitted translations of Chapters 99-103 and 105-112, since they were not edited in CCAG VIII.4. However, I had not noticed that Chapters 99-102 and Chapter 104 had been edited either wholly or in part in CCAG II from the Venetian MS Marcianus 335. Also, David Pingree has edited Chapter 103 and Chapters 105-108 in an Appendix to his edition of the Arabic version of Dorotheus. Thus, only Chapters 109-112 now remain unedited.

Since completing the second edition, I received Giuseppe Bezza's masterful work *Arcana Mundi* (Milan: Biblioteca Universale Rizzoli, 1995. 2 vols boxed 1147 pp.), which contains translations into Italian of several excerpts from Rhetorius's *Compendium*, most notably Chapter 57, the "Significations of the Twelve Houses of the Chart," and Teucer's *Natures of the Planets* (cf. my own translation in Appendix II of the present volume). And later, at my request, Mr. Bezza very kindly sent me photocopies of the pages of the MS Parisinus Graecus 2425 containing the Chapters 99-(118) of Rhetorius's *Compendium*, including those chapters just mentioned that were not edited in the CCAG or by Pingree.

I had hoped that I would be able to read the few chapters that had not previously been edited and translate them. Unfortunately, as mentioned above, MS 2425 is written in a miserable semi-cursive hand that sometimes degenerates into a mere scribble. Since I am not a trained paleographer, I have only been able to decipher a portion of the words in the MS. Consequently, I have not been able to profit from it as much as I had hoped. I have, however, prepared preliminary translations of those chapters, but since I was not able to read all of the Greek words, the translations are incomplete, and I was undecided whether or not to include them. However, it seemed better to include something in the way of translations rather than nothing at all.

In July 2004 at the Conference "Horoscopes and History" at the University of Amsterdam I spoke with Prof. Pingree about his long-awaited edition of Rhetorius. He told me that he had identified some Greek MSS containing a superior text of Rhetorius. However, he did not offer to provide any advance excerpts, nor did he say when he might be able to get his edition published. We hope that it will be soon.

James Herschel Holden
Phoenix, Arizona
2005

Preface to the Fourth Edition.

David Pingree unfortunately passed away on 11 November 2005. Earlier that year I had obtained what was probably his last paper on Rhetorius[1]. It contains his opinion on the *Ueberlieferungsgeschichte* of the Rhetorius text. Some of his conclusions are as follows:

1. The version of Porphyry's *Introduction* that has come down to us goes back to a patchwork recension of various MSS made about 990-1000 by the Byzantine astrologer Demophilus.

2. In a diagram at the end of his paper, Pingree gives his opinion of Rhetorius's sources. Chapters 1-53 are from Antiochus (second century), Porphyry (third century), and Paul of Alexandria (fourth century). Chapters 54-112 are from an anonymous compiler of about 400 who combined material from Critodemus (first century), Dorotheus (first century), Ptolemy (second century), and Vettius Valens (second century), and from some late tracts attributed to Hermes. Books 113-117 are from a compilation by the astrologer of the emperor Zeno (426-491) around 500, who also had access to Dorotheus.

3. Pingree continues to believe that Rhetorius wrote in the early seventh century, but this is incorrect, as noted in the Preface to the First Edition of this translation (see above, p. x).

---

[1] "From Alexandria to Baghdâd to Byzantium: The Transmission of Astrology" (*International Journal of the Classical Tradition*, Vol. 8, No. 1 (Summer 2001): 3-37, a paper that had previously escaped my attention. It contains some useful information about the MS tradition of Rhetorius's astrological works.

4. Pingree thinks that the archetypal MS of Rhetorius's *Compendium* was acquired by Theophilus of Edessa (c.695-785), the court astrologer to the Abbasid Caliphs, between 765 and 770, and from him a copy of the text passed first to the astrologer Stephanus and then in several lines of descent to later MSS, the oldest of which (the Laurentianus) contains Chapters 1-53, and principally to Demophilus, who put together the recension of Porphyry and also a version of Rhetorius (Pingree calls it Epitome III) that contains Chapters 1-117, and from that (or from a copy of it) was derived MS Parisinus graecus 2425, which contains all of those chapters.

Recently, Stephan Heilen has undertaken the laborious task of preparing for publication Pingree's edition of the Greek text of Rhetorius's *Compendium* as it is contained in Books 5 and 6 of MS 2425. In early December 2008, he very kindly furnished me preliminary copies of Chapters 108-112, so I have now been able to translate those Chapters directly from his forthcoming edition.

I have also made some improvements in my translation of other chapters in the Third Edition, and I have corrected several typos that were in that translation. Therefore, the present translation of Chapters 1-118 is now complete. However, it does not reflect other changes that Pingree may have made in his edition of the earlier Chapters, since I have not yet seen the complete edition being prepared by Heilen, which is expected to be published in the latter half of 2009.[1]

The American Federation of Astrologers has undertaken the publication of this translation. And I want to thank the Executive Director Kris Brandt Riske for her devotion to the task of preparing the translation for publication. And I also want to thank the Operations Manager Jack Cipolla for designing the covers of the book.

James Herschel Holden
Phoenix, Arizona
13 January 2009

---

[1] It is expected to be published as *Rhetorius, Qui dicitur. Compendium Astrologicum*. (Munich & Leipzig: K. G. Saur Verlag, 2009).

Rhetorius's Explanation and Narration of the Whole Art of Astrology.

Preface.

On what account, the twelve signs being circular, have we made the beginning from Aries and not rather from Cancer, since it is the ASC of the World,[1] or from Leo because it is the solar sign; but rather than [either of those] of the two luminaries, the house of Mars, Aries, has been preferred? We say then that since the ancients made the twelve signs bodily according to the parts of man, making the beginning from Aries, affirming it to be the head, Taurus the throat, and so on down to the feet, on account of this from the more ruling part of the commander, the brain, and all that which is proper to the head, they have made the beginning from Aries.

And in particular they have made the seasons in agreement with the tropics, taking the beginning from the vernal sign, i.e. from Aries; for spring signifies the suckling; summer, the youth; fall, middle age; and winter, old age. Four of these signs, then, are called tropical, and four solid, and four bicorporeal. And the tropical [signs] are so called because when the Sun is in them the changes of the air are altered; e.g., when it is in Aries, a tropical sign, it brings the vernal and equinoctial change and thenceforth the air becomes more serene; the day grows longer from the equal hours. When it is in Taurus, a solid and vernal sign, it makes the air calmer and unalterable, and it increases the day further. When it is

---

[1] See the 'Chart of the World' in Firmicus, *Mathesis*, iii. 1, where the ASC is the sign Cancer.

in Gemini, a bicorporeal sign, it equalizes the air and makes the blending together of it between spring and summer, and it increases the day further. In this quadrant, then, is completed spring, which is air.

Again, when the Sun is in Cancer, a tropical sign, it brings the summer tropic,[1] and the air begins to become hotter, and from then it takes away from the magnitude of the day and it adds to the magnitude of the night. Again, when it is in Leo, a solid and summer sign, it makes the air steadier and unalterable, taking away from the magnitude of the day and adding to the magnitude of the night. Again, when it is in Virgo, a bicorporeal sign, it equalizes the air and makes the blending together of it between summer and fall, and it increases the night further and decreases the day. In this quadrant, then, is completed summer, which is fire.

Again, when the Sun is in Libra, a tropical sign, it brings the autumnal and equinoctial tropic, and from then the air turns colder, and the night grows longer from the equal hours. Again, when it is in Scorpio, a solid sign, it makes the air of fall calmer and unalterable, taking away the magnitude of the day and adding to the magnitude of the night. Again, when it is in Sagittarius, a bicorporeal sign, it equalizes the air and makes the blending together of it between fall and winter, and it takes away further from the magnitude of the day and adds to the magnitude of the night. In this quadrant, then, is completed fall, which is earth.

Again, when the Sun is in Capricorn, a tropical sign, it makes the winter tropic,[2] and from then the air turns more wintry and the day begins to increase and the night to abate. Again, when it is in Aquarius, a solid and wintry sign, it makes the air of winter calmer and unalterable, taking away from the magnitude of the night and adding to the magnitude of the day. Again, when it is in Pisces, a bicorporeal sign, it equalizes the air and makes the blending together of it between winter and spring, taking away from the magnitude of

---

[1] The summer solstice.
[2] The winter solstice.

the night and adding to the magnitude of the day up to the equinoctial hours. In this quadrant is completed the wintry air, which is water.

1. Masculine and Feminine Signs and Houses, and Stars That Become Masculine and Feminine.

There are six masculine signs—Aries, Gemini, Leo, Libra, Sagittarius, and Aquarius; and six feminine—Taurus, Cancer, Virgo, Scorpio, Capricorn, and Pisces. The houses from the MC to the ASC are masculine; those from the ASC to the IMC[1] are feminine. Again, the houses from the IMC to the DSC[2] angle are masculine, and those from the DSC to the MC are feminine. Of these four quadrants, then, two become masculine and two feminine. Again, the masculine stars are the Sun, Saturn, Jupiter, Mars, and Mercury; the feminine are the Moon and Venus. But these stars sometimes become masculine and sometimes feminine. And these stars become masculine if they are with the Sun in their morning rising, i.e. posited in the signs going before the Sun within 15 degrees. But they become feminine whenever being vespertine they are posited with the Sun within 15 degrees.

Again, the stars become masculine when they are posited in masculine signs and are northern; but they become feminine when they are in feminine or southern signs. Again, the stars become masculine when they are posited in masculine quadrants, from the MC to the ASC and from the IMC to the DSC; but they become feminine in the feminine quadrants, i.e. from the ASC to the IMC and from the DSC to the MC. The stars which become masculine in the masculine signs or the masculine quadrants contribute to masculine genitures, for they make willful, bold persons, having manliness in themselves; but they make women undignified, shameless, bold, unruly, and in sexual relations taking a masculine role or even being *tribades*.

---

[1] Literally, the 'under-earth'.
[2] Literally, the 'setting'.

But when the stars become feminine from phases and signs and quadrants, they make men soft, faint-hearted, cowardly, afraid of everything, effeminate and generally [either] castrated or doing women's work; and the women with downcast eyes, bashful, prudent, solemn, subject to men, and those who were taught womanly ways. And we have said these things about the morning and evening risings of the stars, for the settings and retrogrades[1] of the stars are inactive and weaker and uneven in their action, except the stars that are *in the heart*. And the stars that are *in the heart* are said to be those that are conjoined partilely to the Sun, either in the same degree or an adjacent degree.[2] None of the ancients have made mention of this phase, but, since we have found [it] by experiment, we have added it to the list, because even Ptolemy spoke of conjunction as a phase but didn't mention its force.[3]

2. The Sects of the Stars.

In diurnal nativities, the Sun, Saturn, and Jupiter are rulers of the sect; but in nocturnal ones, the Moon, Venus, and Mars are the rulers of the sect. For Mercury was appointed to be common to the sects. And the Sun, Jupiter, the Moon, and Venus are considered as benefics, but Saturn and Mars as malefics. For Mercury was ap-

---

[1]Accepting Kroll's emendation *aphairetikoi* 'retrograde' for the MSS's *aphairetai* 'it takes away' (*cf.* Ptolemy, *Tetrabiblos*, i. 24, who uses the same phrase, *dytikous kai aphairetikous* '... setting and retrograde ...').

[2]That is, within an *orb* of 1 degree. This would appear to be the Greek origin of the Arabic astrological term *cazimi* 'in the heart of the Sun'. The Arabs cut the orb down to 16′ or 17′ so as to put the planet within the extent of the solar semidiameter. See al-Bîrûnî's *Book of Instruction in the Elements of the Art of Astrology*, Chapt 481, p. 296, "If a planet should be within less than 16′ of conjunction with the sun or have passed it by less than the same amount, it is designated as 'samim'." The translator Wright suggests that the word *cazimi* derives from the Arabic *ka samim* 'as if the heart'. Note the similarity between the Greek and Arabic phraseology.

[3]Ptolemy discusses the aspects briefly in his *Tetrabiblos*, i. 13 "The Aspects of the Signs.", but he doesn't mention the conjunction in that chapter. He does mention the conjunction elsewhere in the book, and he mentions a planet's being *under the Sun beams*, which is a conjunction within 15 degrees orb (see, for example, *Tetrabiblos*, iii. 10 and iv. 5), but he does not mention any closer conjunction, nor does he say anything about the astrological quality of a conjunction.

pointed to be common, being good with the good, and malefic with the malefics. Of the benefics and malefics he said that they are considered [so] because many times in certain nativities the malefics well placed by phase and sect and house magnify the good fortunes, but the benefics badly placed damage them. For Dorotheus, in his chapter on this subject, says ". . . for the malefics are blunted three ways; a star [is] no longer evil when it finds a good house, nor a house bad when it embraces something useful."[1]

3. The Natures of the Twelve Signs.

We have said that Aries is fiery, Taurus earthy, Gemini airy, and Cancer watery. Again, Leo is fiery, Virgo earthy, Libra airy, Scorpio watery. And again, Sagittarius is fiery, Capricorn earthy, Aquarius airy, and Pisces watery. And so the triplicity of Aries, Leo, and Sagittarius is fiery; the triplicity of Taurus, Virgo, and Capricorn is earthy; the triplicity of Gemini, Libra, and Aquarius is airy; and the triplicity of Cancer, Scorpio, and Pisces is watery. This was not said by the ancients without due consideration. For since all materials are made up of these four elements or bodies, it is also necessary that man, since he shares the same nature, should partake of these four elements. And they have assigned the four angles of the nativity according to the four mixtures of these four elements; e.g., if Aries is the ASC, i.e. a fiery sign, and Capricorn is the MC, i.e. an earthy sign, and Libra is the DSC, i.e. an airy sign, and Cancer is the IMC, a watery sign, it will be the best kind of mixture. Again, if you examine the succedents of the angles, you will find the same four elements disposed accordingly.

4. Rough-skinned, Leprous, Mangy, and Scurvy Signs.

The Moon afflicted in Aries, Cancer, Scorpio, Capricorn, or Pisces makes those who are mangy, rough-skinned, scurvy, or leprous. And not only the Moon but also the Lot of Fortune or of the

---

[1] Pingree associates this quotation with Dorotheus, *Pentateuch*, i. 6, "The Power of the Seven Planets." But it does not agree with it especially well.

Daemon posited in these signs and beheld only by malefics. They also make those born thus to be humpbacked.

5. Licentious Signs.

The licentious and indecent[1] signs are Aries, Taurus, Capricorn, Pisces, and also Libra in part. But you will find out specifically about these things further along.[2]

6. Signs Harmful to the Eyes.

The signs harmful to the eyes are Taurus, because of the Pleiades; Cancer, because of the Nebula; Scorpio, because of the Sting; Sagittarius, because of the Point; Capricorn, because of the Thorn; Aquarius, because of the Pitcher; and also Leo in part. And you will find out about these things in more detail further on.

7. Exaltations and Falls.

Having said then all the physical mixture of the signs, we will come to the causes of the exaltations and falls and the opposites of the stars; for what reason is the Sun exalted here, Saturn in its fall there; and Saturn exalted here, and the Sun in its fall there? For we say that the Sun is the storehouse of fire and light and the lord of the day, but Saturn on the other hand is cold signifying darkness. Here then is exalted the light of day, there is in its fall the darkness and the night, and the cold is warmed; and here the darkness is exalted, there the light is in its fall, and the day becomes shorter. Again, for what reason is Jupiter exalted here, Mars in its fall there; and Mars exalted here, and Jupiter in its fall there? We say that Jupiter is the ruler[1] of life and of abundance, but Mars of

---

[1] The two Greek words *aselgê* and *pathopia* do not have exact equivalents in English. They both refer to persons who indulge in immoderate and illicit sex. The former designates individuals who take an active part in sexual activities, either heterosexual or homosexual, while the latter indicates passives.

[2] See also chapter 76.

death. Here then does the breath of life increase, there is the quality of death in its fall; and here does death increase, there is life in its fall. Again, for what reason is Venus exalted here, Mercury in its fall there; and Mercury exalted here, Venus in its fall there? We say that Mercury is the lord of words, but Venus is the ruler of desire and sex. Here then does the rational increase, there is desire and the enjoyment of sex in its fall; and here is longing and pleasure exalted, there is logic in its fall. In which then is the Moon exalted here, none is in its fall there; and the Moon is in its fall there, none is exalted there? We say that the Moon is the fate of all; and the one that fate exalts, none reduces; and the one that fate makes humble, none is able to exalt.[2]

8. The Oppositions of the Stars.

For what reason are the domiciles of the Sun and the Moon opposite to the domiciles of Saturn? We say that the Sun and the Moon are the luminaries of the world, but Saturn is the lord of darkness. Then always is the light opposite to the darkness and the darkness to the light. Again, on what account are the domiciles of Mercury opposite to the domiciles of Jupiter and the domiciles of Jupiter opposite to the domiciles of Mercury? We say that Jupiter is the ruler of wealth and abundance, but Mercury is always the lord of words; for logic is always opposed to and contemptuous of the desire for wealth, and abundance is opposed to logic. Again, for what reason are the domiciles of Mars opposed to the domiciles

---

[1] Here I have translated the word *ephoros* as 'ruler', thus equating it with *kyrios*, but in Greek *ephoros* is a lesser dignity than *kyrios*; *ephoroi* were elected or appointed and their rulership was usually for a designated period of time, while *kyrioi* achieved their position by heredity or by acclamation, and their rulership was usually for life. Sparta, for example, was ruled by two kings and two ephors, but the kings were kings for life, while the ephors were elected for a single year like the Roman consuls. The use of the word 'ephor' here seems old-fashioned and perhaps indicates that this chapter goes back to the early days of astrology.

[2] This chapter offers an explanation of the exaltations and falls in terms of the general planetary rulerships. Ptolemy, *Tetrabiblos*, i. 19, while using the principle of polarity, confines his discussion to the weather. But actually the exaltation signs were assigned by the Babylonians, who called them "the secret houses of the planets." *Cf.* Firmicus, *Mathesis*, ii .3.4.

of Venus? We say that Venus is the ruler of all desire and enjoyment and pleasure, but Mars of all fear and war and anger. Always then are enjoyment and longing and pleasure opposed to dread and irascibility and hostility. Because this is the case, it is also necessary in truth to judge thus in all the chapters the natures of the stars with regard to their mutual configurations. For why else does Mars with Venus prognosticate adulteries? Is it not clear that all adultery is composed of pleasure and fear, i.e. of Mars and Venus? Again, observe Venus conjoined with Saturn, how it makes those born thus to be sterile, unfortunate in their children, [contracting a] sordid [marriage] or even unmarried.[1] When you have mingled the natures of both, you will find the cause, for it has obtained the cold and dry nature of Saturn which was mentioned previously,[2] and, with it cooling and drying the pleasure-loving and generative spirit, how will there be produced child-bearing or how will there be marriages that are not sordid because of the oldness and sordidness of the nature of this star?

9. The Sect of the Rulers of the Triplicities.

Now [I shall speak] of each triangular side.[3] By triangular I mean the numbering through 5 signs, e.g. from Aries to Leo, and from Leo to Sagittarius, and from Sagittarius to Aries, are 5 signs, and they make up a triangular side or line of 120 degrees in the zodiacal circle, for three times one hundred and twenty make 360 degrees, which number of degrees the whole circle has. Now by day the Sun and by night Jupiter rule this triangular side; and a third and common [ruler] along with these is Saturn. Again, by day Venus and by night the Moon rule Taurus, Virgo, and Capricorn; and a third and common [ruler is] Mars. Again, by day Saturn and by night Mercury rule Gemini, Libra, and Aquarius; and a third and

---

[1] Disregarding the false punctuation of the Greek text and ending the sentence here.
[2] Perhaps a reference to the chapter "The Nature of the Planets" in Appendix 2.
[3] That is, *triplicity*. These are mentioned by the Babylonians, but the rulers of the triplicities were assigned by the Alexandrian inventors of horoscopic astrology.

common [ruler is] Jupiter. Again, by day Venus and by night Mars rule Cancer, Scorpio, and Pisces; and a third and common [ruler is] the Moon. You will find the uses and the astrological significations of these triplicities in the succeding [chapters].

10. The 36 Decans and the Paranatellonta and the Faces.

Since the zodiacal circle is divided into 12 sections, i.e. into 12 signs, the ancients suggested another 36 sections, which they called *decans*, and they distributed these by sign to govern 10 degrees, whence they are called decans.[1] The previously mentioned *paranatellonta*[2] in the zodiacal circle lie under these decans, and they have the faces of the seven stars, which have sympathy with the stars that are placed upon them.

For example, suppose the Sun to be in 10 degrees of Aries, in the first decan, the face of Mars. Now since we have said that the Sun signifies the mental characteristics, you will find the mind of this individual to be manly, irascible, delighting in war, fond of weapons, and such like. But suppose again the Sun to be in 20 degrees of Aries, in the second decan, the face of the Sun. It signifies this individual to be magnanimous and loving fame and fond of honor and no longer delighting in war. But suppose again the Sun to be in 30 degrees of Aries, in the third decan, the face of Venus. It signifies this individual to be womanly in spirit, womanish in appearance, shameful, lustful, and such like.

See how in one sign three differences of the mind followed one at a time. And within the decans and their *paranatellonta* and the faces are the astrological influences set forth by Teucer of Baby-

---

[1] The *decans* were originally 36 asterisms identified by the Egyptians and used to tell time at night. The Alexandrians regularized their lengths to 10° each (whence the name *decan* which means "a ruler of ten"), assigned planetary rulers to them, and parceled them out three-each to the 12 signs.

[2] The Greek word *paranatellonta* refers to fixed stars that are "rising along with" the signs of the zodiac.

lon.[1] And we shall recall it in part thusly:

You must know that each individual sign has three decans; and each decan was allotted ten degrees; and in each degree the Sun makes 24 hours or one day and night.

In the first decan of Aries it makes dangers, plots, fluctuations; in the second, rich, honored persons, but dying early; and in the third, maladies, groans, ill health in youth, but cheerfulness in old age.

In the first decan of Taurus it makes the native rich from others and well-known; in the second it makes the youth wretched and those who escape[2] the dangers of military service; and in the third it makes soldiers, well-provided, steadfast, consistent, long-lived.

In the first decan of Gemini the married man will not be lucky, will not be friendly, and he will be grieved over children; in the second, he will have an unsuitable marriage, and it signifies the endurance of armies; and in the third, it makes rich, honored persons, ruling, but dying early.

In the first decan of Cancer it makes those engaged in public business, and they are grieved over children, exceedingly sorrowful in youth, but very fortunate in old age; in the second, the married man will be wealthy, and he will be benefited from the affairs of others, and he will be grieved by his wife; and in the third, the native [will be] eloquent and exceedingly sorrowful in youth, but he will enjoy himself in old age.

In the first decan of Leo it makes commanding and rich individuals, and in the end he will have plenty, and he will bury his wife first; but in the second and third, it makes depravity, and it prognosticates wickedness, and it brings harm to the one living abroad.

---

[1] The chapter title and the text down to this point are equivalent to Porphyry, *Introduction*, Chapter 47.
[2] This could refer either to a soldier who was fortunate enough to escape injury or to an individual who avoided the dangers altogether by avoiding military service.

In the first decan of Virgo it makes dangers, and the natives swiftly become orphans; but in the second and third, it makes those who will become rich through connections with women, but they will be grieved over parents and children.

In the first decan of Libra the native will be in danger in youth, but afterwards he will acquire [property] underground through some pretext or from things found; in the second, he will become rich in quadrupeds, but he will die early; and in the third, he will undergo maladies and groans in youth, but in old age he will have enjoyment in a variety of ways.

In the first decan of Scorpio he will be benefited by windfalls, and, an heir, he will become conspicuous [because] of honored actions; in the second, he will withstand dangers in youth; but in the third, the native will serve as a soldier, and he will live very long, and he will bury his wife, and he will be rich in his old age.

In the first decan of Sagittarius the native will not take a wife, and he will be grieved over children; in the second, he will lead a life without grief, but he will come to his end among foreigners; but in the third, it makes rich and honored persons, and he will get an inheritance from his wife.

In the first decan of Capricorn he makes those engaged in public business, and they will be grieved over children, and they will experience dangers in youth, and they will be fortunate in old age; in the second, it makes useful persons and those who are benefited by the deeds of others; but in the third, a sharp individual is born, eloquent, losing the paternal wealth; in youth, he will be distressed, but in old age he will enjoy himself in old age.

In the first decan of Aquarius he will be born good and will be well-nourished and well-matched in wives; in the second and third, it makes depraved persons and wickedness in youth, a destroyer of things and one who suffers loss from fire and at sea.

In the first decan of Pisces the native [will be] wicked, suffering loss at sea, a liar, but dying swiftly; in the second and third, it makes fortunate individuals and those who are benefited from the deeds of others, and fortunate in their marriages, and grieved over their children.

11. The Bright Fixed Stars and the Powers of the Paranatellonta.[1]

The type of the signs and the *paranatellonta* is established from the combination of the stars. And they have among themselves bright stars, and dim ones, and darker ones. The ancients, observing these [classes], said that the brightest of them were of the first [magnitude], the dimmer ones of the second magnitude, the darker ones of the third, and so on in order as they found them down to the sixth magnitude, and they have shared in the mixture of the planets, as we have stated previously, and those of them that are in the zodiacal circle, those more northerly than the zodiac, and those more southerly.

Observing then the brighter stars among them, they found that there were 30 bright ones of the first and second magnitude. Now when these are found partially in the ASC or in the MC or aspecting the Sun or the Moon or [in conjunction] with one of the stars, they alter the nativity according to the mixture belonging to them; e.g., if it is of a benefic mixture, the acts of fortune are better; but if it is of a malefic mixture, they are worse.

12. The Terms According to the Egyptians and Ptolemy and the Bright and Shadowy Degrees.[2]

Again, the ancients, cutting each sign into regions[3] or places they named *terms*, not according to equal [spaces of] degrees, as

---

[1]This chapter is equivalent to Porphyry, *Introduction*, Chapter 48.
[2]This chapter is equivalent to Porphyry, *Introduction*, Chapter 49.
[3]The Greek text has *eis emiseis chôras* 'into half regions', which makes no sense, since there are five terms in each sign, not two. I have omitted the word 'half' in the translation.

we said in the case of the decans, but different [numbers of degrees] according to another scheme, that they based on the full periods of the stars; and those periods, I mean, [that] you will find in the [chapters] hereafter;[1] and these same degrees of the terms are disposed according to sign. Some of them are found [to belong] to Jupiter, some to Venus, some to Saturn, [and some to the remaining planets].

Now, whenever one of the stars is found in the domicile of a benefic and in the terms of a benefic having significance for the nativity, it benefits the [native's] fortune; and if it is found in the domicile of a benefic but in the terms of a malefic, it reduces the good of the fortune; but if it chances to be in the domicile of a malefic and in the terms of a malefic, it hurts and darkens his luck. Now the force of the terms alters [the pattern of] astrological influences of the stars, as was said, also in connection with the faces of the decans. Now Ptolemy did not agree with the Egyptian ones in several terms; therefore, he was also obliged to make mention of those. And combining his terms in those alone of the astrological influences.[2] And those [influences] of the bright and shadowy and dark degrees have no small force, if indeed the stars are found posited in bright degrees; therefore, he was also obliged to describe these later on.[3]

13. The Rising-times of the Signs.

Ptolemy established the *rising-times* of the seven climes accurately, having examined them to the minute, and we will want these in all genethliacal methods as he established [them in] his

---

[1]In Chapter 49 below.
[2]The Greek text is defective. I have translated it as it stands in MSS **LY**, but Pingree emends *symballontôn* 'combining' to read *symballontai* and translates the phrase as 'But his terms alone contribute in their influences.' An alternative translation would be, 'And his terms correspond to the individual astrological influences.'
[3]Neither Ptolemy's nor Porphyry's text has such a table, but Firmicus, *Mathesis*, iv. 22, has a table of "empty" and "full" degrees from Nechepso, which is their basis. Among the Arabs, see al-Bîrûnî, . .. *Astrology*, Chapter 458, p. 270, where the degrees are divided into four gradations, two light and two dark, rather than three as above.

Handy Table. But the Egyptians[1] and Valens[2] established the seven climes more roughly;[3] and in practice we will want these for the simultaneous risings of the signs and the stars in each clime, as Valens says in his interpretations of astrological influences.[4]

14. The Parts of the Body Ruled by the Signs.[5]

He[6] established the distribution of [the bodily] parts of man, which parts each of the signs and stars rules, through our knowledge of the injuries and sicknesses that are produced among men from the Lots of Fortune and of the Daemon and of Injury and the rulers of these same. For from them are known expressly in most cases the sicknesses and injuries. Now, having consistently stated all the previously mentioned and having made a clear explanation of the same, I[7] shall set forth below the manifest power of the aspects.[8]

15. Trines and Squares and Oppositions and Those That Are Disjunct with Each Other, as with the Oppositions.[9]

They established differences among the trine and square and sextile aspects. And the first and greatest of all is the taking by de-

---

[1] The early Egyptian astrologers used the rising-times as set forth by Hypsicles in his book *Anaphorikos* 'Ascension' which was written about 150 B.C. These rising-times were calculated by using an arithmetical progression developed by the Babylonians (the so-called "System A").
[2] See Vettius Valens, *Anthology*, i. 7, where Hypsicles's method is briefly explained.
[3] The maximum error in the clime of Alexandria is about 5 degrees.
[4] I suppose the reference is to *Anthology*, i. 2, where the *paranatellonta* are given for each sign.
[5] This chapter is the same as Porphyry, *Introduction*, Chapter 50.
[6] That is, Porphyry, according to Weinstock.
[7] The excerptor, says Weinstock.
[8] The Greek text has '*according to* the manifest power...', but either the phrase 'according to' should be suppressed or some other words have fallen out of the sentence.
[9] This Chapter is nearly identical to Porphyry, *Introduction*, Chapter 51.

gree according to the *Handy Tables* of Ptolemy as we shall point out farther along. The second is the temporal, which Antigonus[1] and Phnaes the Egyptian[2] and some others established and named "equilateral triangle", and the rising of the signs. The third is the zodiacal or common and general into which we all wander. For many times, with the Sun in Leo around the 1st degree [and] Jupiter in Sagittarius around the 5th degree, there appeared to be a trine of Jupiter to the Sun, but [it was] the inactive configured with each other. For neither were they posited platically within the 120 degrees, nor were they placed temporally within the 120 [horary] times,[3] nor within 120 degrees of rising-time. {The rest then comes from the chapters about the planets.}[4] Now the triangular side is always called "zodiacal," which again had force, since neither the degree-wise nor the time-wise embraced it. Now, since we have established the side of the trines and squares and sextiles by degree in what follows through the tables of Ptolemy, now we have indicated the zodiacal, having believed it necessary to add also the temporal by an example.

Suppose the Sun to be in Aries in the 1st degree in the clime of Alexandria, Jupiter in Leo in the 2nd degree, and Mars in Leo in the 5th degree. I do thus: the rising of Aries [is] $21°40'$ [horary] times, and the rising of Taurus $25°00'$ times, and the rising of Gemini $28°20'$, and the rising of Cancer $31°40'$; the times of the four signs make $106°40'$; they are less than $120°00'$ by $13°20'$,

---

[1] That is, Antigonus of Nicaea, who lived after the death of Hadrian (138 A.D.) and before Porphyry wrote his *Introduction* (c. 295 A.D.). He wrote at least one treatise on astrology (the author of a chapter on the "Division of Time" [CCAG VIII.1, 242] says ". . . as Antigonus set forth in the fourth chapter of the fourth book."). From this book apparently, Hephaestio of Thebes extracted the famous horoscope of Hadrian (*Greek Horoscopes*, L 76) and two other early horoscopes (*Greek Horoscopes*, L 40 and L 113,IV); the extracts appear in Hephaestio, *Apotelesmatica*, ii. 18.

[2] Evidently an early astrological author. He is mentioned in another chapter by the same compiler cited in the previous note. Cumont (CCAG VIII.1, 238 n.2) thinks he may have been one of the sources of Antiochus of Athens (2nd century A.D.).

[3] A *horary time* is 1 degree of sidereal time or right ascension.

[4] Weinstock says that this is an excerptor's marginal note that has been incorporated into the text.

which I will find around 11 1/2 degrees of Leo. For doubling the 35 times, they make 70 times; doing 11 1/2 times these, I will find 805 times, which I divide by 60; they make 13°25′ times. I combine the 106°40′; the sum is 120°05′ times. And so the 11 1/2 degree of Leo in the clime of Alexandria is found to be [the side of] an equilateral triangle prognosticating for the first degree of Aries. And we say that Jupiter is beheld by the Sun zodiacally and temporally.

Since there remains 21°35′ times of Leo, I add these to the second equilateral triangle thus: of Leo 21°35′ times, Virgo 38°20′ times, Libra 38°20′ times; the sum is 98°15′ times; there remains again of the 120 times 21°45′; these I find around the 18 1/2 1/7 of Scorpio. For doubling the rising-time of Scorpio, i.e. the 35 times, they become 70 times; multiplying these times the 18 1/2 1/7, I find 1305 times, which I divide by 60; they become 21°45′, which same I add to the 98°15′; the sum is 120 times. And so the 18 1/2 1/7 degree of Scorpio in the clime of Alexandria is found to be the second equilateral triangle prognosticating for the 11 1/2 degree of Leo.

Again, since there remains 13°15′ times of Scorpio, I add to these the third equilateral triangle: of Scorpio 13°15′ times, Sagittarius 31°40′, Capricorn 28°20', Aquarius 25, Pisces 21°40′; the sum is 119°55′ times, which same prognosticate the third equilateral triangle of the zodiacal circle. For the remaining 5 degrees were assigned to the 120 times in the first triangle. And by the same method you will find the sextile and square aspects, which are called temporal.

16. Disjunct Signs and Those Having Sympathy with Each Other.

Signs that are *disjunct but having sympathy for each other* are all the equal-rising signs, and those having equal power, and those of like zone. For example, equal-rising are Aries and Pisces, Gemini and Capricorn, Cancer and Sagittarius, Virgo and Libra; of equal power are Gemini and Cancer, Virgo and Aries, Libra and Pisces, Sagittarius and Capricorn; of like zone are Taurus with Libra, Aries with Scorpio. And most of the other disjunct signs they established [as being] wholly ineffective as regards sympathy. This chapter is combined with the joint risings of the signs and the joint ascensions of the stars, and with the friendships and sympathies of men and women, and parents and brothers, and friends and slaves.[1]

17. Squares That Are Sympathetic and Those That Are Not.

Now the signs *having sympathy with each other by square aspect* are these: Taurus with Aquarius and Leo with Scorpio because of equal-rising; again, Leo with Taurus and Scorpio with Aquarius because of equal power; and Gemini with Virgo and Sagittarius with Pisces because of like zone. But all the other squares are ineffective in sympathy. Every square aspect was established through 90 degrees, and every sextile through 60, for 4 times 90 [is] 360, and 6 times 60 [is] 360; but the opposition through 180 degrees, for twice 180 makes 360, which [number of degrees] the whole circle has.

18. The Dodecatmories of the Stars.

The ancients set forth the *dodecatemories of the stars* in three ways: Paul, in his *Introduction*,[2] said to multiply the degrees of a star by 13 and cast [the product] from [the beginning of] the sign itself by 30 degrees [per sign], and wherever the number comes to, in that sign is the dodecatemorion of the star. But Dorotheus says in the 11th book[3] to multiply the degrees by 12. And Ptolemy says

---

[1]*Cf.* this chapter with Paul of Alexandria, *Introduction*, Chapters 11 & 12 and Porphyry, *Introduction*, Chapter 34.

[2]In Chapter 22.

[3]This perhaps indicates an Arabic source, since the reference is presumably to Dorotheus's *Pentateuch*, which was in five books in Greek but eleven in the Arabic translation cited by Mashallah (CCAG,I,pp. 81-2, "Dorotheus 11 books, viz. 4 of nativities, 3 of questions, 3 of calculations, and 1 of conjunctions."). Al-

in the 26th chapter of the 1st book[1] to cast the degrees by 2 1/2 per sign.[2] But I from trial have found further that the method of Dorotheus agrees with that of Ptolemy; and further from the agreement of these, I mean from the [multiplication] by 12 and the [distribution] by 2 1/2 [degrees]. For thus the two methods leave off in the same sign; for instance, as in this example: let the Moon have been in the 25th degree of Taurus; multiplying these by 12, I found 300 degrees; I cast these from Taurus by 30 degrees [per sign], and it left off in the 30th degree of Aquarius, in the completion of the signs. Again, I cast these same degrees from Taurus by 2 1/2 [degrees per sign]; it left off in Aquarius, in the completion of the sign as regards the 2 1/2 degrees. But if I multiply the 25 by 13, the number leaves off in 25 degrees of Pisces, and this is established [to be] a large difference. And the method of dodecatemories is a necessity in nativities; and I also put down the astrological significations of these so that some might use them not just as in a secondary work.

---

though al-Nadîm, *Fihrist*, VII. 2, says under Dorotheus "Among his books there was a large one embracing a number of sections. This book was entitled *The Book of Five*..." Al-Nadîm gives the contents of the first five books, then mentions a sixth, seventh, and sixteenth [!] book. Two Arabic MSS are known; one contains five books and the other has the first four. However, Boll, who edited the Greek text, thinks it should be emended to read "... in the 10th book..." But if we are going to emend the text, it would be better to make it read "... in the 1st book..." Pingree refers it to Dorotheus, *Pentateuch*, I. 8, where he translates from the Arabic version "Count the dodecatemoria according to this manner: in a masculine sign two and a half 'days' [i.e., degrees] masculine and two and a half 'days' feminine..."

[1] Rather, in *Tetrabiblos*, i. 22, "Of Places and Degrees," where Robbins translates "... the twelfth part of a sign, or 2 1/2°, they assign the domination over them to the signs in order." [If "26th chapter" is not simply a blunder, it would be instructive to determine in what MSS the chapter is actually numbered 26. I do not have the Greek text of Proclus's *Paraphrase*, but in Ashmand's translation of it, the chapter is numbered 25.]

[2] The idea of dividing a sign into twelve dodecatemories of 2 1/2 degrees each is Babylonian. And, curiously enough, surviving cuneiform documents show that two different methods of determining into which dodecatemorion a planet falls were used. These amount to multiplying the degree of a planet by either 12 or 13 and casting the product from the beginning of the sign in which the planet is posited. So far no Babylonian explanation of this difference in procedure has been found. See Ulla Koch-Westenholz, *Mesopotamian Astrology* (Copenhagen: Museum Tusculanum Press, 1995), pp. 168-169.

19. Hearing and Seeing [Signs].

The *hearing and seeing signs* are also useful in flights and dangers, and reports together with messages, of the Moon toward the [star] of Mercury or the benefics by the way moving at the first of the inquiries into this part. And the signs that see each other are these: Gemini sees Leo, and Leo sees Gemini; similarly too, Scorpio sees Virgo, and Virgo Scorpio, and so on accordingly.[1]

20. Beholding.

Of these things being interpreted thus, *beholding* is said either when the one leading bears witness to the one following or else [aspects it] by sextile or square or trine or opposition; for moving along it goes away into those that precede; for the planets move with the opposite motion to [that] of the signs; yet certainly they make for themselves the same course, and they revolve with it[2] each day and night.

21. Casting a Ray.

The one that follows is said to *cast a ray* to the one that leads according to the previously mentioned 4 aspects; for the ray of fire itself hastens to those that follow while it is sending forth [a ray] to those that lead. For example, the one in Aries beholds the one in Cancer, and the one in Cancer casts a ray to the one in Aries.

22. Dexter and Sinister Aspects.

Dexter aspects are those in the leading signs of the zodiac, and

---

[1] Here Rhetorius confuses the *seeing* signs (Gemini & Leo, etc.) and the *commanding and obeying* or the *hearing* signs (Virgo & Scorpio, etc.) rather like Vettius Valens, *Anthology*, i. 7. Those that he mentions are the original pairings of the Alexandrian founders that are given by Manilius, *Astronomica*, 2.485-519; and Paul of Alexandria, *Introduction*, Chapters 8 and 9. They were supposed to be signs that had equal rising times or complementary rising times.

[2] That is, the zodiac.

sinister the following; e.g., the 30th degree of Cancer is rising, dexter sextile to the 1st degree of Gemini, square the 1st degree of Taurus, trine the first degree of Aries, and all the hemisphere above the earth; but sinister sextile the 30th degree of Virgo, square the 30th degree of Libra, trine the 30th degree of Scorpio, and all the hemisphere under the earth. Dexter aspects, then, are those which are in the leading [signs] [as seen] from whatever part of the zodiac, and sinister [those that are in] the following.[1]

23. The Doryphory of the Stars.

Doryphory is when an angular star in its own domicile or exaltation is aspected by another [star] in its own domicile or exaltation. For example, with Venus being in Libra and Saturn in Capricorn, it is aspected by Saturn. Or again, with Saturn being in Libra, Mars aspects it from Capricorn or again from opposite Saturn.[2] [Or, with] Venus [in Pisces and Jupiter from Sagittarius]; or again, Jupiter from Sagittarius and Venus in Libra.[3] The contrary situation of the stars to the ASC or the MC will be diurnal in a diurnal nativity, but nocturnal in a nocturnal. And when it is in the domicile or exaltation of another, both the one is in doryphory and the other becomes it. Or, when a luminary is angular in the ASC or the MC, and in the domicile of another there chances to be a star of the sect; it will aspect the Sun in the degree rising before, but the Moon in the one rising after. For example, with the Moon being in the ASC, Venus aspects from Virgo or from Libra. Sometimes too doryphory is said when, with the Sun and the Moon angular, a star of the sect is in doryphory.[4]

---

[1] In a horoscope diagram, consider a point by looking from the center of the diagram; those aspects to the *right* of the point are *dexter* aspects, and those to the *left* of it are *sinister* aspects. (The words *dexter* and *sinister* are simply the Latin words for *right* and *left*.)
[2] That is, from Aries.
[3] Or, delete the word 'Venus' and my bracketed restorations.
[4] The term *doryphory*, literally 'spear-bearing' is variously defined by the astrologers. See, for example, Ptolemy, *Tetrabiblos*, iii. 4 and iv. 3, Porphyry, *Introduction*, Chapter 29 (which explains three different modes), and Paul of Alexandria,

24. The Out-of-sect Doryphory.

[The planets] are in *out-of-sect* doryphory when diurnals are in doryphory with nocturnals and nocturnals with diurnals.

25. [Doryphories With] Harmony.

Harmonious and greater than the others are the *doryphories* by trine and by square, for the sextiles work loosely.

26. Dominance.

Dominance and superiority is when a star situated in the tenth house makes a square to the left. Let Cancer be the ASC: then those [planets] in Aries are superior to one in Cancer. Another kind of superiority is when some one being in a house on the right beholds one by a left trine or square or sextile.

27. Affliction and Ineffective Houses.

Affliction is said when one is aspected by malefics or besieged, or applying to a destructive [star] or becomes in *kollêsis*,[1] or is opposed or is disposed of by one badly situated in the ineffective houses, which are the sixth from the ASC and the third and the second and the eighth and the twelfth.

Introduction, Chapters 6 and 14. In everyday life the term designated an armed guard in attendance upon a ruler. Since the Sun and Moon were the rulers of heaven, astrologers applied the term to the planets that happened to be near the luminaries. Attendance by aspect was probably a later development and may have been suggested by the analogy of rays with spears.

[1] The Greek word means 'gluing' and is sometimes translated into Latin as *glutinatio*, which means the same thing. It is defined in Chapter 34 below. I have decided to retain the Greek word *kollêsis* in this translation.

28. Effective Houses.

Effective houses are the four angles and the two trines on either side of the ASC[1] and the succedent of the MC.[2]

29. Proper Face.

A star is said to be in *proper face* whenever it approaches near to the Sun or the Moon, as its domicile [does] to their domiciles, vespertine to the Sun, and matutine to the Moon. For example, the Sun in Leo, the Moon in Cancer, and Venus in Taurus. Know that when the Sun is in Leo it is in its proper face, for it is in its own domicile and in a masculine sign. And if Venus was in Taurus, similarly it is in its proper face, being matutine to the Moon and in a feminine sign.

30. Joint Possession.

Joint possession is when two planets are in a single sign or behold it, it happening to be the domicile of one and the exaltation of the other.

31. Incongruity of Position.

Incongruity of position is when the diurnal [planets] hold the [principal] houses of nocturnal [nativities] and the nocturnals those of diurnal, or when stars are situated in the signs where they would be quite effective, but the rulers of the signs are afflicted, so that they are not effective.

32. Joint Rulership.

Joint rulership is said when the exaltation of this one is the domicile of that one, in those signs in which the stars chance to be.[3]

---

[1] That is, the fifth house and the ninth.
[2] The eleventh house.
[3] As of the Sun and Mars in Aries, the Moon and Venus in Taurus, etc. This consid-

33. The House-ruler.

[A planet] is said to be the *house-ruler* when it has the greater modes of rulership in one of the signs; I mean by domicile, exaltation, triplicity, term, phase, or aspect.[1]

34. Kollêsis.

Kollêsis is the most important application when a star moves towards a star, the swifter to the slower, if it is not more than three degrees away.

35. Application.[2]

Application is the *kollêsis* of the Moon when it is a day's motion distant from the degree of the conjunction.

36. Intervention.

Intervention is when a star casts its rays into the middle degrees of an application.[3]

37. Separation.

Separation is when one of the stars has passed by, either corporally or by aspect, the degree of the other star.

---

sideration defines the pairs of planets referred to as having *Joint Possession* in Chapter 30 above. Porphyry speaks of the same thing (at considerably greater length) in his *Introduction*, Chapter 7, but he uses the longer term *synoikodespotai allêlôn* 'jointly ruling with each other' instead of Rhetorius's simpler *despotai allêlôn* 'ruling with each other'.

[1] The *oikodespotês* 'house-ruler' This is not just the ruler of a sign, and consequently of a celestial house, but a planet which is predominant in a particular case. It can be the ruler of a chart or a horoscope. *Cf.* Ptolemy, *Tetrabiblos*, iii. 2, in particular p. 232, ll. 1-8 Robbins's ed.

[2] *Kollêsis* in Chapter 34, Application in Chapter 35, and Separation in Chapter 37 are all discussed at length in Chapters 109 and 110. The earlier chapters merely give the definition of the terms.

[3] This is one of the varieties of *prohibition*.

38. Bonding.

The Moon is said to be brought under *bond* when it has become 15 degrees from the Sun, and to unbind itself when, having passed it by, it is distant the same [number of] degrees from the Sun; and this is also said in the case of the full Moon. For being 15 degrees before the full Moon, it goes into bond; and, having separated to the back [side], it unbinds itself.[1]

39. Void of Course.

Void of course is [said] of the Moon when it joins with no [planet] either corporally or by aspect.[2]

40. Juxtaposition.

Juxtaposition is when stars are in the same terms either corporally or by aspect, or they see each other in the terms of the same star.

41. Besieging.

Besieging is when two planets have another one between them according to some aspect pattern, with no other casting a ray in between, within 7 degrees to the front or the rear.[3]

42. Fortified Stars.

Each one of the stars is said to be *fortified* when [it is] in its own domicile or exaltation or terms or in proper phase or well-configured or in one of the stronger houses of the chart.

---

[1] See also Chapter 111. *Cf.* Paul of Alexandria, *Introduction*, Chapter 35, where the degree limit is 5 degrees.

[2] See also chapter 112, which discusses *Void of Course* in more detail. Modern astrologers have tightened the definition given by Rhetorius by adding "...before it leaves the sign it is in."

[3] This chapter is similar to Porphyry, *Introduction*, Chapter 15. The definition is broader than in modern astrology, which only recognizes corporal besieging.

43. Chariots.

The planets are in their own *chariots*[1] when they are found in their own domicile or exaltation or terms; and they rejoice in these places even when they are found under the Sun beams, for the benefics increase their good and the malefics are changed into a good influence.

44. When the Stars Rejoice.

The stars Saturn and Jupiter and Mars are said to *rejoice* when they are *matutine* and configured; but the Moon and Venus when they are *vespertine*. Sometimes Saturn and Jupiter and Mars rejoice when they are configured in the quadrants from the ASC to the MC and from the DSC to the IMC; but the Moon and Venus in the other quadrants; and Mercury with both the sects through his being common. And the diurnals rejoice by day when they are above the earth and the nocturnals when they are under the earth. And again, the nocturnals rejoice by night when they are above the earth and the diurnals when they are below the earth.

45. Stars under the Sun Beams.

Those which happen to be under the beams of the Sun are said to be *under the Sun beams*, being ahead or behind. And this will be known from the calculation of the phases.

---

[1] The Greek word *lampênê* 'covered chariot' designates a four-wheeled vehicle with a cover rather than the *harma* 'chariot', which was the usual two-wheeled war chariot. The covered chariot was used for the transportation of rulers, especially on formal occasions. In modern terms, it was a 'limousine' rather than a 'car'. By analogy, then, a planet in its own zodiacal subdivision was like a ruler in his own special vehicle.

46. Times [Of Life] of the Angles and Succedents and Cadents.[1]

The ASC shows the first age, the MC the middle age, the DSC the last age, and the IMC angle death and the honors or dishonors occurring after it. And again, the succedent of the ASC[2] signifies the pains of childbirth and the things happening to the mother when the native was in the womb; and the ASC the act of birth and the times immediately after it; and the cadent of the ASC[3] the final times of the first age.

The succedent of the MC signifies the first [parts] of the middle age; the MC the middle of the middle age; the *epanaphora* the last [parts]. The succedent of the DSC signifies the first [parts] of the final age; the DSC itself the middle; and the cadent the last [parts]. The succedent of the IMC signifies the time [immediately] before death; the IMC itself death; and the cadent the time after death.

47. Signification of the Lots.

The Lot of the Moon [or] of Fortune signifies all those things in the body of men and the actions and praises arising from his way of life and the sicknesses of the mind and companionships. The Lot of the Sun [or] of the Daemon signifies the things of the mind and of character and rulership and worth and glory and religion. The Lot of the ASC [or] of the Basis was established as an accessory cause of life and breath. For the Basis itself is giving of breath from the ASC and it signifies bodily things and dwelling abroad.

The Lot of Saturn [or] of the Retribution was established over daemons of the underworld and all things hidden and display and manliness and flight and destruction and misfortune and the kind of death. The Lot of Jupiter [or] of Victory, faith and good hope and assembly and fellowship, and also treachery and success. The

---
[1] This chapter is equivalent to Porphyry, *Introduction*, Chapter 52.
[2] That is, the 2nd house.
[3] The 12th house.

Lot of Mars [or] of Boldness is indicative of rashness and treachery and strength and every sort of villainy. The Lot of Venus [or] Love signifies the desires and lusts and loves made in the same sense and it is indicative of gratification. The Lot of Mercury [or] Necessity signifies anguish and wars and hatred and judicial sentences and all the other violent actions happening to men.

48. Signification of These [Lots].

The Sun aspecting the Lot of the Daemon makes childless persons. The Sun disposing of the Lot of Injuries makes injuries to the heart. Jupiter beholding the Lot of the Daemon makes the individual to be instructed by the gods and in dreams, and he will have all the divine favors, even by square or opposition. The ruler of the Lot of Fortune being under the Sun beams makes those dying violently according to the nature of the signs of the Lot of Fortune. But if it escapes the Sun beams a little, those dying violently are no longer produced, but [rather] vagabonds and those who are sentenced many times. But if the benefics are in aspect, no longer [will he be] dying violently, but he will have moderate luck. The ruler of the Lot of Fortune and of the Daemon being under the Sun beams makes those dying violently according to the nature [of the sign], not good and not particularly evil, but always honorable when angular.

If the Lot of Children falls in a domicile of Saturn and a malefic aspects the lot, it destroys the first-born [children]; and if the Lot of Children falls in [either of the] domiciles of Mars and a malefic aspects the lot, it destroys the middle-born; but if the Lot of Children falls in [either of the] domiciles of Mercury, and a malefic is in aspect, it destroys the youngest-born.

But if the Lot of the Daemon falls in Capricorn, it makes the native forbearing and changeable, but if in Aries or Leo or Scorpio irascible and stubborn. The Sun aspecting the Lot of Fortune and having its ruler under its beams makes exiled persons. If the ruler of the Lot of the Father is found opposite to its own domicile, where the Lot of the Father happened to be, this [native] is said [to be] suppositious. The ruler of the Lot of Fortune being an infortune and aspecting the lot says [that] this aspect is bad, especially if it is also under the Sun beams or it is aspected by malefics.

If the Moon happens to be in [conjunction with] the Lot of Marriage and [Venus ?][1] aspects the Lot of Marriage by opposition or square, it gives marriage with a relative or with [the native's own] sisters. If the ruler of the Lot of Marriage is found setting, he says the marriage will be accomplished secretly. If Saturn is found [to be] the ruler of the Lot of Marriage and is in the DSC house, the female [native] is seduced by an old man. And if the DSC is found [to be] a domicile of Saturn, this one[2] is made to be born of the father's or the mother's family, or even to be an uncle; and this one will not be a foreigner. If the ruler of the Lot of Marriage is setting, the husband is quite undistinguished and this [marriage will be] made secretly. But look also at the phases of the stars, that they are not exalted or depressed and consequently saying the destructive things if they are high or low in their luck. If Jupiter is found ruler of the Lot of Marriage and setting, this will be accomplished from [members of the] family, and they will be rich or famous. If Venus is found ruler of the Lot of Marriage, and she is found in the descending angle, it signifies that this will be accomplished through deceit and jest. But if Mars is in aspect, this was done for the sake of an attack resulting from a dispute. If the Lot of Marriage happens to be where [Venus][3] is, with Mercury ascending or being angular in a masculine sign, it prognosticates pederasts. But also, if Mercury aspects the Lot of Marriage, it makes the same thing; and if Mercury happens to be in a masculine sign aspecting the lot, it will make relations with males; but if Mercury is found in a feminine sign aspecting the Lot of Marriage, he will have unnatural relations with women.

If you find the ruler of the Lot of Brothers in the ASC, say that this one is an only child. If the ruler of the Lot of Brothers falls in a

---

[1] Boll says the name of a planet is missing here and suggests Venus.
[2] That is, the seducer.
[3] Boll's conjecture. The name of the planet is missing in the Greek text.

bicorporeal sign, say that this one will have other brothers also from another husband or from another mother, by which I mean, for example, if the Lot and its ruler fall in a feminine sign, say the brother is from another mother, but if in a masculine sign, from another father.

If the Lot of Fortune falls in a masculine sign, it destroys the father first, but in a feminine sign, the mother, according to Dorotheus.[1] If Saturn first casts a ray on the Lot of the Father, or by aspect or by transit first beholds the Lot of the Father, it destroys the father first. But if similarly it beholds the Lot of the Mother, it destroys the mother first. If a malefic beholds the Lot of the Father or of the Mother, he[2] says that one will be destroyed.first.

49. The Complete and Least Years [Of the Stars].

The complete years of the Sun are 120, their twelfth 10; of the Moon 108, the twelfth is 9; of Saturn 57, the twelfth is 4 3/4; of Jupiter 79, the twelfth is 6 1/2 1/12;[3] of Mars 66, the twelfth is 5 1/2; of Venus 82, the twelfth is 6 1/2 1/3; [and] of Mercury 76, the twelfth is 6 1/3. The least years of the Sun are 19, the twelfth is 19 months; of the Moon 25 years, the twelfth [is] 2 1/12; of Saturn 30 years, the twelfth 2 1/2; of Jupiter 12 years, the twelfth 1; of Mars 15 years, the twelfth 1 1/4; of Venus 8 years, the twelfth 8 months; of Mercury 20 years, the twelfth 1 1/2 1/6.[4]

---

[1]Pingree refers this reference to *Pentateuch*, i. 15,1, but the resemblance is slight. Here is his translation: "If you wish to know which of his parents will die before his companion, then look at the lots of these two; that in which the malefics are or which they aspect from opposition or quartile, that is the one who will die first." Considerably closer to Rhetorius is Firmicus, *Mathesis*, vii. 9,8-9 "[Calculate the Lot of Fortune, and if the sign it falls in] is masculine the father will die first, if feminine the mother." Firmicus seems to attribute this to his *Myriogenesis*; he does not mention Dorotheus here.

[2]Dorotheus, says Boll.

[3]That is, 6 7/12. The ancients preferred to work with unit fractions except for 2/3 and 3/4.

[4]The "complete" years of the planets go back to the early days of western astrology. They do not have any obvious astronomical significance, but they are simply the sums of the terms of the planets "according to the Egyptians," and consequently they add up to 360. The figures assigned to the Sun and Moon, 120 and

50. How One Calculates the Increment of the Signs and the Hours of the Climes.

For example, in the third clime,[1] when the greatest of the times, i.e. from Cancer to Sagittarius, become 210 years, and the least time of it is from Capricorn to Gemini, 150 years.[2] These [years], then, if you divide them by 15, they are equinoctial horary times, [and] there is the greatest day of 14 equinoctial hours, the least day of 10 equinoctial hours. We shall take then the sixth of each of the greatest and least times: they become then of the greatest time, of the 210, the sixth is 35; of the least, [of the 150], 25. The difference of these is 10; of this, the third is 3 1/3, which is the increment of each sign. By this same method you will know [the increment] in the other climes.[3]

---

108 are also unexplained unless one wishes to accept Neugebauer's assumption (HAMA, ii, p.958) that their sum (120+108=228) is equal to the 228 calendaric months of the 19-year luni-solar cycle. But Neugebauer does not explain why months would be equated with years or why the figure of 228 would have been divided into 120 and 108. In Hindu astrology the 120-year period is called *vimshottari dashâ* and the 108-year period is called *astottari dashâ*.

The "least" years of the planets are related to their periods. The 19 years of the Sun is the luni-solar cycle, in which 19 revolutions of the Sun are very nearly equal to 235 lunar months and 254 revolutions of the Moon; the 25 years of the Moon are a recurrence period in the old Egyptian calendar, for 25 X 365 = 9125 days and 334 X 27.3216 = 9125.4 days; the years of Saturn and Jupiter are simply their periods of revolution in the zodiac; the 15 years of Mars are a recurrence period when Mars returns to nearly the same place in the zodiac, for it is slightly more than 7 synodic periods of Mars; the 8 years of Venus and the 20 years of Mercury are likewise recurrence periods when the planets return to nearly the same place on the same (Egyptian) date.

[1]That of Alexandria.

[2]He speaks of "years" rather than "degrees" because of the common equation of 1 degree of arc to 1 year in primary directions. Firmicus, *Mathesis*, ii. 11, does the same thing when he gives tables of the rising of the signs in various climes in "years," rather than in "times" or degrees.

[3]Rhetorius forgets to tell his reader what to do with the "increment" once he has found it. The 25 and 35 times that he mentions are the rising times of Taurus and Leo respectively. To find the others, add or subtract the increment successively. For example, if Taurus rises in 25 times, then Aries rises in (25 - 3 1/3 =) 21 2/3 times; Gemini rises in (25 + 3 1/3 =) 28 1/3 times, etc., up to Virgo, which rises in (35 + 3 1/3 =) 38 1/3 times. The same numbers apply to the other half of the zodiac, from Libra to Pisces, but in reverse order. This is the so-called "System A" of the Babylonians as adapted by the Alexandrian mathematician Hypsicles (c. 150 B.C.). Similar instructions appear in Vettius Valens, *Anthology*, i. 7, and Manilius, *Astronomicon*, iii. 395-442.

51. The Greatest Years and the Complete Revolutions of the Seven Stars.

Saturn makes his greatest return in 265 years; Jupiter in 427 years; Mars in 284 years; the Sun in 1461 years; Venus in 1151 years; Mercury in 480 years; and the Moon in 25 years. The *cosmic return* occurs in 1,753,200 years, and then there occurs a conjunction of all the stars in the 30th degree of Cancer or the 1st degree of Leo, and a fulfillment occurs; but in Cancer a cataclysm occurs, in part of the world.[1]

52. Stars Disjunct with the Lights.

The Moon being *disjunct* the Sun prognosticates separation or inconstancy or alienation of the parents. The Moon being disjunct Saturn I have found [to be] the cause of good nativities and of accidents and suffering. The Moon being disjunct Jupiter makes ineffective, humble persons, unable to cope with their daily lives. The Moon being disjunct Mars makes moderate persons, not rash, listless, and withdrawn from their parents. The Moon being disjunct Venus makes graceless persons, and unsuccessful in both marriage and love affairs. The Moon disjunct Mercury makes quite inactive

---

[1]These are all recurrence periods of the celestial bodies after which they return to nearly the same zodiacal position on the same (Egyptian) date. Neugebauer notes (HAMA, ii, p. 605) that these recurrence periods were known to the Babylonians. The Sun has a recurrence period because in the old Egyptian calendar there were only 365 days. Hence, in 1461 Egyptian years (of 365 days) there were 1460 tropical years (of 365 1/4 days). Kroll (CCAG I, p. 163, note to line 19) suggested that *ekplêrosis* ' fulfillment' was an error for *ekpyrosis* 'conflagration'. This seems possible, for Leo is a fire sign and Cancer is a water sign. *Cf.* Firmicus, *Mathesis*, iii. 1,9, who speaks of a *...maior apocatastasis...per ecpyrosin aut per cataclysmum...* '...greater restoration...through conflagration or through deluge...'. The number 1,753,200 is the product of 1200 and 1461. It is evidently intended to be what is often called the "Great Year"—a period of time after which all the celestial bodies would return to their original position. The number is given in the MSS as 1,750,000 + a smaller number that is corrupt. In Lydus, *Months*, iii. 16, the first number is the same and the second is 3,200. The same numbers appear in two later Byzantine writers. Plato set the Great Year at 10,000 years, and the Hindus ran it up into huge numbers. Ptolemy, *Tetrabiblos*, i. 2, derides the whole idea, and, while it died out in the West, it unfortunately came to dominate Hindu astronomy.

and rather foolish persons. And I say these things [of] all the aspects of the homozone and equal-rising and equal-powered signs.

53. Influences of the Doryphories of the Sun.

Saturn being *in doryphory* makes reasonableness and deceit and happiness from the father's name and great wealth. Jupiter makes justice and kindliness and boastfulness and illustriousness and command and great wealth and success. Mars makes manliness and heat and boldness recklessness and violence and causing fear and abjectness in their accomplishments (?). Venus makes good fame and charm and shrewdness and sweetness and shamelessness and happy marriage and success. Mercury makes cleverness and logic and enterprise.

And it must be known that if the [stars] in doryphory of the Lights, which are themselves posited in angles, are cadent, they bring forth nothing less than royal rule or tyrranical rule [for] those so born. And [if] the Lights have doryphories, but they themselves are cadent, then neither kings nor tyrants will be born, but they will be friends of such persons. And judge the same also in the case of the out-of-sect doryphories.

54. Topical Examination [Of the Horoscope].[1]

The topical examination is made as follows. At the outset, it is

---

[1]Here begins the edition of Rhetorius's text from **MS** 2425 in CCAG 8.4, p. 118. I don't know any good way to translate the title of this chapter. The Greek word *Episkepsis* is easy enough: it means 'inspection' or 'examination' or even 'investigation'. The other word, *pinakikê*, presents a problem. It can mean 'tabular' when it is used to describe an astronomical table where the numbers are arranged in columns. But Ptolemy twice uses it (*Tetrabiblos*, ii. Introduction and iii. 6) merely to refer to earlier chapters in his book. In that sense it refers to text formatted into sections dealing with individual topics rather than to running text divided only into larger sections called "books." The present chapter presents seven methods of interpreting a horoscope. I think "topical" is as good as I can do. It is certainly better than "tabular." This entire chapter was translated into Latin in the 12th or 13th century from a fuller Greek text than we now possess. It appears as Chapter 16 of the *Book of Hermes* under the title *Consideration of the Figure*.

necessary to examine good births and bad births and consequently the doryphories of the lights, whether they are in doryphory with those of their sect or with those of the opposite sect, and whether they are in masculine signs or in feminine quadrants of the chart, whether the lights are well-connected or disjunct with each other and with the ASC, whether the one [is] in a masculine [sector] and the other in a feminine, or vice versa; for there is a considerable effect from these [positions].

And then examine the rulers of the triplicity of the light of the sect and of the ASC and their dispositors, and the rulers of the terms of the Sun and the Moon, and the dodecatemories of the stars, where or with which [stars] they fall.

Also, examine the Lot of Fortune and of the Daemon and their rulers; for when these have fallen under the Sun beams and are beheld by malefics or are opposed to each other and are badly placed, they make those that are born to be non-viable, especially when the lights are beheld by the malefics[1] <or besieged and making a conjunction with malefics, especially with those that are not of the same sect. For with these so placed, one should consider nativities of this sort to be non-viable and without years. Along with these, one should examine the rulers of the triplicity of the preceding conjunction or opposition and its ruler and the ruler of the terms.>

<In the second consideration, one should again examine the rulers of the triplicity, and especially of the luminary of the sect and of the ASC and of the MC, lest perchance they are in their fall or under the Sun beams for seven days also. For this sort of figure is significative of error and contrariety. But if the rulers of the triplicity, especially of the luminary of the sect, are well placed but aspected by malefics, they make misfortune or a violent death; also, if the rulers of the sect are opposing each other, they are made very unlucky and debilitated in life.>

---

[1] The remainder of this "examination" is missing in the Greek text, as are all of the second "examination" and most of the third. I have supplied the missing text in angle brackets from the Latin version.

<They also investigate the bright fixed stars and the bright degrees. Therefore, when they are present in the ASC or in the MC or in the DSC or in the IMC in the same degree with one of the seven planets, they signify great and unexpected nativities, and especially with the Sun and the Moon, although they are some of the planets. Look too, lest perchance the ruler of the Moon in a nativity does not aspect her, and similarly lest the ruler of the ASC be remote from it. For then it is not a human that is born, but a monster or a quadruped.>

<The third consideration is that you investigate the Moon and her ruler, and the ruler of the terms, and the ruler of the triplicity, and her [position on the] third day, and the seventh, and the fortieth, and her conjunctions and separations and apparitions, and the "latitudes of the winds," and her nodes, and the revolutions and courses through the nativity, and if she is increased or [made] less in course or light, and her dodecatemories, and if she runs slow or fast, and if she is in the last degrees of a sign. Since the separations of the Moon signify those things which pertain to the body and to the elder brothers; the conjunctions, business activities and financial circumstances; her "latitudes of the winds" and greater or lesser motions, increases or decreases of course, void of course, and the nodes, errors and disturbances of life; but besieging of the Sun and Moon and the ASC by benefics signifies good, but by malefics, evil. Their dodecatemory signifies the same things. And falling on the ecliptical nodes, they make illnesses both for the child and the mother;> or say the mother is wanton, unless it is with the Descending Node. But when it is in the last degrees [of a sign], it signifies low birth of the mother, except in Libra because the last degrees of Libra are called "Increase," and except in Cancer because the last degrees of Cancer are called "Land of the Gods."[1]

<Moreover, they also investigate the ruler of the triplicity and the IMC because the former signifies the kind of death, the latter

---

[1] The Latin version has "Marriage of the Gods."

sicknesses. If, therefore, these are unfortunate, they make death and sickness unfortunate, also if they are made unfavorable by position.>

In the fourth examination, it is necessary to examine the new Moons and full Moons, in which houses they are, and to which [stars] they join themselves after the new or full Moon. Also, look at which ones rise before the lights and which after. And if they happen to be benefics, the [circumstances] of luck and of the parents will be good. But if [they are] malefics and out-of-sect, say that the parents are foreigners, or of another race, or low-born, or humble. Similarly too the malefics alone dominating the Moon or the Sun by sextile or square are especially indicative of dangers, sometimes even of violent death.

Look also at the rulers of the new or full Moon and the rulers of their triplicities, how they are situated, and by whom they are beheld, and what phases they have, and if they are not averted from the new Moons and full Moons, or are in opposition to these places. The new and full Moons and their rulers being beheld by malefics, and being averted from or opposed to the rulers of the new or full Moons, are indicative of violent death. And if the ruler of the radical place of the Moon is found being averted from her, and the ruler of the ASC is averted from it, the native will not be a man but rather a monster or a quadruped. And if benefics aspect the angles, the native will be manageable or worshipped, e.g. a dog or a cat or a bird and such like.[1] But if the malefics aspect the angles, while the benefics are averted [from them], the life form that is born will be savage.

In the fifth consideration, it is necessary to examine the Lot of Fortune and of the Daemon and of the Basis and of the Exaltation of the Nativity and their phases and the house positions. For if they happen to be averted from the ASC, angular with respect to the Lot of Fortune, together with the benefics, they signify fine things for

---

[1] Cumont thinks that Antiochus, Rhetorius's source, might have read "...a cat or an <ape or an ibis> bird . . ."

the luck if indeed they are under the Sun beams. But if, with these situated thus, only one malefic beholds the eleventh house of the Lot or of the ASC, the so-called wealth-bringing, or the eighth house of the ASC, or the Lot of Fortune, or the ruler of the eighth house, the aspect shows together with exile also a violent death. But if the Lot of Fortune and its ruler happen to be dignified, but the Lot of the Daemon and its ruler happen to be afflicted and beheld by the malefics, they bring about loss of position for the native, especially in nocturnal nativities, because according to Ptolemy the Lot of Fortune is the Lot of the Daemon.[1]

But if also the ruler of the Exaltation of the Nativity is afflicted or beheld by malefics, it will make destruction of the dignities or the actions, idleness and laziness. But if, with the Lot of Fortune well situated and beheld by the benefics, its ruler (or the ruler of the [Lot of] the Daemon) is found in the ninth house of the ASC, this one will achieve success from sacred matters or sacred places. But if the ruler of the lot happens to be in the IMC, this one will be a treasury guard. But if the Lot of Fortune and its ruler happen to be in a moist sign, this one will be successful in watery or nautical affairs.

And plainly, [either] happiness or dejection must become manifest in accordance with the nature of the sign and the house position [in which][2] the Lot of Fortune and its ruler chanced to be.

If Mars or Saturn happens to be in the 12th house of the lot and the [light] of the sect is found in its own house or triplicity or exaltation, it will make acquisitions from violence or robbery and wrongdoing. And some that have the configuration in the sixth [house] of the Lot of Fortune also suffer injury from servile per-

---

[1] *Cf. Tetrabiblos*, iii. 10, where Ptolemy says to calculate the Lot of Fortune, both by night and by day, by measuring from the Sun to the Moon and adding the distance to the ASC in the order of the signs. This is the only one of the lots mentioned by Ptolemy. His procedure, however, has the effect of equating the Lot of the Daemon in a nocturnal horoscope with the Lot of Fortune, which is exactly what Rhetorius says.

[2] Adds Cumont.

sons and are betrayed as [you would expect] from the sixth house. For the twelfth house of the Lot of Fortune being aspected only by malefics, and especially by those out of sect, signifies losses of position—by Mars, from conflagrations or from rulers or military affairs or piratical attacks or similar things; but by Saturn, from shipwrecks or decrees or elderly persons and those in authority[1] or eunuchs or from some removals on account of old matters or from deceased persons. The Lot of Fortune and its ruler averted from the Sun make abject individuals unless [they are in] homozone or equal-rising signs or those having equal power. But also the ruler of the new Moon or full Moon in the twelfth or eighth from the ASC make abject individuals; and similarly too, the new Moon or full Moon in the twelfth or the eighth.

And if most of the configurations and their rulers are found in order as to nature and arrangement, the things of life and honor will be long-lasting; but the long duration of good fortune or bad fortune or alternation [of fortune] from the bonding of the progressions which occur from all the stars and the Lot of Fortune and of the Daemon. But it is necessary too from the rising of the sign, according to the Egyptians, and from the cyclical period of each star, i.e. from the complete and middle and least years, according to the third and a half and the half of the times together with the risings of the signs ...[2] and the transitions in rulership[3] of the stars; also, if the stars are badly configured with respect to the eastern horizon,[4] but well configured with the Lot of Fortune and its ruler, the first things will be unsuccessful, but afterwards successful. But if the configuration is vice versa, both as regards the ASC and the Lot of Fortune and its ruler, say that the result or the outcome will be reversed.

---

[1] Accepting Cumont's suggestion of *exousiastikôn* 'authorities' for the MSS's *ekklêsiastikôn* 'ecclesiastics'—a natural mistake for a Christian copyist.
[2] What this means is not clear. Cumont thinks something is missing. The Latin version has simply "... in the third clime."
[3] Literally, 'the handing over and giving up [of rulership]'. The reference is to the sequence of planetary rulers generated by a progression through successive signs. *Cf.* Vettius Valens, *Anthology*, v. 1 (p. 209,2).
[4] That is, the ASC.

Similarly, the lots signify the first age [of life], but their rulers the last; for Fortuna signifies the bodily ailments as well as acquisitions, especially the 11th house of it and its ruler; but the Daemon mental things and business transactions and honors and character. And the ruler of the Basis is the foundation of fortune.

Therefore, when dividing the years of the native, it is necessary to cast the years not only from the ASC but also from the Sun and the Moon and the Lot of Fortune. And if he has a father and a mother, the years are cast from the Lot of the Father and [the Lot] of the Mother, and thus look at the years of the parents.

And examine lest in any manner the [star] having the most authority for the nativity fall out badly or be beheld by malefics; and this is an evil scheme, for it will make a bad death for the native.

And with all of the aspects, look also at the influences of the terms and the judgments of the houses and the mutual configurations of the stars and the faces of the decans along with their *paranatellonta* and the forms of the circle of twelve animal figures.

Examine also the ruler of the twelfth house and of the sixth from the ASC lest they happen to be angular; for, when they are in the ASC, they injure youth, but, when they are in the DSC, old age.

And also examine the Moon lest she see the Lot of the Anaeretic Star, [for] this signifies a violent death. And the Lot of the Anaeretic Star is taken from the ruler of the horoscope up to the Moon, and the result [is cast] from the ASC, but by night vice versa.

In the sixth consideration it is necessary to examine the Ascending Node and the Descending Node, in which houses and decans they are, and by which [stars] they are beheld; for many times also when stars are well situated, especially the benefics, the Descending Node being with the Sun or the Moon or Jupiter,[1] <it harms the

---

[1] Here the Greek text breaks off. What follows in angle brackets is from the Latin version of the *Book of Hermes*.

nativity considerably and brings disasters. With the Sun, indeed, the Ascending Node or the Descending Node injures the father, but with the Moon it causes the death of the mother or declares her to be ignoble, especially in the angles. And the Ascending Node signifies the same thing with Saturn or Mars, especially in the angles, because the Ascending Node, when it is with benefics, does good, but with the malefics, evil. Similarly too, the Descending Node with Saturn or Mars does good things, but with the rest [of the planets], evil. For it sets aside their virtue, lest . . .>[1]

In the seventh consideration, examine the dodecatemories of the stars, especially of the Sun and Moon and the ASC, in which houses of the ASC they are, and by which [stars] they are beheld; for if their dodecatemories along with the ASC happen to be in quadrupedal signs, say that the native will be a quadruped or a monster, especially when the lights are so placed and also in particular the Lot of Fortune and its ruler. And many times this scheme makes charioteers and horse-couriers or animal caretakers when the benefics are in aspect. But if also the Moon is averted from its dispositor or opposed to it, it signifies the same thing. Nevertheless, the third day of the Moon[2] chancing to be in a quadrupedal sign and beheld by malefics signifies the natives to be monsters or quadrupeds; but if, with these situated thus, the third day is found beheld by malefics, and the ruler of the preceding new Moon or full Moon is averted from the ASC and its ruler,[3] it signi-

---

[1]And here even the Latin version fails, but perhaps not much of the original was lost, for the basic theory of the nodes has been stated.
[2]That is, the position of the Moon on the third day. Cumont cites Bouché-Leclerq, *L'Astrologie grecque*, p. 487 n. 2., where the "third day of the Moon" is discussed and the following references given: Firmicus, *Mathesis*, ii. 29,16, iii. 14,10, iv. 1,7, iv. 1,10, and iv. 8,1. To these can be added Hephaestio of Thebes, *Apotelesmatics*, ii. 24, 10-13, which Pingree relates to Dorotheus, *Pentateuch*, i. 12,1-8; and Hephaestio, Epitome IV, 26,40-41, and 31,1-3. Presumably, by "third day" all these authors mean what we would call the "second day." The Moon would generally be in the next sign after its birth sign, and this may lie behind Firmicus's method of selecting the ruler of the chart itself (*Mathesis*, iv. 19).
[3]Reading *oiko<despotê>n* 'sign-ruler' rather than simply *oikon* 'sign'. (Actually, 'house-ruler' and 'house', but the reference is to the "houses" of the planets in the zodiac; i.e. the signs.)

fies[1] the same thing.

Examine also the Causative Lot, the one taken from Saturn to Mars and the result [cast] from the ASC, but by night vice versa; for this lot beheld by the malefics is perilous and especially dangerous, making the nativities destructive. It beholds the configuration of the signs according to the equal-rising [signs]; for it is necessary that Virgo and Aries be considered to be an opposition, and Libra and Pisces, and the rest of the equal-rising and *homozone* signs.

Also, it is necessary in each nativity to examine the influences of the decans as regards the stars and the *paranatellonta* and the faces of the decans and the bright degree areas of the signs.[2] For, by reviewing thus all seven of these considerations, you will not go wrong on the fundamentals of the nativity.

Examine also the influences of the eleventh [house] of Fortuna and watch out for the triplicities of the eclipses.[3] Examine also the degrees of the angles, for many times, when the stars of the nativity have fallen aside [from the angles], the bright ones of the fixed [stars] are found in the degrees of the angles, and they make the natives to be great and surpassing.[4] For many do not know the power and efficacy of the fixed stars. But they are also very effective in the bondings of the progressions, especially if the star of the bondings runs [towards] the wind of the fixed [star].[5] And simi-

---

[1] The Greek text has *skopei* 'sees' or 'see'! But I think this is a mistake for *sêmainei* 'signifies' (*cf.* 124,2).

[2] See Chapter 81 below.

[3] The two parts of this sentence do not appear to be related. I think something is missing in the middle. The "triplicities of the eclipses" is reminiscent of Ptolemy, *Tetrabiblos*, ii. 5, but that chapter relates to mundane astrology rather than to nativities. I suppose the phrase could be translated "trines of the nodes", but why we should watch out for those is not immediately obvious.

[4] *Cf.* Guido Bonatti, *Introduction...*, Consideration 145, where the efficacy of the 1st magnitude star Cor Leonis (Regulus) in close conjunction with the ASC or MC is noted.

[5] He means, if both the planet and the fixed star have the same *direction* of latitude, i.e. both North or both South. Since in classical antiquity the winds that blew from different directions all had names, the word 'wind' could also imply 'direction'.

larly, the fixed [stars] are again effective if they happen to be in the same degrees with the planets according to the same *wind*.[1]

55. Childbirth.

In masculine nativities, the lights being in masculine signs and the ASC beheld by benefics makes a favorable birth; but in feminine nativities, it makes an unfavorable birth, and especially if the lights are in trine to each other and in masculine signs. But in masculine nativities, the lights trine each other and in feminine signs along with the ASC makes an unfavorable birth. For this phase of the lights is called *gibbous*.

Jupiter in the ASC gives a favorable birth, and, if the ascending sign is masculine, it causes the father to be better born than the mother, but if feminine, the mother [rather] than the father. Saturn in the ASC causes an unfavorable birth, especially in the feminine signs. Mars in the ASC, especially in feminine signs, makes the birth to be sudden and quick, especially while on the road or in the bath. And they also say that the straight and the crooked signs contribute much to the matter of childbirth. The straight signs are [those] from Cancer to Sagittarius, and the crooked are the remaining ones from Capricorn to Gemini. Now the Moon chancing to be in the crooked signs and located between[2] the malefics prognosticates an unfavorable birth, especially also when the malefics chance to be in crooked signs and bear witness to the non-angular Moon.

---

[1] Cumont notes that this same information is found in the treatise on the fixed stars by the so-called Astrologer of the Year 379. The Greek text of that work is edited in CCAG, V, Part 1.

[2] Literally, 'embraced by'. This term can mean 'besieged', but here it means simply a situation where Mars is on one side of the Moon and Saturn on the other. *Cf.* Vettius Valens, *Anthology*, vii. 2 (p. 268,20).

56. [The Kinds Of] Natives [Indicated] by the Day-ruler and the Hour-ruler.

When Saturn is day-ruler and the chart [is set for the] 1st, 3rd, 8th, or 10th [hour], those born are low-born, injured, and dying violently.

When Jupiter is day-ruler and the chart [is set for the] 1st, 4th, 10th, or 11th [hour], those born are rulers, honored, and charming.

When Mars is day-ruler and the chart [is set for the] 1st, 5th, 6th, or 8th [hour], they meet their end from iron or fire or the wrath of a noble or the bursting forth of blood.

When the Sun is the day-ruler and the chart [is set for the] 1st, 2nd, 3rd, 6th, or 8th [hour], [those born are] illustrious, honored, friends of great men, and beloved of the gods.

When Venus is day-ruler and the chart [is set for the] 1st, 2nd, 5th, 8th, or 10th [hour], [those born are] charming and capable.

When Mercury is day-ruler and the chart [is set for the] 1st, 4th, 6th, 7th, or 8th [hour], [those born are] effective, active, and well-informed.

When the Moon is day-ruler and the chart [is set for the] 1st, 3rd, 6th, 7th, or 8th [hour], those directing important matters.[1]

Similarly too in the case of the nocturnal hours. If the ruler of the hour-ruler of the hours is in the twelfth house, it makes those eaten by wild beasts.[2]

---

[1] The hours given for each day-ruler are, in general, the hours of the day when the day-ruler is also hour-ruler or when a planet of similar nature is hour-ruler. Thus, in the case of Saturn, Saturn itself is hour-ruler of the 1st and 8th hours, while its fellow malefic Mars is hour-ruler of the 3rd and 10th hours. And, in the case of Jupiter, it rules the 1st hour, while Venus rules the 4th and 11th hours, and the Sun rules the 10th hour. Variations occur. For example, in the case of Jupiter as day-ruler, one would have expected Jupiter ruling the 8th hour rather than the Sun ruling the 10th. There may be additional rules or the Greek text may be corrupt.

[2] Reading *thêriobrôtous* instead of the meaningless *thyriobolous*. *Cf.* Chapt. 57, Twelfth House (CCAG VIII,4, p. 128,23). But I think some mention of Mars has dropped out of the text at this point.

57. Significations of the Twelve Houses of the Chart.

The Twelfth House.

The twelfth house is called *Bad Daemon* and "rising before the ASC" and *metacosmic*.[1] It signifies things concerning enemies and slaves and quadrupeds, and all the things that transpire before the hour of birth, both to the mother and to the one that is about to be born, since this sign[2] rises before the expulsion of the fetus.[3] And it is chosen as the house of Saturn, inasmuch as through the pouring out of the waters the fetus is expelled, and because the new-born is placed in the midst of life and death, being beheld by Saturn and Mars by opposition.[4]

Now the malefics chancing to be in this house make unfavorable births and bodily sicknesses and cuttings or injuries to the feet or the mouth or the toe, and the destruction of slaves and enemies. But if the Lot of Fortune occurs in this house and the malefics aspect the lot, they bring about the greatest evils, always doing [physical] injury at the same time.[5] And similarly, the benefics do injury in the 12th [house] and do not bestow their good. For the Sun being present in the house declares the native to be born of a father who is a slave or an outcast or low-born, or he is expelled from his father's kindred, or the father is injured. And the Moon shows similar things for the mother. And Jupiter being present in this house makes uprisings of enemies. And Venus [makes] bad

---

[1]See p. 61, n .4.
[2]The use of the word 'sign' where we would expect 'house' reflects the use of the original "sign-house" system of house division.
[3]Cumont says this is the reason why Rhetorius begins the series of houses with the twelfth, rather than with the ASC as is customary.
[4]MSS **AV** omit '...is placed–opposition', perhaps correctly. But if the phrase is part of the original text, then presumably it refers to the house rulerships–Saturn being the natural ruler of the 12th house as just announced and Mars of the opposite house, the 6th (these are the houses in which they "rejoice"–see Chapter 44 above).
[5]*Cf.* Shakespeare, *Hamlet*, Act. 4, Sc. 5, "When sorrows come, they come not single spies, /But in battalions."

marriages or marriages with slaves. And Mercury [makes] malignant persons and evil-doers.

But if the rulers of the new Moon or full Moon [preceding the birth] are found in this house, say that the scheme will be bad, for it makes outcasts or those dying violently. If the dodecatemory of the Sun or the Moon is in this house, say that the parents are low-born or outcasts or that whatever is received from the father is destroyed. And if the Sun and the Moon are in this house, with the malefics being angular, and with no benefic in aspect, they make the natives to be *cynanthropoi*.[1] And if Mars and Venus are found in this house, they make wife-slayers.

And if the ruler of the Lot of Fortune is found in this house beheld by Saturn or Mars and aspecting the Lot of Fortune, they make bad luck. And if the ruler of the third house is found in the twelfth, he will have brothers and friends as enemies. And if the ruler of the IMC angle is found there, predict his end abroad. And if the ruler of the twelfth house is found in the fifth and the ruler of the fifth in the twelfth, they make these [natives] to be step-fathers of others' children. And if the ruler of the seventh house is in the twelfth, it prognosticates bad marriages or slave marriages and those who endure damage and harm on this account.[2] And if the ruler of the eighth house [is] in the twelfth, it makes harm for this one from something to do with the dead or he will die abroad. And if the ruler of the ninth house is in the twelfth, it prognosticates that

---

[1]Literally, 'dog-men'. Cumont (*L'Égypte des Astrologues*, pp. 169, 187) says these may be lunatics whose madness takes the form of imagining themselves to be dogs. A modern instance is King Otto of Bavaria (1848-1916), who succeeded to the throne in 1886. He lived for more than 30 years in a padded room of Castle Fürstenried, where his food was served on dishes placed upon the floor to the accompaniment of his furious barking. However, the MSS disagree. The reading 'dog-men' is found only in MS **P**. MS **V** has 'a bad thing for men', which seems to be corrupt. And MS **A** has 'dog-leaders', i.e. 'masters of the pack'. Still another possibility is that the reading should be 'those eaten by dogs', which would refer to unwanted infants who were abandoned in cemeteries outside the cities, where they were sometimes devoured by wild dogs.

[2]The reference is to marriage with a unattractive woman, one of low degree, or even a slave. Obviously such wives would involve the husband in social difficulties.

these will wander about abroad. And if the ruler of the twelfth house is found in the ASC, it makes the [native's] youth more toilsome. And if the ruler of the twelfth house is found in the DSC angle, it will make the old age of this one more miserable.

And if the ruler of the nativity is found in the twelfth, say that the native is a slave or low-born or an outcast or that he is injured. And if the ruler of the twelfth house is found with the Sun, say that the father is cheap or the patrimony is destroyed. And similarly also in the case of the Moon, the things of the mother.

And if Saturn or Mars is found to be ruler of the twelfth house and it is in the ASC, it prognosticates those who are eaten by dogs or by wild beasts or those who are fond of hunting with dogs. And if the ruler of the ninth house is in the twelfth and if it is with Saturn, it makes shipwrecks for this one or dangers in the sea if a benefic does not aspect the scheme. And if it is found with Mars in the twelfth house, it makes attacks by soldiers or pirates against this one abroad or on the road.

And if the Ascending Node is in the twelfth house and the Sun and the Moon are found there with Mars and Mercury, he will fall into misery or a bone of his will be broken or he is blinded or he is burned in a fire or ill-fated in his end or he is destroyed by enemies, especially if Saturn is also with them. But if Jupiter and Venus are there, he is delivered to some extent from evils, but [he is] ill-fated in his end. But if Jupiter and Venus are there alone, he may not suffer the worst, but he [will] acquire cheap[1] property or he will have good luck from slaves.

If the Descending Node is in the twelfth house and Mars and Saturn are there or they aspect it, it will be best of all. For he will find a windfall, or he will be given a share in the property of others. And if Jupiter and Venus are there alone, without [any] aspect of Saturn or Mars or Mercury, he will be insistent [in his behavior] towards his wife and children, and he will have an internal in-

---

[1] The text seems a bit shaky here.

jury or [one] in the spleen. And if the Sun and Mars and Mercury aspect each other and Saturn is found there, he will be very unfortunate in his whole life.

Saturn being in the sign of the Bad Daemon by night shows the loss of the inheritance and dangers and plots on account of slaves, and those who are [mentally] disturbed or perverts. But by day, the god[1] will be more moderate in these [matters]. And if he squares or opposes the Moon, it will be indicative of inconstancy and decline unless Jupiter aspecting either the Moon or Saturn causes a partial overturn of the rulers. And they experience severe illnesses, and they have internal pains.

Jupiter being in the sign of the Bad Daemon prognosticates fights and dangers and litigation[2] against superiors. And always this god in these signs[3] is not benefic, especially by night.

Mars being in the signs that constitute the Bad Daemon is the cause of sicknesses and injuries. And they also experience dangers and treacheries, [and] not few [either] on account of slaves or condemned persons and associated persons, especially by day. But by night the evils become more moderate. For this god being angular in the IMC by day is generally destructive.

The Sun being in the sign of the Bad Daemon makes the parents lower-born or slaves or captives, and some experience injuries or sicknesses.

Venus being in the sign of the Bad Daemon by night makes those who are distressed by the pretenses of women, but, if she is aspected by Saturn and Mercury or Mars, those involved in mental illnesses, that is [those of an] erotic [nature]. Some of them too marry slaves or courtesans, on which account they remain childless. And being in this house by day, it signifies those who are

---

[1]Saturn. (It is interesting to note that this term was not altered by the Christian copyists of the middle ages.)
[2]The Greek term *krisiologias* is found only in this passage of Rhetorius.
[3]That is, in the 12th house.

badly and violently ruined by women, according to the physical nature of the signs. For the goddess has various and hard-to-find ways of doing business, through which also the affairs of life are guided.

And if Mercury chances to be in the sign of the Bad Daemon, it begets those who take care of major affairs or even employees of the state, those who are endangered by others' affairs but who also are happy in them. Being vespertine in this house, he becomes a busybody.

For not without cause and just as it happened, but rightly Hermes marked the house for childbirth, while the fate of the one giving birth was at hand, if she was pregnant [and] with the opposite sign sympathizing with it, from which house the stars in combination render the actions less effective.[1]

The star of Mercury being in this house will produce grammarians, orators, geometers, [and] students that have used words, or those becoming benefactors of men in distress[2] through speech, and those who are considerably wiser than the rest. But if it is opposed by Mars, becoming evil, it will condemn [the native] on account of state-secrets or forgeries or [mis]management or on account of slaves, or it will force [him] into a judgment.

If the Moon is in the sign of the Bad Daemon . . .[3]

---

[1]This paragraph is an interpolation, or at least it is misplaced, for it has nothing to do with Mercury's signification in the 12th house. However, it is found in exactly the same place in the *Mathesis*, so it goes back to the common source, presumably Antiochus of Athens. Two items in it are noteworthy. First, it attributes the assignment of this particular house rulership to Hermes, thus perhaps pointing to the origin of this whole set of house rulerships. Second, the word *moira* 'part' or 'share' is here used in the sense of 'fate', common enough elsewhere but unusual in astrological Greek, where its usual meaning is 'degree'.

[2]The Greek text has *homoiôn*, literally 'of the same', which could mean 'of the same rank'. But Bidez thinks *homoiôn* is corrupt, noting that Firmicus has *laborantibus* 'toiling' or 'suffering'. I have assumed the Greek should read *poneontôn* with similar meaning. (Bidez suggests *kindyneuontôn* 'venturesome'.)

[3]MS **P** preserves the beginning of this section; MSS **AV** omit the entire section.

The Ascendant (First House).

The first house is called the [house] of life; and on account of this [fact] it is so-called: because after the rising of the [house] of the Bad Daemon this very sign rises and after the passing of the climacteric it is examined closely and the one giving birth and the newborn, and because they have both gone from dangers and shadows into the light and life. And it is called *tiller*, and we term it the "first house" because the beginning of the investigation[1] becomes known to the mathematicians[2] from there; and also it is indicative of both breath and *basis*.[3] The [star] of Mercury rejoices when it is present in this house because breathing was established through speech.

And whenever one of the benefics is in the ASC without the aspect of the malefics, and with the ruler of the ASC well situated and the rulers of the triplicity of the ASC [likewise], the native will be well nourished, and he will have a fine first age [of life]. But if one of the malefics is in the ASC and it aspects the Sun and the Moon, say that those that are born will not be reared or will be short-lived or injured or sickly or ending up in orphan hood. But when the Sun is in the ASC in his own triplicity, say that the natives are first-born or first-raised; and he will bestow rulership and advancement without the aspect of the malefics. And Saturn in the ASC declares the natives to be first-born or first-raised. And Venus in the ASC declares the natives to be cheerful, agreeable, fond of the arts, promiscuous, and not marrying well. And Mercury in the ASC makes the natives intelligent, prudent, [and] ingenious. And Mars in the ASC makes them hot-headed, reckless, daring, and foolhardy; and sometimes too they are injured or sickly. And he makes a quick birth or one on the road[4] or in the bath. And the

---

[1] That is, the interpretation of the horoscope (and also the construction of the houses of the horoscope).

[2] That is, the astrologers.

[3] The *foundation* of the horoscope (because it is the principal house and because the other houses are reckoned from it); hence it is the foundation of the native's life.

[4] This sort of thing happens. I myself have two cousins who were born in taxicabs

[star] of Jupiter, if he is in the ASC without the malefics, always makes famous persons, commanders,[1] [or] rulers[2] of their own fatherland.

And the Lot of Fortune and its ruler in the ASC, lying in the house, matutine, oriental, unaspected by the malefics, will make such persons fortunate [and] long-lived. The ruler of the ASC being under the Sun beams and [also] the Lot of Fortune and the rulers of the lights will make short-lived persons. But if the ruler of the Good Daemon[3] is in the ASC, it makes [the native] wealthy in youth and the scheme [of the nativity] good. And Mercury matutine in the ASC with the Sun or the Moon in a feminine sign and feminine degrees will make such persons to have their necessary [parts] cut off.[4]

The ruler of injury and the ruler of the Lot of Injury in the ASC in tropical signs make both him and his parents crippled. If the ruler of the 7th house is in the ASC such a one will take a wife hostile to himself. If the ruler of the 9th house is in the ASC without the ray of the malefics, such a one will live well in a foreign land. If the dodecatemorion of the lights is in the ASC, proclaim that the parents are well-born. If the Lots of the Parents are in the ASC by night, the parents are well-born.

Venus in the ASC in a feminine sign makes the mother to be more well-born and richer and longer-lived than the father. And in the case of Jupiter, consider from the ASC: if Jupiter is in the ASC in a feminine sign, say that the mother is more well-born; Jupiter in the ASC in a bicorporeal sign makes the native to have two fathers

---

on the way to the hospital. An ancient instance is the Roman poet Virgil, whose mother was seized with birth pangs while walking along the road with her husband one day.

[1] The Greek word *hêgemonas* 'leaders' designates high officials, either military or civil.

[2] The word *archontas* 'rulers' generally designates a high municipal official, such as a city councilman.

[3] The 11th house.

[4] The 'necessary parts' are the male genitals. "That is, eunuchs," add MSS **AV**.

or two names; and Venus in the ASC in a bicorporeal sign also makes these same things.

Mercury in the ASC, if in a feminine sign, gives advancements and status to the native through his wife. Mercury in the ASC in a bicorporeal sign makes guardians of children belonging to others.[1] And Saturn angular with the Sun while the Sun is eclipsed in a day birth makes the native [to be involved] in captivities and imprisonments and slavery; and if Venus and Mercury are with [them], they become eunuchs. {The Sun and Venus in the ASC in Leo in a day birth make such ones to be eaters of forbidden foods beyond the needs of life.}[2] But Saturn and Venus in the ASC in a house of Saturn or Venus make such ones to have intercourse with their own daughters or sisters. But if the Moon is also in aspect, it will make those committing incest with their mothers or their aunts.[3] But if the Moon is not in aspect, but Mars aspects the configuration, it

---

[1] In MSS **AV**, the passage " Jupiter in the ASC . . . belonging to others." is as follows. "With Venus or Jupiter in the ASC in a bicorporeal [sign], say that the native has two fathers or two names. And with Mercury in the ASC, if it is in a bicorporeal sign, there will be advancements and status for the natives through the wife."

[2] The sentence in braces is found in MS **P** but not in MSS **AV**. The eating of forbidden foods is also noted by Ptolemy, *Tetrabiblos*, iii. 13 (Section 159); Vettius Valens, *Anthology* IV, xv (p.184,4-6); and Manetho IV, 564. But in these references it is mentioned in connection with impiety, which arises from Mars and Saturn afflictions, especially when involving the third or ninth houses, which are the houses of religion. The Sun with Venus in Leo in the ASC has nothing to do with impiety, so either this is an inept citation of positions in an actual horoscope or else the passage as it stands is defective (e.g., "day birth....make such ones"). The phrase "beyond the needs of life" is a conjecture of the meaning of the Greek *hyper chromt biou* with some word such as *chreian* 'need' in place of the meaningless *chromt* 'colors' (?) of the MS. Cumont inserted the "doubtful" conjecture *bromata* 'foods' in his text, but it doesn't seem to make much sense.

Cumont (*L'Égypte des astrologues*, pp. 150-1 and p. 150, n.4) suggests that these "eaters of forbidden foods" are religious ascetics who frequented the temples (and presumably ate some of the food offerings). But Ptolemy describes a character type who was a law unto himself, eating whatever he wanted to eat, and Vettius Valens evidently had in mind a person who rejected religion and the rules associated with it, possibly in favor of another religion with a different set of rules. For example, a Jew who turned Christian and began to eat pork, or a man who turned away from the old gods and showed his disdain for them by eating the sacrificial offerings.

[3] Similar indications are found in Dorotheus, *Pentateuch*, ii,4,20.

produces a buyer of women or it makes damages among these same [natives] from a cause of this sort.[1]

If the Ascending Node chances to be in the ASC, and Jupiter and Venus chance to be there without [the presence of] Saturn and Mars, [the native] will be a man great and fortunate in his city. And if the Moon is configured with them, the good will be better. And if the Sun is also present in this house or if he aspects them, he will be even more fortunate; for such [natives] will become magnates or tyrants[2] But if both Saturn and Mars aspect them or are also present in the ASC, he will have a miserable youth and [will experience] loss, and he will have pains in his eyes, and he will not be successful in anything until he passes his 36th year. But when he has passed [that age], he will be delivered from all the evils. But if Saturn and Mars along with the Sun and the Moon encounter Jupiter and Venus by presence or by aspect, his bones will be broken[3] or he will be blinded or he will have a cut from an accident, and whatever he gets he will lose, and sometimes in fact [the native] will die violently.

If the Descending Node chances to be in the ASC and Saturn and Mars chance to be there without any aspect from the benefics, the scheme [of the nativity] is entirely satisfactory, for [the native] will be well-known and noble and wealthy. But if both Mercury and the Sun are present with them, the scheme is evil for the father, for he will endure damages and controversies and entanglements. But if both Jupiter and Venus chance to be there alone with the Descending Node, this is the worst [condition] for the native, especially if the Moon is also present with them, for he will be ordinary and will acquire nothing.

When the [star] of Saturn chances to be in the rising sign by day, it will produce a loud outcry and those things that are done for the

---

[1] MSS **AV** have "they marry slave girls or the they incur damage from a cause of this sort."
[2] That is, absolute rulers of a city or state.
[3] Literally, 'injured'.

native through sound.¹ And it also makes those who are first born or first reared or a lack of brothers before him; and always this god being present in the angles makes those who are first born or first reared or it destroys the brothers before him. But by night it brings about damages and opposition and hardships, and by night also actions in wet <places>.

Jupiter being in sect in the ascending sign will make notable persons, ingenious, leaders in war, those living pleasantly, and also those of good courage. But when he is out of sect in this house he will make those who are first born or first reared [or] he destroys the brothers [born] before them; and in addition he makes those who grow up well and in happiness with their parents, but those who destroy the things of their parents and lose their own. And always this god, when he is angular, makes those who are first born or first reared or he makes the destruction of the elder brothers.

The star of Mars being in sect in the ascending sign will produce military commanders, soldiers, troop commanders,² rulers of life and death, terrible [in their actions] against cities and countries. But when he is out of sect in this house, he prognosticates hot-blooded, reckless individuals, those living abroad, fickle in their opinions and failing in their undertakings, and mostly craftsmen in fire or iron, or those who get their living from military service.

The Sun being in the rising sign, in the same angle [with Saturn],³ will produce kings or commanders; but if the [star] of Mars is with them or aspects them by square or opposition they will have

---

¹I don't know what this means. Firmicus, *Mathesis* iii. 2.1, has simply *cum summo clamore edi partum* 'to be born with the loudest outcry', which I take to be the first cry of the newborn.

²I have translated *polemarchous* as 'military commanders' and *stratopedarchas* as 'troop commanders', but both terms obviously refer to individuals with authority over important military forces. In my present state of knowledge it is not possible to define the terms more precisely, or for that matter to distinguish between them.

³Adds Cumont from Firmicus, *Mathesis*, iii. 5.2.

their kingdoms or their commands [beset] with jealousies and dangers and wars. But by night this god being in the ascending sign indicates that the parents will be lower class. And in the said house, aspected by Saturn or Mars by square or opposition or conjoined to them, he [the Sun] will become the destroyer of the elder brothers, either of their life or of all their possessions and their actions.[1] But always the Sun, when he is in the angular parts of the signs will become the destroyer[2] of the elder brothers, but it also indicates that some [of the natives] are first born or first nourished.

Venus being in sect in the ascending sign will produce demigods in thought, magnates, those having great friends, friends of kings, and those who are entrusted with the business affairs of princes, worthy professors according to the particular nature of the sign, for in the signs of human form they will be high priests adorned with gold,[3] bearers of golden objects, possessing a dignity derived from the gods, predicting the future, the greatest in the world.[4]

And in the half-voiced signs[5] [she makes] crafty[6] hunters, very agressive, friends of kings, those who construct marvelous things fit to be displayed to kings, those who receive allowances from kings and who become wealthy thereby. And in the earth or water

---

[1] Firmicus, *Mathesis*, iii. 5, makes the phrase "...either...actions." apply to the native rather than to the brothers. Rhetorius's text is ambiguous, but it seems to apply to the brothers (where I have written 'their' it actually says merely 'the').

[2] Reading *anairetikos* 'destroyer' instead of *achrêstos* 'useless'. Firmicus, *ibid.*, "he destroys the older brothers."

[3] The Greek text is shaky here: Cumont adopts *chrysokomêtoi* 'golden-haired' from MS **P**, but in *L'Égypte des astrologues*, p. 177n.4, he emends it to *chrysokosmêtikoi* 'adorned with gold'; MSS **AV** have *chryson kosmoumenoi* 'adorned with gold'. Firmicus agrees with **AV**, for he has *auratis vestibus induantur* 'dressed in golden garments'.

[4] We have here a picture of the pagan clergy dressed in cloth of gold and carrying golden religious objects in procession—a picture faithfully copied by the Christian priests who supplanted them.

[5] Presumably the "ruminant signs"—Aries, Taurus, Sagittarius, and Capricorn.

[6] The Greek word is *poikilous* which means 'spotted' (like a fish), which suggests a hunter in what we would call *camouflage*, but most likely it was used metaphorically here.

[signs] it prognosticates perfumers, or else those with a good wardrobe,[1] or dyers. And in the quadrupedal [signs] it will make haughty individuals, fond of praise, good, fond of nurturing animals, or in charge of animals. But when she is out of sect in the rising sign she will make sexually promiscuous persons, reprehensible, lustful, indecent. But they also become linen-weavers or makers of clothes or of pigments or dyes, and inventors of some foods or drinks.[2]

The [star] of Mercury being in the rising sign by day will produce philosophers [and] grammarians, and sometimes also orators or geometers or those who know the secrets of the heavens or take care of the revenues of the gods or those who know about secret transactions. Aspected by any of those [planets] of the sect, it indicates magnates, those crowned with a wreath, [and] those entrusted with the transactions of kings. And when Mars is casting an aspect by opposition or square or by partile conjunction, it becomes thrice evil; but [if] by a trine aspect, you must judge the result to be more effective and better. And being in the ascending sign by night he produces persons who are semi-divine in their thoughts and capable in their efforts and elegant in their way of living, and those who take care of governmental departments or disbursements or accounting or tax revenues,[3] accomplished according to the nature of the sign.

The Moon being in sect in the ascending sign, making application to none [of the planets], will be judged to be not good. But being in the same angle of the ASC, she will produce those in command, rulers, magnates, [and] kings, when Mars is not posited in opposition to her, and when Saturn is not with her and is not joined

---

[1]Firmicus has 'those who make fine clothes', what we would call couturiers. A third possibility is 'those who offer fine clothes for sale'.

[2]Firmicus has '. . . linen-weavers or embroiderers or inventors of pigments and dyers or inn-keepers or tavern keepers'.

[3]MSS **AV** have the interpolation *daimonikôn* 'of those possessed [by a demon]', their scribes having misunderstood *telonikôn* 'of taxes', a word derived from *telonion*, which was a 'custom-house' in Classical Greek but a 'demon' in medieval and modern Greek.

to her either by opposition or square aspect. For in those same configurations, aspected in that way by them or by either one of the two, she will make short-lived [infants] or else those that are exposed or those who die violently, according to the nature of the signs.¹ Being in sect in the ascending sign, she will produce priests who handle temple funds or high priests or those who preside over the sacred games or who have actions and benefits in sacred things, if indeed she happens to be attended by the stars of the sect. And the doryphory is when the Moon is in the preceding part [of the figure], i.e. the western, [and] the stars are following. For the stars make a doryphory to the Sun in their matutine appearances, but to the Moon, as was just said, in their vespertine [appearances].²

And in general, when the Moon is void of course in the important houses of the nativity, no good will be produced. You are helped to decide [by noting] in which house of the nativity she is [and] what phase she was allotted, for in the ascending sign by day, being angular, she will produce ship-masters or pirates or those in charge of places that are difficult to traverse.³ But when she is seen by the [star] of Mars by conjunction or by opposition or square aspect, she will become the cause of injuries and sicknesses, or in

---

¹Accepting the reading of MSS **AV**.
²Here we have a partial definition of the term *doryphory*. A doryphory is an attendance upon the ruler of the sect by one or more of the planets. The term is variously defined, and indeed the definition given in Chapters 23-25 above does not seem to fit the present case, which agrees better with the definition given by Paul of Alexandria, *Introduction*, Chapter 14. What Rhetorius is saying here is that the Moon in the ASC is especially favorable when she is ruler of the sect and when Venus and Mars (and possibly Mercury) are lower down in the first house, so that they will rise after her. [Cumont notes that MSS **AV** omit this definition, which may therefore be an interpolation. This would explain why it doesn't agree with the earlier definition, but we must remember that Rhetorius was a compiler, and the ultimate sources for Chapters 23-25 and the present chapter may have been different.]
³Literally, 'commanders of hard-to-pass places'. Firmicus, *Mathesis*, iii. 13.2, translates it as *inaccessorum locorum praepositos iudices* 'judges in charge of inaccessible places', where the word 'judges' refers to civil authorities who also excercised legal functions in remote places. The famous Texas Judge Roy Bean (1825-1903) "The Law West of the Pecos" comes to mind as a modern instance.

general she will even make [the native] short-lived and dying violently.

The Second House.

The second house is called *livelihood* and *Gate of Hades* and *idle* house. The benefics dwelling in this house are more idle; however, they denote fine things that are hoped for, and they grant hopes from things of the dead, since the house is established as the succedent to the ASC. But when the malefics are present in this house, they make impractical and lazy individuals and injuries around the eyes. And if the Lot of Fortune is there, and its ruler and the ruler of the ASC, and if these are malefics and behold the house, they make guardians of the dead and those who spend their lives outside of town;[1] and these also are eaten by dogs; sometimes too they are cast out by their parents.[2]

Similarly, when Saturn is present in this house and is the ruler of the Lot of Fortune and/or the ASC, it makes listless, sickly persons . . .[3]

[When Jupiter is present in this house]. . . ,[4] or it will make receipt of money.

When the [star] of Mars is ruler of the Lot of Fortune or else of

---

[1] 'Guardians of the dead' are what we would call 'cemetery caretakers'. The cemeteries of ancient towns were outside the walls. Guards were employed to ward off grave-robbers, both human and canine, for packs of starving dogs surrounded the cities. These caretakers were shunned by the citizens, and either chose to or were obliged to live outside the town.

[2] This is not quite clear. The first phrase seems to refer to caretakers caught unaware and devoured by dogs, but the second phrase refers to the practice of exposing unwanted infants. These unfortunate babies were carried out into the cemeteries and abandoned, where in some cases they were promptly seized and eaten by wild dogs.

[3] The Greek has *nekropsychous* 'dead-spirited', probably referring to acute depression. The rest of the signification of Saturn is lost (Vettius Valens, *Anthology*, ii. 14, says they will experience imprisonment (in the beginning of the signification of Jupiter).

[4] Something is missing in the Greek text.

the ASC and is present in the second house, it makes the greatest losses for the native; and sometimes too it makes injuries around the eyes. But if Venus is found in the house, he will also have injuries from women, and let the [particular kind of] evil be chosen according to the nature of the star whose sign it is. And if Mars is found in his own face,[1] sometimes too they become prison guards or those who gain their livelihood from prisons.

If the Sun is present in this sign, ruling the Lot of Fortune or the ASC, partilely in his own face, with Mars in the ASC in a sign of Saturn, the native loses his eyesight in the period of Mars and he will beg, or else he will be deprived of his inheritance.

If the [star] of Venus is present in this house, ruling the Lot of Fortune or the ASC, the natives will leave their native country; or they will have acts having to do with wet things if she is matutine. But if she is vespertine, they take refuge in the temples of female gods, abounding in necessary things, or they preserve the mysteries of the gods and their rites. They will have a good old age.

If the [star] of Mercury, being under the Sun beams, is present in this house, he makes those who are uninitiated and unlettered. But if he is oriental,[2] such persons are intelligent and inquisitive, and they take up those things which they have not learned about, and they become skilled in astrology.

If the Moon is present in the second house, and Saturn is in the ASC, such a one will have cataracts in his eyes.

If a malefic beholds the second house by square or opposition or conjunction,[3] it signifies the loss of livelihood for the native. And if the second house is the domicile of Venus, such a one will sustain losses for the sake of women or through the agency of women.

---

[1] 'Face' is another name for 'decan'.
[2] Literally, 'rising', but here it means "rising before the Sun." Valens also has 'oriental' and Firmicus has 'matutine', which amounts to the same thing.
[3] Note that the aspect is not to a planet in the house but to the empty sign constituting the house. This type of aspect was also employed by the French astrologer J. B. Morin in his *Astrologia Gallica*.

And if [it is] the domicile of Mercury, for the sake of learning or calculations or inheritances or separations. And if [it is] the domicile of Jupiter, he will have his loss from magnates or public affairs. And if [it is] the domicile of Mars, say that the loss is from military affairs or suchlike persons, or from war, or burning, or a fight or from robbery or from highway robbers.[1] If [it is] the domicile of Saturn, say that the loss is from old people or slaves or freedmen, for the sake of land or inheritance, or from tombs or the affairs of the dead, or from worthless persons. If it is the domicile of the Sun, it will make the loss to be from the father, or from paternal relatives or elders, or on account of loans, or some monies, or business affairs. And if it is the domicile of the Moon, on account of the mother, or the maternal kindred, or the step-mother, or suchlike persons.

And it seems to me[2] that in each domicile and house that is damaged by a malefic that the loss is shown forth by the nature of the ruler of the sign, if it is a malefic, and the significations by the house. And if you want to cast the Lot of Livelihood, according to Dorotheus take always by night and day [the distance] from the ruler of the second house up to the second house itself,[3] and cast the result from the ASC; and wherever it leaves off, [there is] the lot. Look at the ruler of the lot and the sign itself in which the lot fell. And if the lot and its ruler chance to be in a good house without any aspects from the malefics, say that his livelihood will be good. But if the ruler of the lot is found making its morning setting seven days after the birth . . .[4] but if [instead it is in its] morning rising, it will make hidden and secret wealth.

---

[1] I have so translated ê *lêstrikôn* ê *ephodikôn prosôpôn*, lit. 'or robbing or traveling persons'. The roads were not secure in ancient times, and travellers were frequently assaulted by roving bands of robbers. *Cf.* Cumont, *L'Égypte des Astrologues*, pp. 65-68.
[2] Rhetorius himself is speaking.
[3] That is, count the signs from the planet to the 2nd house, and then count off the same number of signs from the ASC. All of the lots were originally determined by counting the signs from one point to the other. Counting from the degree of one point to the degree of the other was a later development.
[4] The effect produced by this configuration is missing.

If the Ascending Node is found in the [house of] livelihood, and Jupiter and Venus and the Sun and Mercury happen to be there, he will acquire property, and he will be trustworthy and fond of money. But if Saturn and Mars and the Moon behold them, he will be unstable in youth, and he will reverse himself, and he will be in a bad state until he comes to his 35th year, after which he will be delivered and will acquire property. But if Saturn and Mars happen to be there alone without the aspect of Jupiter and Venus, he will be unlucky; and sometimes too, ill-fated in his end.

But if the Descending Node is found in [the house of] livelihood, it will be very bad for his father, for he will have penalties and false accusations. But if Saturn and Mars happen to be there, it is the best configuration, for he gets property for himself from unpleasant activities, and from murders, and from activities having to do with the dead or from the destruction of a house by some unexpected action. But if Jupiter and Venus happen to be there, whatever he gets will be bad luck for him.

Saturn[1] happening to be in the succedent of the rising sign [by night][2] will make the loss of children and sizable disturbances and reduction of livelihood and being put to shame[3] and loss of the paternal and maternal [inheritance]; and it prognosticates those who are lazier in their actions and also some who are stricken by bodily illness. But by day it prognosticates those who experience increase in their livelihood with the passage [of time], but who are undistinguished and poor in spirit, and some getting their living from watery things.

Jupiter chancing to be in the succedent of the ascendant by day or by night prognosticates inheritances from other than his family,

---

[1] And here Rhetorius begins a second set of significations for planets in the 2nd house. He does this for each house, evidently having found two different sources for the significations.

[2] Added by Cumont, having compared Firmicus, *Mathesis*, iii. 2.4, which also omits "by night," but gives the contrasting effects of the diurnal position in *Mathesis*, iii. 2.6.

[3] *Cf.* Vettius Valens, *Anthology*, p. 43,26 et al.

and those who are adopted by someone, and lords of lands and buildings.

The [star] of Mars chancing to be in the [house] of livelihood by day makes estrangements from one's own [country] and dwelling abroad; and it makes injuries and cuts from iron for the natives. But if the Moon happens to be in an angle or in a succedent, it will injure the natives by a fall[1] from a height or from a quadruped, but [it makes] some who experience exposure[2] or captivity or enslavement; they also become abandoned and [find themselves] in straitened circumstances, not in anything favorable. But if the [star] of Jupiter or the [star] of Venus is bearing testimony to this [star], the ensuing dangers are traversed [safely] and they escape [from their] enslavement. They will not lack the necessities of life, but sometimes they will have [them] and at other times they will be pinched. But by night the god[3] is ready for military campaigns and for combat, but it also prognosticates dangers for them in these activities and glories(?).

When the Sun chances to be in the succedent of the ASC, it prognosticates private owners [of property] and a pleasant existence.

When Venus chances to be in the [house] of livelihood by day, it prognosticates contrarities and or late marriages and disputes with female persons; but some also see the death of their wives, however, it does not bring about living poorly in old age. But by night, it signifies those who are both more prosperous and who with the passage of time are more fortunate, and who are delightful in making love and are [generally] pleasing.

When Mercury chances to be matutine in the [house] of livelihood by night, it will produce foolish persons, those who are devious, strangers to letters,[4] and lacking [a sufficiency] in their liveli-

---

[1]Reading *ptôseos* 'fall' instead of *phyxeos* 'flight'. Cf. Valens, *Anthology* i. 20.6.
[2]That is, exposure as an unwanted infant.
[3]Mars.
[4]That is, 'only semiliterate'.

hood. But when it is vespertine by night in this house, it will produce money-lenders, merchants or managers of others' [property], [and] clever trustees; but by day, those fond of learning or singleminded or peculiar [in some way], learning those things which they have not been taught, living in filth and those who punish themselves. If the ruler of the preceding conjunction chances to be in this house, it makes losses of livelihood.[1]

{And he will encounter sickness, and he will be in straitened circumstances. But if Saturn and Mars happen to be there and they bear witness to the house, he will suffer severely in youth, and after that he will be in good [circumstances], getting possessions from princes and kings, and he will be notable and a tyrant. And he will be a worthless sort of person, and he will not consider anyone, because Mars and Saturn rejoice in [conjunction with] the Descending Node. But if Saturn chances to be there with Venus, he will be unstable in [his relationships with] women. And after this, he will be in fine [circumstances], and he will live 70 years.}[2]

The Third House.

The third house is called [the house] of the *Moon Goddess*.[3] overshadowed, authoritative, [and] *metacosmic*.[4] It signifies the topic of foreign [things] and that of dreams and religious observance and banking and friends and brothers and the queen.

---

[1] Cumont thinks the sentence 'If the ruler....livelihood.' is an interpolation.

[2] In MS **P**, this paragraph enclosed in braces is found in place of the latter part of the preceding paragraph (from 'but by day, those fond of....livelihood.') It does not appear in MSS **A** or **V** (nor in Firmicus). Cumont says it may belong to the section on the Moon in the 2nd house, although it is not found in Firmicus. I think not. It mentions the Descending Node, and therefore belongs to one of the sections detailing the influence of the node in the houses, which are only mentioned in connection with the third house.

[3] It is the house in which the Moon rejoices and is usually called "the House of the Goddess." *Cf.* the 9th house.

[4] The word *metakosmios* 'metacosmic' is unusual. But the term 'metacosmic' is applied to all of the cadent houses, so it probably simply means 'after the cosmic [house]', i.e. 'after the angular house', since the word *kosmikos* can refer to the angular houses (*Cf.* Vettius Valens, *Anthology*, ii. 18.6, *kosmika kentra*).

If then the Moon chances to be in the 3rd, having the rulership of the ASC or the Lot of Fortune, especially in her own face, and of the sect, and full, and adding to her numbers,[1] the native will be great, rich, one who gives advice from the gods, and he will have various moneys from sacred places, and he will rule cities. But if the Sun is with the Moon following the new Moon, he will be a priest. But if the [star] of Saturn is with the Moon, he will be a haruspex, a person fond of lawsuits, one causing damage, suffering from the wrath of a god, [or] a blasphemer against the god;[2] if Jupiter is with the Moon, a soothsayer, an interpreter of oracles, [or] a rich person; if Mars is with the Moon, he will be energetic and a robber of things belonging to others, but if they are in their own places[3] faces, especially by night, there is produced a general, a perjurer for the sake of gold, sometimes too he is killed because of the wrath of the queen.

But if the Lot of Fortune is present with the [star] of Venus in her face, especially by night, and the Moon, ruling the Lot, is there with [her] in her own face, the native will be great, rich, and he will receive kindness from a woman, and some too spend time in positions of authority, and they also deal in spices. But if the [star] of Mercury happens to be there with the Moon in [one of] his own faces and ruling the ASC or the Lot of Fortune, the native will foretell the future like a god, and he will take part in secret mysteries,[4] and he will be a participant in celestial things, and experienced, and those receiving divine warnings in dreams, and like a prophet. But the Sun being present with the Moon will make those dwelling abroad. And the ruler of the ASC being there will cause dwelling abroad.

But the ruler of the third well situated by phase or house [or] ex-

---

[1] That is, "swift" in motion.
[2] Vettius Valens, *Anthology*, ii. 14.3, has *theous* 'gods' instead of *to theion* 'the god'.
[3] Cf. Valens, *Anthology*, ii. 14.5, 'if [Mars] chances to be in domicile in his own face'.
[4] That is, he will be a participant in one of the secret rites called *mysteries* by the Greeks.

altation, aspected by a benefic, will make such persons to be friends of great men and will give benefits from friends and brothers, especially if a benefic chances to be in this house. But if a malefic chances to be in this house, they make damages from friends and on account of brothers.[1] Sometimes too, they make blasphemers and dangers abroad.

Saturn and Mercury being in the third make revelations from dreams, and mysterious things. The Lot of Marriage being in the third says the marriage will take place abroad or with a foreign woman. Venus being in the third bestows favors from women and gifts on the native.

The ruler of the 6th or the 12th being in the 3rd makes hypocrisies and betrayals by friends and damages from enemies; sometimes too they make injury and sickness [when the native is] abroad. The ruler of the 3rd being in the 2nd or the 6th makes assaults by bandits on the road.[2] The ruler of the 5th and the 11th being in the 3rd makes good and profitable sojourns abroad and friendships. The ruler of the 7th being in the 3rd makes foreign marriages. If the 3rd is found encompassing a bicorporeal sign and the ruler of the 3rd is in a bicorporeal sign, say that the brothers are born of others and other parents and not of the same father or the same mother. If the two Lghts are found in different cadent [houses], say that the parents are of another race.

If the 3rd is in Cancer [or] Leo and Jupiter is with in aspect with Venus or Mercury, it signifies good luck. If Saturn and Mars aspect this house, they make vagabonds and bad friends; but if a

---

[1] Or, possibly, 'damages along with friends and for the sake of brothers'.
[2] The Greek text has *klêmatikous en odô* 'vine-twigs on the road', which is an obvious blunder. Cumont suggests *ktêmatikous* 'property-owners', which is no better, but in his *L'Égypte des Astrologues*, p. 66, n.2., he calls attention to a similar prediction for a 12th house position ...*lêstrikas ephodous...en odô* 'assaults by bandits on the road'. He points out that the countryside was not secure in classical times, and inter-city travelers were often robbed or murdered by highwaymen or other attackers. These hazards are frequently mentioned by the astrologers. Another possibility is *klimaktêrous en odô* 'critical (illnesses or accidents) on the road'.

good [star aspects], trusty friends. If the 3rd is in Sagittarius being aspected by Jupiter [and] Venus, he will be very lucky, if it is [a] day[time nativity]; but if Mars is configured with them, it makes military commanders. If Saturn [and] Mercury aspect this house, [they make] grammarians, orators, sophists. If Saturn is well-configured, it makes administrators and trustees; if Venus, a secret, rich, and fortunate marriage, especially if it is rising by night. Venus and Mercury in the faces of Jupiter, and the malefics being of the sect in those signs in which they rejoice, produce good things. Jupiter and Saturn in the 3rd without Mars show good fortune.

If the 3rd is in Aries [or] Scorpio with Mars and Venus in aspect, they make those who commit adultery with their own friends or siblings,[1] especially with Mars and Venus in each other's terms. If in Aries or Scorpio or Libra with Mars in aspect, [they make] adulterers, especially in the terms or faces of Venus; but if aspected by Mars, he will have adulterous wives. If the 3rd is in Gemini or Virgo with Mars in aspect, it makes this [native] miserable because of his friends or along with his friends. If the ruler of the 3rd is found in a fertile sign aspected by a benefic, he will have many brothers. If the ruler of the 3rd is found in the 2nd or the 11th or the 10th or the 9th, it shows younger and elder brothers; but if it is in the ASC, [the native is] first-born or an only child. If the ruler of the 3rd is found in a good house or in its exaltation, it makes [the native] to enjoy feasting with his friends and it makes his life and skill to be lacking in nothing.

If the Ascending Node chances to be in the [house] of brothers and Jupiter and Venus and the Sun are there with the Moon or are aspecting [her], he will be grieved over a brother or lose one or will injure one. If the Descending Node chances to be in the [house] of brothers and Jupiter and Venus are there or are aspecting [it], this is the worst configuration for the parents. And if Saturn and Mars happen to be there, the evil is weakened by them, but the father at least is injured.

---

[1] Reading *moichous* 'adulterers' instead of *mochthous* 'hardships'. Cumont suggests *moicheias* 'adulteries'.

Saturn chancing to be in the [house] of the God[1] by day [makes] initiates, chiefs of the Magi, philosophers, prophesying portents from the gods; but it surrounds some of them with hindrances; but by night, recluses, inventors of apothegms, philosophers.

Jupiter chancing to be in the [house] of the God by day [makes] those predicting the future. Some too are consecrated and make portents; but by night unstable in their dreams and speaking falsely of the Gods, fond of gold.[2]

Mars chancing to be in the [house] of the God by day or by night [makes] those who are unpunished, sophists, fearful to the Gods, even if they swear falsely, those having an opportunity for deliverance. And they become fearful to daemons.[3]

The Sun chancing to be in the [house of the] Goddess [makes] God-fearing persons, those inspired by the gods, those having ignoble or servile duties in temples.[4] Venus being in [the house of] the God or the Goddess in sect denotes those involved with demons or those wearing rags in temples, speaking from God,[5] [and] philosophers. Such things are produced especially when Venus is

---

[1] Cumont notes that beginning with this paragraph most of the interpretations that follow apply to the 9th house (the House of the God) rather than to the 3rd house (the House of the Goddess). They are repeated in the section on the 9th house below. The missing interpretations were presumably similar to those found in *Mathesis*, Book iii.

[2] Cumont conjectures *philochrêsmous* 'fond of oracles' instead of *philochrysous* 'fond of gold'.

[3] The translation of this paragraph might need to be improved. Cumont notes in *L'Égypte des Astrologues*, pp. 136-7, that the Egyptians not only cast powerful spells that compelled demons to obey them but sometimes even directed such spells against the gods themselves.

[4] The Greek is awkward: 'those in temples who are ignoble in service or who have servile [duties]'. Firmicus (*Mathesis*, III.v.15) has 'ignoble duties in temples [or] a servile function'. Cumont, *L'Égypte des Astrologues*, p. 144, n. 2, mentions the care and feeding of the sacred cats as an example of the duties of some temple servants.

[5] Firmicus, *Mathesis*, iii. 6.17, says dirty, long-haired individuals haunted the temples and gave forth oracular utterances that were assumed to be divinely inspired. These were either demented persons or ascetics who had abandoned interest in such worldly things as their personal appearance. *Cf.* Cumont, *L'Égypte des Astrologues*, pp. 150-1.

aspected by Saturn. But by night Venus out of sect in these houses [makes] good prophets, [those who explain] prodigies, God-fearing persons, divines; some of them [are] in sacred orders or they have gifts.[1] When Saturn or Mars are in conjunction with her or in square or opposition, it makes disputes on account of women and quarrels and misfortunes and ingratitudes, especially in the tropical signs, for these signs have affinity with most of these things. But if the [star] of Jupiter is with this [star] or is in trine or square or opposition, it makes charming persons, successful, rulers of the goods of the wife.[2] Some become managers of women and live in [the households of] great men for the sake of feminine persons,[3] on account of whom they also advance.[4]

The [star] of Mercury chancing to be matutine in the [house of the] God [makes] haruspices, holy seers, augurs, physicians, astrologers, those who are inspired by the Gods, from which [activities] they also have their livelihood. In opposition to Mars it makes sacrilegious persons [or] temple-robbers; but, when it is vespertine, priests, mages, physicians, [and] craftsmen who contrive those things that they have not learned.[5]

---

[1]*Cf.* Firmicus, *Mathesis*, iii. 6.18, 'But on some she bestows offices or gifts from temples'.

[2]The last phrase seems to refer to the wife's dowry, which, under Roman law, was owned by the husband but could not be disposed of without the wife's consent. Firmicus, who was a lawyer by profession, has *qui in re dominentur uxoris* 'who own the wife's property', which is virtually an exact translation of the Greek. Since this was a normal condition of marriage, it seems pointless to mention it. And the following phrase speaks of 'managers of women' in the sense of 'business managers' or 'major domos'. Perhaps in Egypt women normally retained control of their own property after marriage, and this is a survival from the earliest days of astrology, when it dealt with Alexandrian society. Alternatively, the phrase may refer to wives with large dowries.

[3]The text has *thêlykôn prophaseôn* 'feminine pretexts' and the corresponding passage in the 9th house has *gynaikeôn prophaseis*, which amounts to the same thing. But Ptolemy, *Tetrabiblos*, iv. 4 (Sect. 179), has *thêlykôn prosôpôn* 'feminine persons', and this same phrase occurs elsewhere.

[4]Firmicus, *Mathesis*, iii. 6.19, speaks of those who 'stay in the palaces of kings or in the houses of powerful men in order to make those things which are needed by women...and on account of these things they gain advancement'.

[5]That is, those who are inventive and can devise new techniques.

The Moon being in the [house of the] Goddess[1] by night [makes] those who live abroad in honor [and] acquisitive persons. Some of them are also entrusted with the business affairs of women; and they are God-fearing. But by day, those who live abroad in dishonor, leading a life of wandering and danger. Some of them too have some ignoble [function] or servile duties in temples, or they embrace the god,[2] or they confess [their sins], and especially when Venus is aspected by malefics.

The Fourth House.

The fourth house is called the *Under-earth* angle and the time of old age. It signifies the topic of parents and property and hidden matters and the house in which one is born and foundations and the things happening after death. In horary charts or elections it signifies the action of the astrologer according to the aspect of the stars. For either Jupiter [or] Venus will bestow gain and praises or Saturn [or] Mars losses and condemnations on the astrologer.

Now a good old age and death [will result] from Jupiter or Venus being in this [house], but Mars or Saturn chancing to be there give not only a miserable death to the native, but also injury and suffering. And they totally destroy the ancestral [possessions]. Venus there makes bad marriages, but old age [will be] free from toil and trouble. The Moon aspected by Saturn or Mars makes hardships in secret places or on account of some secret matters, for it brings restrictions and imprisonment. These [natives] bury their wives and children. Aspected by the benefics, it brings profit from secret works. But if the Moon is in a domicile of Mars, aspected by a malefic, it signifies banishment and the loss of the paternal [inheritance], if in fact it is not in a domicile or in the exaltation of Jupiter.[3]

---

[1] As Cumont notes, this is wrong, since these presages belong to the House of the God (the 9th). *Cf.* Firmicus, *Mathesis*, iii. 13.8.

[2] Cumont, *L'Égypte des Astrologues*, p. 146, explains this phrase as meaning 'those who seek sanctuary in temples'.

[3] Something is wrong with the text, since the Moon cannot be at the same time in a

Saturn being there in sect in a domicile or in the exaltation of Jupiter shows finders of treasure, and, especially when it is stationary, loss of the parental [inheritance], but it will certainly give hidden things and it will destroy the children.

Jupiter being there makes profit from forbidden activities or from inheritances or the finding of treasure. But if this [native] is middle-aged, it shows loss, but gain in old age; and it shows the rising of good fortune and an easy death.

Venus being there aspected by Saturn or Mars, he will see the death of his wife. But if it is in a tropical [sign], it will destroy not just one, but many. And if she is found [there] alone [and] stationary, it makes not only adulterers, but also effeminates.

Mercury being there with Venus injures the matter of brothers and children. It makes prudent persons and false accusations and charges, but especially when it is aspected by Mars and posited in signs other than its own, but it will also give female sorcerers. In a house or the exaltation of Jupiter, he becomes the father of others' children and he begets children by a cripple.[1]

The Moon being there says that the mother is of lower birth, but if the ruler of her [sign] is cadent it certainly makes [her] a slave and [one who suffers] a miserable death. And understand these same things also in the case of the father [judging] from the Sun.

Saturn being with the Sun there, when the Sun is eclipsed, in a diurnal nativity, [the native] becomes a captive or is placed in detention. If Mercury and Venus aspect [Saturn], he becomes a eunuch. These same things happen also [when these configurations occur] in the other angles. Mars out of sect in the sign of another

---

house of Mars and a house of Jupiter, but perhaps he means '<if the malefic> is not in a domicile or in the exaltation of Jupiter'.

[1]Literally, *hypo tinos sesinomenou* 'by someone injured'. The participle has a masculine ending, which must be a mistake if my interpretation is correct. If the Greek text is correct, then perhaps 'begets' should be replaced by 'adopts'.

[planet] makes [the native] struck by a poisonous animal. The ruler of this opposing the house or in the 6th or the 8th or the 12th, he will meet his end abroad. Saturn and Mars and Venus there destroy his wives through miscarriages or madness. Venus there in tropical [signs], especially in Cancer or Capricorn, [the natives] marry whores and through this fall into debt.

The Ascending Node there with Jupiter or Venus, with the Moon and the Sun in aspect, the house in which he is born will be fortunate. The Sun with Saturn there [says] he will be childless, and the house where he was born is abandoned or alienated from its owner. The Sun there with the Ascending Node, the father will be a great man. But if it is with Saturn and Mars, the house in which he was born is abandoned, and his father will die or he will suffer the loss of his possessions, and the native will be short-lived or he will be unstable in his wife and children. But if the Moon and Venus chance to be in [conjunction with] the Ascending Node, he will be an astrologer, and from this art he will acquire wealth. But if Saturn and Mars and Mercury are there without Jupiter or Venus, he will suffer, and he will have sickness and injury and cuts, and he will die miserably, and the house in which he was born is eradicated. But if the Sun chances to be with them, the father dies quickly. And if the Moon is with Saturn, Mars, [and] Mercury, the native and his mother die quickly.

The Descending Node chancing to be there with Jupiter or Venus, the native will be unhurt. But if the Sun or the Moon are there, both of the parents die miserably or are blinded or fall down a precipice.

The [star] of Saturn being there by day makes those who pile up wealth and guard their gold, but by night destruction of the parents and danger to the father and illnesses to the native and makes his youth ignoble. Aspecting the Moon by opposition or square or being with her, he makes childlessness and fathers or guardians of the children of others. And it makes severe illnesses internally and affecting the stomach, and widowhood to the mother and distress from feminine [complaints].[1] Jupiter there in sect [makes] great commanders,[2] persons known to rulers, those in charge of public affairs, God-fearing, trusting in the Gods and receiving guidance from the Gods concerning the future.[3] Some also have positions of importance in temples, and some are deemed worthy of windfalls.[4] Wherefore they will also lead an enjoyable old age. But being out of sect it makes moderate individuals [who become] more fortunate and better known with the passage of time.

The [star] of Mars being there by night [makes] generals, toilers, those who travel in the desert, those in charge of wild animals,[5] foot-soldiers, royal messengers; but by day, epileptics, sickly persons and those who take the risk of surgery because of sickness,[6] and those who are wronged by women and suffer from their ingratitude. But if it is also aspected by the Sun [and] Saturn is either with it or in square or opposition, it denotes those experiencing many dangers, some too are lunatics and epileptics particularly if it is the ruler of the Lot of Fortune or of the ASC or of the [Lot] of the Daemon.

The Sun being there destroys the native together with his par-

---

[1] Firmicus, *Mathesis*, iii. 2.9, has *ex muliebribus graves ei valitudines* 'serious illnesses for him from females', which, if the *ei* 'him' is correct, predicts the illnesses for the native rather than for his mother. The Greek does not say explicitly, but it seems to me to refer to the mother. Both the Greek and the Latin have 'feminine' rather than 'women' as the source of the illnesses.

[2] The Greek word *hêgemôn* 'leader' could designate the *chief* of anything from a gymnasium to the Roman Empire. In Latin, the equivalent word is *dux*, although Firmicus often translates it as *iudex* 'judge'. The same range can be seen in the 20th century, where we see the term range from *Der Fuehrer* and *Il Duce* to *Scout-leader*. It would appear that the classical astrologers were referring to some post such as provincial governor, in which the incumbent excercised civil, military, and judicial authority. The lexicon says the word was often used to designate the *Prefect of Egypt* under the Roman Empire.

[3] Cumont conjectures '... from the Gods, [those having foreknowledge] concerning the future', but it seems unnecessary.

[4] Firmicus, *Mathesis*,iii. 3.6, has 'some...will find treasures'.

[5] Zookeepers, for example.

[6] I have translated *tomes siderou*, literally 'cutting by iron' simply as 'surgery'. Surgical operations were painful and hazardous prior to the 20th century and were usually undertaken only as a last resort.

ents or destroys his livelihood ... according to the diversity of the stars in aspect with it.¹

If Venus is there, it denotes those who become more fortunate with the passage of the years, and those who are friends of magnates, and charming persons, becoming in their manner of life in youth, lacking for nothing, but strongly emotional. And in a tropical or bicorporeal [sign] it denotes widowhoods and damages and fights over women. In fixed [signs], they are well thought of [and] benefitted by women, unless Venus is in Aquarius opposed by the Moon, for this denotes those without posterity and persons who are sterile and those who are unhappily married and homosexuals.

The [star] of Mercury chancing to be there matutine indicates participants in forbidden mysteries. And when Saturn or Mars aspect it thus placed, they make those participating in judgments or restraint or condemnation.² But when vespertine it will make those who pile up money or find it, or initiates in secret [rites],³ or [experts]⁴ in numbers, or those in charge of wrestlers.

The Moon [being] there in sect makes the mother honored, and it increases the native's standard of living; but out of sect it makes the mothers low-born but wealthy; and they become involved in exchange,⁵ if indeed the Sun is not in the ASC. But if the Sun is in the ASC, they are thought worthy of praise and presidency and sovereignty or of a kingdom, with Saturn or Mars by day and also by night with the Sun moreover being absent from the ASC.⁶

---

¹Part of this section has been lost. *Cf.* Firmicus, *Mathesis*, iii. 5.17.
²Firmicus, who was a lawyer, takes this (*Mathesis*, iii. 7.7) to refer to those who get into trouble with the law and wind up being sentenced.
³The text actually has *apokryphôn ktistas* 'founders of secret [rites]', but Cumont conjectures *apokryphôn mystas* 'initiates in secret [rites]' because this phrase appears several times in Vettius Valens.
⁴Supplied by Cumont from Firmicus.
⁵Literally, 'in giving and taking', or 'selling and buying', referring to some sort of business transaction.
⁶The last part of this sentence appears muddled. MSS **A** & **V** have 'with the Sun either in the ASC or absent [from it]'.

The Fifth House.

The fifth house from the ASC is called *Good Fortune* and *Course*. It is the house of Venus, for she rejoices there. When therefore Jupiter or Venus chance to be there and are rulers of the Lot of Fortune or of the ASC, the native rules through the people; and especially Venus....being in proper face [and] not under the Sunbeams.[1] For such a [native] will rule nations, and he will be charming and handsome, and he will have honors in the presence of all, if it is not aspected by a malefic. But Jupiter also makes a good indication for those things [just] said.[2]

Mars there [makes] a tyrant [or] general.

The ruler of the ASC or the ruler of the Lot [of Fortune] there in their own faces make rulers of life and death.

Saturn there [makes] very rich persons, rulers of lands, founders of buildings or countries or cities.

The Sun there in its own face [makes] friends of kings and those ruling sacred and divine [persons and] things.

Mercury makes secretaries of wide experience, advancing through words and entrusted with money,[3] especially if it is not under the sunbeams and is in proper face, not beholding Mars or Saturn.

The Moon there well situated makes good fortune, especially when she is ruler of the Lot of Fortune or of the ASC and is in proper face and increasing her motion. But the benefics being with her will give good things, while the malefics will shatter [them].

---

[1] Valens, *Anthology*, ii. 12, has "Venus rejoices the most when she is ruler of the ASC or of the Lot [of Fortune], [and] especially when she is in proper face or in her own house, she denotes wealthy and honored persons."
[2] Translation uncertain. Jupiter is omitted in Valens's text.
[3] That is, department heads or personal secretaries of important persons with power to direct affairs.

If the ruler of the 12th is in the 5th or the 8th, or the ruler of the 5th is in the 12th, [the native] will be a step-father or foster-father of the children of others. If the ruler of the 5th or the ruler of the Lot of Children is in the 8th, it makes childless persons or those burying children. If the ruler of marriage or of the Lot of Marriage is in the 5th, it makes a happily married man and one who takes [to wife] a widow having a son.

If the Ascending Node is there with Jupiter, Venus, [or] Mercury, or they are aspecting the house, he will be blessed with children, and he will have notable children. But if Mars or Saturn behold the house, it will destroy the first children or one of them will die violently.[1] If the Sun chances to be there or is in aspect, he will be delivered from these evils, but his children will be injured.

If the Descending Node is there with Saturn, Mars, [or] Mercury, it will destroy the first children, and he will have good fortune from women. But if it is with Jupiter [or] Venus [or] they are in aspect, his son will not return from a trip abroad.

Saturn [there by day]...drawn near gives kingships and positions of command but with considerable delay.[2] And if the Sun is in the ASC and is receiving the conjunction of the waxing Moon, it gives rule with good. But if the Sun is not in the ASC, but Saturn is there [in the 5th], it denotes those obtaining their ends in the course of time. In youth he will suffer ups and downs, and it diminishes the possessions of the young. By night, it makes those who are delayed in their projects and sluggish in their actions, some too are deprived of their possessions.

---

[1]The Greek text has *en autô* 'in the same', which doesn't make sense. Cumont emends it to *en eniautô* 'in a year', which is not much better. I think it should read *en autôn* 'one of them'.

[2]Adding 'there by day' from Firmicus, *Mathesis*, iii. 2.10. Something else is missing, as Cumont noted, and the word *eggisas* 'drawn near' is the tag end of it. Note that Rhetorius indicates delay for the diurnal position, whereas Firmicus only mentions it in connection with the nocturnal position.

Jupiter there by day and by night is strong, for [the native] will become...having authority for their own good.¹

Mars there by night will make the possessions [consist] of many good things, [the natives will be] renowned as [well as honored] by the people,² and they rule their acquaintances. And if the Moon is present with it in the same domicile or degree or decan, [it makes] great dynasts, terrible in the army. But with the Moon not present, if the [star] of Venus is there or her trine or sextile, it makes fortunate persons and careful in their actions and charming. But if it is there by day, it makes foreign travel hurtful and very dangerous. However, Jupiter or Venus beholding [Mars] help [the situation] with regard to travel, and the declines will be quicker.³

When the Sun is there, they are more moderate in their fortunes, and childless or unfortunate in their children.

Venus there [makes] good prize-fighters, victors in rich contests, masterful, those having good luck in everything, prophesying the future, ruling their acquaintances, subsidized by women, or advanced by amorous endeavors, and acquiring [property] with the passage of the years.

Mercury chancing to be matutine in the 5th makes those piling up gold and finders of good things or managers of other people's money and long-lived and blessed with children. But vespertine he will not become a custodian or a guardian of money, but one who squanders [money] deposited in secret. And it makes professional

---

¹Much is missing in this description of the action of Jupiter in the 5th. Firmicus has nearly three pages on this position in the Teubner edition.

²I have added 'the natives will be', and Cumont has added 'well as honored', having compared Firmicus, *Mathesis*, iii. 4.12 'honors by the people' and iii. 3.18, where the same phrase is used of Jupiter in the MC, with Rhetorius's text at the latter point.

³The word *hyponosteseis* 'declines' seems to be corrupt. Firmicus, *Mathesis*, iii. 4.14, has *cito de peregre revocabitur ad patriam* 'he will be recalled quickly from abroad to his native land'. Perhaps the Greek should read *epanaklêseis* 'recalls' or something of the sort.

men or teachers or geometers or calculators[1] or masters of wrestlers. Receiving the conjunction of the waxing Moon, it will make the native to have white spots [on his skin] or he will have sickness. But [if the Moon is] waning, it makes unseemly injuries, or else it damages the mind.

The Moon there by night will be most gracious. For she makes leaders, fortunate, illustrious, presidents, [and] those having good things from their parents, if indeed she is not aspected by Saturn or Mars. But by day she denotes foreign travel, estrangement of parents or orphanhood, but with the passage [of time] [the native] will become fortunate.

The Sixth House.

The sixth house is called *evil, cadent,* and "pre-DSC," and "first to fall," and *metacosmic*[2] and *Bad Fortune*. It has signification of injuries and slaves and enemies and quadrupeds, sometimes also of actions because it is in right trine to the MC, but it is also the house of the feet and of sicknesses involving the feet. The malefics there make sicknesses or injuries involving the feet and the loss of money.

The Sun there, [the native] will be oppressed by superiors, and he will be in subordination; wherefore, it makes the father a slave or low-born or crippled, always a foreigner, especially if in addition the ruler of the Sun is there or the Lot of the Father or the dodecatemory of the Sun or the triplicity rulers of the Sun. For these configurations indicate that the parents are low-born, or crippled, or banished, or they are foreigners. Understand the same things from the Moon in the case of the mother and from its ruler and dodecatemory. And especially if the luminaries happen to be in the Descending Node, say that the parents will be ill-treated. And if Saturn is also present in the house, it makes wandering and

---

[1] In Greek, *arithmêtikoi* 'arithmeticians'. Firmicus, *Mathesis*, iii. 7.9, has 'astrologers', as if his source had read *mathêmatikoi*.
[2] See the discussion of this term under the 3rd house.

losses [and] the native leaves his things [behind] with sorrow.

Jupiter there, he will suffer loss in civil affairs.

Venus [there], he will suffer loss because of a woman or for a woman, and he will have disputes over birth; he has intercourse with slave-girls or servant-girls[1] or cripples, but they will be lacking in desire and charm.

Mars there makes injury to the feet, and it is also harmful in matters concerning slaves; and it gives uprisings of enemies and dangers abroad and injury [in the part of the body ruled] by the sign Mars is in.

Mercury there [gives] ill-advised persons, thieves, those wanting other peoples' possessions, slanderers, incompetents, and those who get a bad reputation.

The Sun and the Moon in conjunction there [make] madmen, epileptics, deranged persons.

Saturn there makes injury and sickness arising from wetness and cold and black bile, sometimes too paralysis, gout, gout in the feet,[2] gout in the hands, according to the nature of the sign, especially by night.

Mars there makes cuts, burns, those bitten by wild animals, attacks, wounds, attacks by robbers, especially if it is matutine; but if it is under the Sun beams, [it makes] hidden sicknesses in the internal organs or hemorrhage according to the [nature of] the sign, and more so by day.

Jupiter ruling the 6th, impeded by Saturn or Mars, badly pos-

---

[1] Hired servants, not slaves.
[2] The Greek word *podagra* 'gout in the foot' (lit., 'foot-trap') and its companion *cheiragra* 'gout in the hand' refer to painful inflammation of the joints of the foot or hand, not necessarily due to the specific disease we call gout. The common modern term for this condition is 'arthritis'. When the classical astrologers mention 'gout', we should probably understand 'osteoarthritis, rheumatoid arthritis, or gout'.

ited in the 6th or in the 12th, makes those suffering from liver complaints and impairments from wine.

Venus ruling the 6th, badly situated and aspected by Mars or Saturn, will make those who are mad for women, but if [Venus] is in a masculine sign, lovers of boys, who suffer many bad things because of this. And they will have sickness in the lungs.

Mercury ruling the 6th, aspected by Saturn or Mars, will injure the hearing or the speech or the throat.

The Sun, Mars, and the Moon badly configured [and] situated there damage the vision.

The Moon also makes those diseased in the spleen. The full Moon moving toward Mars [makes] lame persons and those with club feet or bandy legs.

The Sun there in the domicile of Venus will injure [the native] through a woman.

The [ruler] of the 4th in the 6th, or the [ruler] of the 8th or the [ruler] of the 9th [in the 6th], [makes] wanderers who die abroad. The ruler of the 7th in the 6th, or the Lot of Marriage or the ruler of the Lot of Marriage, they have intercourse with slave-girls, cripples, or wretched women.

Saturn, Mars, and Venus together there destroy the wives in some evil fashion. The ruler of the 3rd in the 6th causes ill-treatment [of the native] by his friends or brothers, or it injures the brothers.

The dodecatemory of the Moon in the 6th injures the native, and says that his mother is low-born. But the Sun also does the same in the case of the father.

The Ascending Node being in the 6th with Mars and Saturn, or aspected by them, [the native] will fall into water or into a well, or it injures his bones. Jupiter, the Sun, and the Moon there, [or] if they aspect Saturn or Mars there, they deliver [him] from all evils; however, let him guard himself up to age 26 and [again] up to age 35, and then he will be free from fear.

The Descending Node in the 6th, he will be seriously ill in his youth. Jupiter and Venus there, he will have a hidden sickness. But if Saturn and Mars [are there], he will be delivered from evils; however, they injure some part of his body.

Saturn there by night will bring about the extinction of his inheritance, and it will make dangers and plots for the sake of slaves; and some are also injured. But by day, the evils will be moderate. And if it is square or opposite the Moon, it makes unsteadiness and consumption.[1] But if Jupiter is in aspect with either the Moon or Saturn, it will help to some extent, but it still makes sickly persons.

Jupiter in the 6th makes fights and disputes with those in authority. And Jupiter always become evil in the 6th and 12th, especially by night.

Mars in the 6th makes sicknesses and injuries and dangers and plots on account of slaves or of persons convicted or arrested, especially by day. Mars being angular by day in general produces those in danger of [sudden] death.

The Sun in the 6th makes the father to die miserably or to be condemned, and it injures [him] and destroys his property, if indeed there is no star in the 10th; but if one is found in the tenth, it makes those [receiving] good fortune from their parents.

Venus [there] by day and by night, [the native] has intercourse with lower-born women or widows or cripples; and it makes those who are treated unkindly by their wives, especially if nothing is in the 10th. But if the chart is that of a woman, she will have difficul-

---

[1]The Greek has *astasias kai phthiseis*. Firmicus, *Mathesis* iii. 2.12-13, has *erraticos ... phthisicos* 'unsteady persons ... consumptives', but the former epithet is due to Saturn in bad aspect with the Moon, and the latter epithet is due to Saturn in bad aspect with Mars. Rhetorius's text, as we have it, does not mention Mars. Perhaps there is a lacuna between the two Greek words.

ties in childbirth or embryotomies. But if there is a star in the 10th, especially by night and of the sect, it denotes fascinating and charming persons and good fortune through women and [generally] successful. But [if Venus is] declining from the angles,[1] with the malefics holding the angles and impediting the Moon, it makes [the natives] short-lived or exposed.[2]

Mercury in the 6th by day [makes] those having some advancements and good fortune from talking or speech-making or business or from [actions] of the gods, especially if any star happens to be in the 10th. But Mercury being in the 6th by night, matutine, makes interpreters, fishermen, bird-catchers, and carvers, if indeed any star is in the 10th; but if no [star] is there, it makes evil-minded, idle, unsuccessful, conceited persons. But if it is vespertine, [it makes] intelligent, sensible, discerning persons, [and] those in charge of offices, or banking, or storehouses, or documents, or merchants, and from which activities they prosper. And if it receives the application of the Moon, it makes public scribes,[3] or instructors of kings,[4] or financial administrators, especially if there is a star in the 10th.

[The influence of the Moon in the 6th is missing in the MSS, which is all the more unfortunate because it is also missing in Firmicus.]

---

[1] Reading *apoklinasa* 'declining from' instead of *prosklinasa* 'inclining towards'. (Firmicus, *Mathesis* iii. 6.13, has *aliena...a cardinibus* 'alien from the angles'.) But Pingree, *The Yavanajātaka of Sphujidhvaja*, II, p. 341, cites an explanation of the Sanskrit word *lagnabhimukha* 'facing the ascendant' as referring to a planet in the 12th house, so perhaps also to the Greek mind 'inclining towards the angles' might be equivalent to 'declining from the angles', in which case the text is correct as it stands.

[2] The Greek text actually has *ekbolimous* 'ejected' or 'aborted' where we would expect *ekthetous* 'exposed'. (*Cf.* above, the Moon in the first house.) However, Firmicus, *Mathesis* iii. 6.13, has *expositos* 'exposed'. The classical astrologers mentioned the exposing of children much more often than they did abortion, so the odds seem to favor 'exposed' rather than 'aborted'.

[3] These functionaries prepared legal documents of various sorts—contracts, wills, etc., thus combining the activities of public secretaries, notaries, and lawyers.

[4] Cumont, *L'Égypte des Astrologues*, p. 31. These were instructors or professors attached to the royal household. Cumont inclines to equate them with the functionaries who supervised the care of the royal children.

The Seventh House.

The seventh house is called *Descending Angle*. It signifies old age and marriage, sometimes too the matter of inheritance and that of injury. In particular, it signifies the fingers or the bladder or the feet. And it makes travel abroad.

Jupiter being there then makes old age fine and free from toil and trouble and windfalls or inheritances abroad and professional activities, but youth more troublesome, [and it makes] unhappily married persons, especially in a tropical sign and unfortunate in their children or childless.

If Venus chances to be there, it makes [the native] pleasing and youthful[1] in old age, and enjoying a good old age, and promiscuous and unstable in marriage. Venus setting there, without any aspect from the malefics, [makes] sensible persons; and in her fall it makes the same thing, the youth unstable, and having intercourse with slave-girls and whores.[2]

Mercury in the 7th [makes] rich, educated, prudent persons, their wives meddlesome or beastly-minded[3] or fond of poisoning.

Saturn there makes not only those making bad marriages or [marrying] widows, but it also makes sicknesses affecting the fingers or hemorrhages or fluxes from the feet. And it always injures the body and causes the birth of bad children, especially out of sect. But if [it is] in sect in its own domicile or exaltation, it makes long-lived persons, rich in old age, but it distresses them in youth.

Mars being there makes a bad marriage, and he marries an adulteress. It injures the eyes and the fingers and the feet and makes

---
[1] The printed text has *neôterizontas,* which would usually mean 'innovating' or perhaps 'being youthful', but compare what is said of Venus in the section below, where it seems that the text should read *neôterais zontas* (or *synousiontas*) 'living with younger women' or something similar.
[2] This sentence doesn't hang together.
[3] MSS **AV** have *thêrapsychous,* which Cumont emends to *thêriopsychous* 'beastly-minded'?, both words otherwise unattested.

persons who tremble. And it always destroys the ancestral [property?], especially [when it is] out of sect and in the domiciles of other [stars], and it makes old age bad. But if [it is] in sect in its own domicile or exaltation, the evil is moderated.

The Moon there [makes] [the native] hospitable, and in a feminine sign, aspected by the Sun and Venus by conjunction or opposition, it makes effeminate homosexuals and those having sexual relations with two sisters. But if the chart is that of a woman, with the Moon in a masculine sign and Venus aspecting from masculine signs, it always makes *tribades*.[1] The Sun there [makes] bad luck with marriage and children but prosperity and wealth.

The ruler of the 7th in the 12th, or the [ruler] of the 12th in the 7th, makes bad luck with marriage or marriage to a slave. The ruler of the 7th being aspected by the ruler of the 8th makes widowers or divorced persons, once if in a solid [sign], twice in a bicorporeal [sign], but many times in a tropical [sign]. The ruler of the 7th in the MC and the ruler of the 12th in the 4th [makes] either those who marry slaves or those who purchase their own wives. The ruler of the 7th in the 9th gives a foreigner or a religious wife. The ruler of the 7th being under the Sun beams or in the 4th or struck by the malefics makes intercourse with whores or slave-girls.

The Ascending Node in the 7th with Saturn, Venus, and Mercury makes the native's wife twice-married. But if Venus and Mars happen to be there or in aspect, he will marry a rich old woman or one with damaged vision. Jupiter, Venus, [and] Mercury there, he will marry a well-born woman and will have good fortune from wifely affection, and he will bury his wife.

The Descending Node there will take away the wife first or injure her. Saturn [and] Mars being there or aspecting will give a practical or frugal woman or a widow as wife.

Venus being there or aspecting will give a young woman as wife. Jupiter together with her there or in aspect, [the native] will

---

[1] Female homosexuals. *Cf.* Ptolemy, *Tetrabiblos*, iii. 14, and iv. 5.

be unstable in his relations with women.

The Sun [and] Mercury being there or in aspect, he will marry a foreigner or a grey-eyed woman.[1]

Saturn there by day makes those who succeed after long delay, long-lived persons, [and] treasurers. But they will have injuries either of the fundament[2] or in secret places; but [these conditions are] worse by night, for it makes sickly persons, those suffering from a flux, [and] those afflicted with a sickness arising from heating.[3]

Jupiter there by day makes long-lived persons and those having few children, rich towards the end [of their lives]. By night, moderate in their circumstances and meeting with success in their middle years.

Mars there by day makes hard-working, wicked, violent, murderous persons, torturers, [and] traitors; some are also short-lived, especially if it aspects the angular Moon. But in general, Mars there by day or by night makes those who die violently, especially if [it is] in signs[4] of other [stars], [for then it makes them to perish] from pains and cuts or falls. But by night it makes sorrows and agitations in everything that they do. And in addition it makes burns or cuts by iron or hidden pains when it is ruling the time,[5] and it gives professional activities from iron or fire or the military or from some violence arising from tortures or obligations or even the killing of men.

---

[1]The lexicon notes that this eye-color was not admired by the Greeks.
[2]Rhetorius, like Ptolemy, *Tetrabiblos*, iii. 12, uses the word *hedras* 'seat' as a euphemism. Paul of Alexandria, *Introduction*, Chapter 24, has *epi tas hedras pathos* 'sickness in the seats'. Firmicus, *Mathesis*, iii. 2.14, is more explicit: *aemorroicos* 'hemorrhoids'.
[3]The text has *pyrotikois* 'heating' or 'inflammation', which is not a Saturnian ailment. Cumont suggests *hydropikois* 'dropsical' as a possible correction.
[4]The text has *topois* 'houses', but *zôdiois* 'signs' or *oikeiois* 'domiciles' is required. *Cf.* Firmicus, *Mathesis* III.iv.18, which has *signis* 'signs'.
[5]That is, when it is the current *chronocrator* or ruler of the 10 year and 9 month profectional period. *Cf.* Firmicus, *Mathesis* iii. 4.19.

The Sun in the 7th becomes the cause of sickness and injuries according to the nature of the star that is in conjunction or aspect with it.

Venus there by day or by night makes, with the passage of time, those marrying younger women[1] and marrying late and good-dispositioned.[2] Impedited in tropical or scaly or servile signs, especially by Mars, it makes lewd and passionate persons. In the [chart] of a woman, if it is impedited by Saturn, it makes indecent persons and whores, especially in Capricorn.

Mercury there by day [is] not good with Venus mediating it, for by passion(?) it gives judgment against those born not from unknowns, for example lewd persons, brothel-keepers and such like. And with Mars in opposition or dominating, it makes short-lived persons, consumptives, fugitives, [and] condemned persons. But by night Mercury there [makes] those managing the affairs of wealthy women and deriving good fortune from sexual matters and numbers or the fine arts, or finders of obscure writings.[3]

The Moon there by day [makes] foreign travel and dangers either from wet places or from robbers or who are ill-treated by slaves or sickly persons, especially if it is also joined to a malefic, for then the evils become unavoidable. The Moon [there] by night makes changes of place and foreign travel and increases in means with the passage of time.

The Eighth House.

The eighth house is called *idle* and *epicataphora* of the ASC

---

[1]The MSS have *neôterous* (**A**, *-ôn* **V**) *zôntas neoterois* (or *–ous*) *zôntas* **P**, which Cumont corrects to *neôterizontas* to agree with Paul of Alexandria. But, I conjecture that both Paul and Rhetorius should read *neôterais zontas* (or *synousiontas*) 'marrying younger women'. *Cf.* Ptolemy, *Tetrabiblos* iv. 5, Sect. 183.
[2]Reading *eudiathetous* rather than the *endiabletous* 'slanderous' of MS **V** or Cumont's conjecture *eudiablêtous* 'easily-assailed'.
[3]That is, "revealed" writings, esoteric treatises, and those with veiled meanings, etc. See Cumont, *L'Égypte des Astrologues*, Chapt. 12.

and *epikatadysis* and *dimming*.¹ It is the sign that is turned away from the ASC; because of this, and because of its meaning of death, it signifies the turning away of life.

If then the Lot of Fortune chances to be there, and its ruler, and the ruler of the ASC, it makes misfortunes and irregularities. And if these [rulers] are malefics, the evil is worse, for it makes unfortunate persons, and if [they are] under the Sun beams, short-lived persons.

Mercury being ruler of the [Lot of the] Daemon, [and] being present in the 8th, [makes] unintelligent, and illiterate, and lazy persons. Mercury being ruler of the 8th or of the 12th or of the 6th, being present in the 8th under the Sun beams with Saturn and Mars, [makes] deaf and dumb persons.

The Moon there by night, adding to her numbers and light, especially if Jupiter is in the 11th, [the native] will profit from matters having to do with the dead and with inheritances.

The ruler of the 4th in the 8th, he dies abroad. The ruler of the 8th makes these same things when it is cadent.

Venus in the 8th makes miserable and shameful persons.

The ruler of the 8th in the 10th or the 11th or the 5th, [the native] will grow rich from matters having to do with the dead, especially in its own domicile or exaltation, and not under the Sun beams, and adding to its numbers. But if it is under the Sun beams, it makes an inheritance, but he immediately squanders it. The ruler of the 3rd in the 8th destroys the brothers first. The ruler of the 5th being there causes childlessness. The ruler of the 12th or of the 6th being there [makes] the deaths of enemies and slaves.²

---

¹The two names I have left in Greek mean respectively 'falling down upon' the ASC and 'falling down upon the DSC'. The reference is to the setting of the stars as they move downwards towards the western horizon. The reasoning behind the phrase '*epicataphora* of the ASC' (if it is not simply a blunder) is similar to that applied to the term 'cadent from the ASC' that is sometimes applied to all the cadent houses, since the ASC is the basis of all the other houses.
²As J.B. Morin points out in *Astrologia Gallica*, Book 21, the 8th house is only the house of death for the native, so some of these aphorisms are inconsistent with

Mars there injures the vision, especially if the Sun or the Moon is in the ASC.

Saturn [and] Mars there without Jupiter [and] Venus make [the natives to be] banished.

Jupiter there in its own domicile or exaltation, adding to its numbers, [the native] profits from matters having to do with the dead, and especially without Saturn and Mars.

Mercury and Mars there [make] forgers.

Saturn, ruler of the 8th beholding destroys him [in some fashion involving] water or abroad, especially in a water sign or impedited in another [sign]; but if Saturn is in an earth sign, it destroys [him] on a mountain. In a word, examine the ruler of each sign of the 8th, in what sign it is, for that one becomes the [significator of] death.

The Sun ruler of the 8th impedited in the sign of another, if the 8th house itself is impedited, it destroys [by a fall] from a height according to the nature of the sign.

Mars ruler of the 8th, with the house impedited, makes those dying violently; sometimes too, it makes huntsmen.[1] Mars aspected by the Sun makes a violent death [caused] by kings or enemies.

Venus ruler of the 8th impedited, and the 8th impedited, makes a violent death from [too] much wine or from poisoning by women.

Mercury ruler of the 8th impedited, and also the 8th itself, makes death [caused] by slaves or by writings.

Jupiter ruler of the 8th impedited along with the house makes the death [to be caused] by kings or magnates, and, if [it is] in its own domiciles or triplicity or exaltation, in the same country, but if in other [signs], abroad.

---

the doctrine of derived houses.
[1]Literally, '(hunting) dog leaders'.

If the Ascending Node happens to be in the 8th with the Sun, Mars, Mercury, [and] Saturn or if they aspect the house, it makes a bad death or a short-lived person.

If Jupiter and Venus [are] in the 8th alone, [it makes] an easy death and great good fortune.

If the Descending Node happens to be in the 8th and Jupiter, Saturn, Venus, and Mars [are] there, they make those dying violently.[1]

Saturn there by day denotes those acquiring [assets] with the passage of time, in order to assist others, but some [other natives] acquiring [assets] from death. Being there by night, it makes those who are banished, consumptives, and those dying a bad death.

Jupiter there by day and by night denotes acquisition and inheritance with the passage of time.

Mars in the 8th by day makes wants and disorders and dangers.

The Sun in the 8th makes the early death of the father, and some [of the natives] are madmen;[2] the stars that are with it or in aspect to it show the cause. But the Sun opposing the Moon, with the bond not yet broken,[3] injures the native.

Venus by day in the 8th [makes] those who marry late and those who have intercourse with lower-born women or widows or young girls. And it destroys the natives through gonorrhea[4] or spasms or apoplexy. But by night, it denotes wealthy and rich persons and those who benefit from the death of women. And it makes the

---

[1] This paragraph is a condensed version of Chapter 77 "General Configurations of Those Suffering a Violent Death."
[2] In Greek, *phrenetikous*, a variant of *phrenitikous*, means someone suffering from inflammation of the brain. Here it refers to the noisy type of dementia - the raving madman.
[3] He means 'with the technical condition of "bonding" still in effect'. This usually means "within an orb of 3 degrees."
[4] That is, through some sort of venereal disease, not necessarily the one we call *gonorrhea*.

death [of the native] quick and painless and easy.

Mercury in the 8th vespertine by day [makes] ineffective, unsuccessful, lazy, toilsome persons; but vespertine by night, those inheriting from unrelated persons, those deserving of windfalls, fortunate, but passive and who easily become sick. Matutine in the 8th, it makes increases of money and those who aim at great actions, and some who share in responsibilities, or fiduciary relationships, or managing, or legal documents, or even those inheriting from unrelated persons.

[The influence of the Moon in the eighth house is missing!]

The Ninth House.

The ninth house is called *God*. It is the house of the Sun. It signifies all things concerning the gods and kings and foreigners and dreams and religious observance. It is the *astronomical* sign and the *metacosmic*.[1] The good [stars] being in this house make good fortune in foreign places and pious persons and righteous in religious observance, especially if the ruler of the house is also well situated and in its own domicile or exaltation and not aspected by the malefics.

And Mercury being in the 9th in its own domicile or exaltation or matutine, if it is not aspected by the malefics, such [natives] are established in making money, leaders of the people through business; some become royal secretaries. It makes these things after the first age. It also makes astronomers.

---

[1] Cumont says the 9th house is called *astronomical* because it is the house of the Sun, and the Sun rules the other stars according to the Chaldeans. He also offers an explanation of the term *metakosmios* that might suit the 9th house or even the 3rd, but Rhetorius uses the term as an epithet of all four of the cadent houses. The *kosmios* part of the word is probably equivalent to *kosmikos*, which means 'mundane'. (*Cf.* Vettius Valens, *Anthology,* ii. 18, who speaks of the *kosmika kentra* 'mundane angles'.) Perhaps Rhetorius had this in mind and thought "if the angles are 'cosmic', then the houses that are next to them in the direction of rotation (i.e. clockwise) are properly called *metacosmic* 'after the cosmic'. But in effect the term merely means "cadent." (See the note to the 3rd house.)

The Sun there and the Moon: say the parents are pious or foreigners. Sometimes too the native is pious. But he always travels a lot.

If Saturn and Mars [are] there matutine or stationary, and they aspect the Lot of Fortune in the ASC, they make a great tyrant, a despoiler of temples, impious, and he will not have wrath from a god[1] through the star of the Bad Daemon or else the star of the Bad Fortune.

Mars being in the [house of the] God, and if the Lot of Fortune is not in the ASC, but it chances to be in the 6th or 12th, with Saturn and Mars in the 9th, he will be very unfortunate and a wanderer and afflicted by demons.

The ruler of the 8th in the 9th, he will die abroad. The ruler of the 9th well situated and not under the Sun beams, in its own sign or exaltation, will give good fortune abroad. But if it is in the 6th or 2nd or 3rd or 12th or 8th, it denotes those who wander about abroad. Venus in the 9th [is] not good for marriage for a man, [nor] Mars [there] for a woman. The ruler of the 7th in the 9th will give a foreign or pious wife to the child.[2]

Mars in the 9th without Jupiter and Venus prognosticates blasphemers.

Saturn in the 9th makes a person knowledgeable about the mysteries and the interpretation of dreams.

Venus in the 9th makes the marriage unstable.

The Ascending Node in the 9th with the Sun and Saturn and Mars [makes] misfortunes abroad or through foreigners or captives or wanderers or persons dying a bad death. But if Jupiter and Venus [are] there without Saturn and Mars, [it grants] friends with great men in foreign countries and good fortune. If the Sun and

---

[1]Reading *menin apo theou* instead of *amynên hypo theou* 'vengeance by a god', as Cumont conjectures.
[2]That is, to the *native*.

Venus and Mercury [are] there, [it makes] pious persons, priests, and those who set up offerings in the sanctum, from the property of the gods or the king or great men...and they are held in honor abroad; from a sacred place and in a dream they receive an answer, especially if the Moon happens to be with Jupiter and they aspect the Ascending Node, they maintain the [native's] livelihood in good circumstances, and [the natives] will be fortunate and long-lived.

If the Descending Node [is] in the 9th with Saturn and Mars or they aspect it, [it is] a good configuration, for they will rule gloriously in a foreign place and they will be fortunate. But if the Sun and Mercury [are] there, they will be much honored.

Saturn in the 9th by day makes initiates, chiefs of the Magi, philosophers, prophesying the future, some too involved with sacred duties or in charge of priests; but by night, recluses, inventors of apothegms,[1] interpreters of dreams, philosophers, some of them long-haired.

Jupiter there by day [makes] those predicting the future with portents from the gods, some too are deemed worthy of the priesthood or they have inalienable privileges.[2] But by night [it makes] those unsteady in dreams and speaking falsely of the gods and those relying on the hope [engendered by] oracular responses and who consider themselves happy.

Mars in the 9th by day and by night [makes] those who are unpunished, sophists, fearful to the gods, even if they swear falsely, those having an opportunity for deliverance. And these [natives]

---

[1]Or perhaps 'speaking from God', reading *apo theou phtheggomenous*, as at Venus in the 3rd house above, instead of *apophtheggomenous* 'inventors of apothegms'. But the latter word is also said of Saturn in the 3rd house above.

[2]Cumont, *L'Égypte des Astrologues*, p. 114 n.2, explains *dôreas anaphairetous* as 'a salary for life that could not be taken away.' Firmicus, *Mathesis* iii. 3.17, merely says 'some gift from temples'. An example of inalienable privileges in more recent times would be the Five Privileges granted in perpetuity by Pope Clement VII in the year 1531 to the House of Borgia (see Frederick Baron Corvo, *Chronicles of the House of Borgia*. pp. 304-305.)

also become fearful to demons.[1]

The Sun in the 9th [makes] builders of sacred things, those who make sacred inscriptions and adorners of the gods and hymn-singers and temple-founders, from which [activities] they become famous. Some too have duties in temples or privileges or positions of authority.[2]

Venus in the 9th out of sect prognosticates those who are afflicted by demons or those wearing rags in temples, shaggy-haired, having something divine to announce from the gods or from dreams, [or] philosophers. Such things are produced especially when [Venus] is in aspect with Saturn. Venus there in sect [makes] good prophets, priests, god-fearing persons, but with Saturn and Mars in conjunction [with her] or in square or opposition, those who are stirred up by women and those who are condemned and those who are unlucky and those who are mistreated by them, and especially in the tropical signs, for these are the signs of multiple marriage. But if the [star] of Jupiter is conjunct this [star] or trine or square, [it makes] those having children by their wives, charming, successful, and having control of the [property] of their wives. Some of them also become business managers of women, and they dwell in royal palaces, being advanced through the pleas of women.[3]

Mercury vespertine in the 9th [makes] priests, wizards, physicians, those who invent those things that they had not learned about. But [if it is] matutine, [it makes] holy seers, sacrificers, augurs, astrologers, those devoted to the gods, from which occupations they also get their living.

The Moon in the 9th by night [makes] notable persons who live abroad; some of them benefit [in some way] from the temples of

---

[1]Firmicus, *Mathesis* iii. 4.27, explains that the reference is to exorcists.
[2]The Greek text has *apostasias* 'revolts', 'defections', etc. This cannot be right unless some words have been lost before it. Cumont suggests *epistasias*, which I have adopted.
[3]See the note to Venus in the 3rd house above.

the gods, some others are entrusted with the business affairs of women, good businessmen, god-fearing. But by day [it makes] inglorious persons who live abroad, having their lives [disturbed] by wandering and dangers; some of them too dwell ingloriously in temples or [they are] temple-servants or those devoted to the gods and those who confess, especially if Mars and Saturn are in aspect.

The Tenth House.

The tenth house is called *angle*, *midheaven*, and *quadrant of the ASC*. It signifies youth and action and marriage and children and the substance of the parents. In this house the rulers of the sect rejoice, and they give actions that are good and useful.

Saturn, then, there by day, in its own domicile or exaltation, makes a rich man and those who are in public service; [the native will be] happy in old age, except that it is bad for marriage and children; but it makes an easy death. He will also be fond of farming. By night, it destroys the ancestral [property] and it is bad for marriage and the children, and it makes lazy persons and gardeners and water-carriers or sailors or fishermen or ferrymen[1] and really poor people and those who dwell around wet woods.[2]

Mars being in the MC by day scatters the [possessions] of the parents and either kills or separates them from their children. And it makes wanderers and poor individuals and a wretched youth; but it is also bad for marriage and the children. By night, these evils are moderated.

Jupiter being in the MC by day [makes] rich persons, those who have good children, who makes fortunate marriages and have distinguished friends, but if it aspects the malefics it will harm.

Venus being in the MC by night and by day, especially not under the Sun beams [and] not afflicted [makes] those who are en-

---

[1] The reading of the Greek text is uncertain. Cumont conjectures *porthm<eis>* 'ferrymen'.
[2] The Greek has *hygras hyl*as 'wet woodlands'?

trusted with state affairs, and those who act as negotiators in the marriage of rich women, those who are loved by women, and [it also makes] a pleasant old age and an easy death.

Mercury being in the MC [makes] resourceful persons, good at everything, sensible, having good children, honored in cities and called "great," and having many friends, for whom they give up their activities.[1]

The Moon and the Sun being in the MC, without any aspect of the malefics, [make] distinguished fathers, and the natives themselves [will have] many friends, and [will be] dear to great men. But if the dodecatemorion of the Sun or of the Moon falls there, say that the parents are very well born.

The Lot [of Fortune] or its ruler being in the MC, not under the Sun beams and not afflicted, [makes] very fortunate persons; the ruler of the 7th being in the MC [makes] good marriages; the ruler of the 8th being in the MC [makes] increases [of wealth] through inheritances; the ruler of the 9th being in the MC gives good fortune abroad.

The Ascending Node being in the MC with the Moon, Venus, [and] Jupiter [makes] fortunate persons, distinguished, and loved.

Saturn and Mars being in the MC, if they aspect Jupiter and Venus and the Sun, [makes] the figure very bad. For the [natives] will be miserable, thieves, or those who live with cheap women. And whatever they get, they will lose, or [their possessions] are confiscated, or they will be short-lived or die a violent death, especially if the Moon is there.

The Descending Node being in the MC with Jupiter [and] Venus, the [natives] will be unstable in their living, and they will be passionate and promiscuous,[2] and whatever they get they will lose;

---

[1] Or, less likely, 'to whom they bequeath their activities.'
[2] The Greek text has *epikindynous* 'endangered', but it seems to me that this is an error for *epikoinous* 'common' or 'promiscuous'.

they will also be moderately unstable and needy. But if Saturn and Mars are in the MC or aspect the house, they will suffer distress in youth, but after this they will be in good circumstances, getting [things] through domination and violence, seizing possessions by force and by tyranny, sons of cheap persons and not caring for anything because Mars and Saturn rejoice in [conjunction with] the Descending Node. But if Saturn is in the MC with Venus, they will be unstable in [their relations with] women, and afterwards they will recover.

Saturn in the MC by day will produce leaders, and especially if the Sun happens to be in the ASC. The [star] of Saturn in the MC by day makes becoming persons and those fond of agriculture and fond of damp. But by night the [star] of Saturn in the MC denotes bunglers[1] and puts them in damp [places]. And the god is not good for things relating to the wife, nor will it be useful in regard to children, if there is no benefic aspecting the [star] of Saturn in some manner, it will help little in the mother's giving birth. And, in general, this god chancing to be angular by night is not good, and it denotes sorrows because of women.[2]

Jupiter chancing to be in the sign of the MC by day denotes athletic contestants, directors of public affairs, those esteemed by the people, famous, well-known, or those who are entrusted by kings and magnates with [the management of] their affairs, [or] those who wear crowns throughout their whole lives.[3] But chancing to

---

[1] Firmicus, *Mathesis*, iii. 2.21, has *infelicitates* 'misfortunes' where the text of Rhetorius has *dyspraktous* 'bunglers'. Perhaps Firmicus's Greek source had *dyspraxeias* 'misfortunes'. Since bungling often begets misfortune, the difference is slight.

[2] So MS **P**, as edited by Cumont. MSS **AV** have 'It makes a bad marriage and childlessness if no benefic aspecting Saturn helps; for, in general, Saturn angular by night', etc. Firmicus, *op. cit.*, 'it will deny marriage, it will deny children, especially if it is found in the sign or house or terms of an evil star. But if a good star, i.e. Jupiter or Venus, aspects Saturn so placed by night with a good aspect, it bestows in some measure those things which we just said would be denied. But in particular the star of Saturn placed by night in all the angles denotes the greatest evils for the nativity, for it destroys the wives, prostrates the children, and it always indicates the bitter pains of bereavement.'

[3] Not royal personages, but rather high-priests and victors in the principal games. *Cf.* Cumont, *L'Égypte des astrologues*, pp. 76 & 117.

be in this house by night, it denotes handsome, dignified persons, but easily overthrown and deprived of their livelihood.

The [star] of Mars chancing to be in the MC sign by night denotes unstable persons, prone to dangers, leaders, rulers of life and death or military commanders, frightful to the districts. But by day the [star] of Mars in the MC is not good, for it makes those who accomplish nothing, or who are hindered in their activities or efforts, and [who suffer] seizures of their livelihood, or even those who become fugitives and meet their end abroad. Mars being in the MC, in the same angle with the Sun, makes kingdoms and rulerships handed down from the fathers to the children.[1]

[The signification of the Sun in the 10th house is missing!]

Venus chancing to be in the MC sign denotes those who are honored,[2] especially when it happens to be unaspected by Saturn and Mars either by square or opposition or by conjunction, it will make [the natives to be involved] in different activities, especially if it also happens to be oriental, for [then] it will make popular persons, musicians honored by the people. But if the [star] of Saturn is present or in aspect in the indicated manner, it will make reprehensible persons, and in these honors not free agents but those who act under [instruction from] others, or else those who entrust their personal [property] to [the management of] others. But if the [star] of Mars also casts an aspect to the [star] of Venus, just as was explained previously, it denotes those who are very indecent and notorious. But if it chances to be a woman who has this configuration, she will be promiscuous, a courtesan, and she will remain in whorehouses throughout her life.

---

[1]This last statement about Mars seems inappropriate. Firmicus, *Mathesis*, iii. 5.34, says something similar about the Sun and Jupiter: 'The Sun...in the MC in its own domicile or in a domicile of Jupiter or in that degree in which it is exalted, will make kings to whom rulership is handed down from the father, or military commanders likewise . . .'

[2]The word *doxastikous*, which I have translated as 'honored', more commonly means 'having opinions' or 'making conjectures', but this is contrary to the nature of Venus. The other meaning derives from the passive 'being thought of', hence 'honored', 'praised', 'glorified'.

But the variations of actions and occurrences come to pass in accordance with the analogies of the signs, for in servile and tropical signs and the signs of Saturn or in fishy signs things of this sort are effected. But if [the native] is a man, he will be very scandalous, and he will be a sodomite, and he will do all sorts of lewd things. But if the Sun chances to be in a feminine sign, in the same angle with the Moon, men become eunuchs or castrates or they will be hermaphrodites performing the acts of women.

Mercury chancing to be matutine in the MC sign will indicate admirable and splendid actions, for they will be, when it is aspected house-wise by one of the [stars] of the sect, great rulers, or those who are entrusted with the affairs of cities or kingdoms or great men, trustworthy, good, discriminating. But with Mars opposing it, they will be unsuccessful in advancement, imagining themselves to be promoted; and they will have their share of flights or convictions or even violent death. Mercury vespertine chancing to be in the MC sign makes changes of place and diverse [experiences of] living abroad. Possibly, it will also indicate those whose acts are made public. But if it is aspected by Saturn by opposition or square, it gives occupations and enterprises beside water; and it will involve the natives in moist illnesses.

The Moon chancing to be in sect in the MC sign with [the MC itself][1] will produce great rulers, kings, rulers of life and death. [But] chancing to be [merely] in the sign of the MC house [it makes] those who are great in their actions and in those efforts with which they are entrusted or which they do for their own benefit, those who receive money. [But if the Moon applies to Saturn or Saturn is in another angle],[2] it will often produce hardships and drudgery. But chancing to be out of sect in this house, [the Moon]

---

[1]The Greek text has *homokentros* 'in the same center (angle) with'. This usually appears with the name of another planet, but here it stands alone. Either the name of the planet has dropped out of the text or we must take it to refer to the MC degree, as did Firmicus, *Mathesis*, iii. 13.9, who has *partiliter in hoc loco* 'partilely in this house'. The more common case, where it is merely in the 10th house, is dealt with in the next sentence.

[2]The words in brackets are supplied from Firmicus, *Mathesis*, iii. 13.9.

will produce those who are middling in their livelihood and actions, and it will produce unsteady persons and those who do not possess [steady] jobs. But if the Sun chances to be neither in the ASC nor in the MC it indicates great rulers, commanding, [and] frightful to kings.[1]

The Eleventh House.

The 11th house is called *Good Daemon* and *epanaphora* of the MC. Consequently, the benefic stars chancing to be in this house in their own faces or domiciles or exaltations or terms signify great wealth and illustrious actions. And the 11th house also shows the 3rd time of life. And it signifies the matters of action and patronage and precedence at the prime of youth.

Every lot and every ruler of a lot or of an angle or a house or a triplicity that chances to be there signifies all good things, but if it is aspected by malefics or chances to be under the Sun beams or in its own fall or in opposition or retrograde, it weakens the goodness of the house. Similarly too, the malefics chancing to be there and having significance for the nativity (I mean, of course, the rulers of lots or houses or triplicities) without any evil positions (I mean, of course, being under the Sun beams or in their fall or in opposition or retrograde) renders the nativity good and increase the good things and lessen the bad things.

The house is called [the house] of Jupiter because Jupiter rejoices when it is in this house. And the house also signifies the matter of children.

If the ruler of the 11th house is in the ASC and the [ruler] of the Bad Daemon is setting, it makes [the native] wealthy in his youth and in moderate circumstances in old age. But if the configuration is reversed, it will also reverse his luck.

---

[1]The last sentence does not agree with Firmicus, *Mathesis*, iii. 13.10, where a similar indication is given for the Moon in the 10th and the Sun in the 1st. As it stands, the Greek text must be wrong. Perhaps it should read *eite . . . eite* 'either . . . or' instead of *mête . . . mête* 'neither . . . nor'.

But if the Ascending Node happens to be in this house and Venus or Mercury is found there, he will have all kinds of good fortune from women or he will acquire property from eunuchs. But in the first part of life he will be unsettled in his wife and children, and he will be loved by women. And if Jupiter is present with them, it will be good, for he will acquire much property, and he will be an important man in his city. But if Saturn and Mercury chance to be there, and no good star is in aspect, he will be condemned and will sue for his life. But if Jupiter and Venus chance to be there with the Moon or with the Sun, it will make fortunate persons and those acquiring much property. And they will live 70 years.

If the Ascending Node chances to be in the 11th house, and Jupiter and Venus chance to be there, he will have instability, and whatever he acquires he will lose, and after that he will be successful. But if Saturn and Venus chance to be there, he will be seriously ill in his youth, and after that he will acquire property, and he will rejoice in wet [places], and he will live the remainder of his life in good [circumstances]. But if they happen to be going from the Ascending Node to the Descending Node, [this will be] the very best of all. In the end of his life he will be fortunate and he will acquire property, and he will live many years, when the stars have gone into light.

Saturn chancing to be in the signs of the Good Daemon[1] by day bestows kingdoms and leaderships more slowly if indeed the Sun chances to be in the ASC, but if it also receives the conjunction of the waxing Moon it bestows the good things in full [and also] positions of greater authority.[2] But if the Sun is not in the ASC, and the star [of Saturn] is posited by day in the sign of the Good Daemon,

---

[1] Cumont notes that what follows really pertains to the 5th house and not the 11th. It appears that Rhetorius accidentally reedited the significations of the house of Good Fortune (the 5th) given by his source instead of editing those of the house of the Good Daemon (the 11th). We have already seen that he made a similar mistake with the 3rd and 9th house significations. Consequently, Firmicus remains the only witness to the text of the common source for the 11th house.

[2] After *ta agatha* 'the good things', the Greek text (based here on MS **P**) has *meizous hairesiarchêtas* 'greater heresiarchies [directorships]', which seems to correspond to Firmicus, *Mathesis*, iii. 2.10 *maiorum potestatum ornamenta* 'distinctions of greater powers'.

it makes those who attain their ends with the passage of time. There is a diminishing of property, and enterprises in youth. But by night, it indicates those who are slower in their enterprises and more sluggish in their actions; some of them too are deprived of their own [property] and lose things they have acquired.

Jupiter chancing to be in the sign of the Good Daemon by day or by night is made stronger, for in contests[1] they will become persons having victory. And it will produce divine doctrines for mortals, and it fashions those who are perfect in their bones.[2]

The [star] of Mars chancing to be in the signs of the Good Daemon by night makes the existence of many good things and those who are deemed worthy of honor by the people, and friends among the powerful.[3] And if the star [of Mars] is also in its own signs or decans or degrees, with the Moon accompanying it, [it makes] great rulers, frightful to the troops, possessing the power of the sword.[4] But with the Moon not present, if the [star] of Venus is present or[5] happens to be trine or square it, it will make happy individuals and those making a profit in their activities, and charming persons. But, chancing to be in these positions by day, it makes changes of place and living abroad on account of strange events that happen to them. And they also become involved in dangers unfavorable to them. But if the [star] of Jupiter or the [star] of Venus is in aspect, it makes the time spent abroad profit-

---

[1]The Greek text has *athlôn* 'deeds' or 'contests' or 'struggles' or 'labors' (as those of Hercules). But the corresponding text in the 5th house has *agathô* 'for good'.
[2]This whole paragraph seems to be badly preserved. Firmicus, *Mathesis*, iii. 8.8, says if Jupiter is configured with Mars *is, qui sic eum habuerit, regali erit semper potestate perspicuus et sententiae eius sic erunt, tamquam ab eo cunctis hominibus divina documenta proferantur. Erit autem, qui sic eum habuerit, fortis corpore validis ossibus* 'he, who has it thus, will always be known by his royal power, and his opinions will be such as if divine documents were offered by him to mankind as a whole . . .' *Cf.* religious leaders who say they are speaking for God.
[3]Reading *hyperechonton* 'powerful' instead of *hyperechousi* 'they surpass'. *Cf.* Firmicus, *Mathesis*, iii. 4.12, *cum potentibus viris....amicitiae gratia coniungit* 'it unites them with powerful men on account of friendship'.
[4]That is, possessing the power of life and death.
[5]The Greek text should read ê 'or' with MSS **AV**, instead of *kai* 'and' with MS **P**.

able, and it indicates those who are soon restored again to their own [country].

The Sun chancing to be alone in the sign of the Good Daemon denotes happy individuals, and it will make those born of a renowned and distinguished father, and those who, with the passage of time, come into good fortune and happiness.[1]

Venus in the sign of the Good Daemon, especially when it is in the matutine phase, and even more when it is aspected by Saturn and Mars, it will produce those with no offspring or sterile persons or those unhappily married or sodomites or lovers of actresses, but this is especially true when [Venus] is in the cardinal signs. And it denotes those increasing in worldly goods with the passage [of time], and those who are advanced by friends, charming, and good-natured.

Mercury chancing to be oriental and matutine or vespertine in the sign of the Good Daemon will produce those who pile up the gold and inventors of good things, or else controllers of other people's money, [and] those having the bearing of a demi-god.[2] They will also be long-lived and have many children. But chancing to be vespertine and occidental in this house, [the native] will not become a guard nor a guardian of money, but a spendthrift of those valuables lying in secret [places]. And it will make agents or those who are seen in accounting offices or teachers or geometers or astronomers or inventors of astronomical numbers or those in charge of wrestling schools. Receiving the conjunction of the waxing Moon, it will mark the natives with white leprosy, or it will involve [him] in easily-contracted diseases according to the nature of the sign; but if the Moon is waning, it surrounds [him] with more unseemly injuries or it damages the mind.[3]

---

[1] As mentioned above, the significations given for Saturn, Jupiter, and Mars in the 11th house are really for those planets in the 5th house. But with the Sun in the 11th, Rhetorius gets back on the right track for a while.
[2] *Cf.* Cumont, *L'Égypte des astrologues*, p. 26.
[3] This set of significations really applies to the 5th house, as can be seen by comparing it with Firmicus, *Mathesis*, III.vii.8-10.

The Moon chancing to be in the signs of the Good Daemon by night will become very gracious, for it makes rulers, presumptive and settled in the first place and receiving good things from their parents, if indeed it happens to be unaspected by Saturn or Mars. But by day it denotes living abroad and estrangements from the parents or it predicts separations or orphanhood, but with the passage of time it will produce happy, prosperous individuals.[1]

58. The Power of the Fixed Stars.[2]

I think it is also necessary to describe both the power of the fixed [stars] and their action, since they are able [to do] many things when they are in the same degrees as the angles or the planets. For they are accustomed to produce strange and unexpected nativities, as the learned Julian says in his *Astrology*.[3] And his [remarks] are as follows:

The Spike of Libra in 0 Lib 20 North 1st magnitude, of a mixture of Venus and Mercury. [Spica or Alpha Virginis]

The Bright [Star] of Lyra in 21 Sag 00 [North] 1st magnitude, of a mixture of Venus and Mercury. [Vega or Alpha Lyrae]

The [Star] in the mouth of the Great Fish in 12 Aqu 00 South 1st magnitude, of a mixture of Venus and Mercury. [Fomalhaut or Al-

---

[1] This is essentially the same set of prognostications as was given for the 5th house. But this may be correct, for Firmicus says that the Moon in the 11th house signifies the same things as it does in the 5th house, and unfortunately there is a lacuna in the text of the *Mathesis* from the middle of the 4th house to the middle of the 9th house, so Rhetorius is the only witness to the common source.

[2] This chapter closely resembles the treatise on the same subject by the so-called Astrologer of the Year 379 (edited in CCAG V.1), but the longitudes of the stars agree with the values given in the chapter on the signs of the zodiac ascribed to Rhetorius (edited in CCAG VII) and are 3°40′ greater than those in Ptolemy's Catalogue of Stars. This corresponds to a date of 504 A.D., which may be indicative of the approximate time when Rhetorius composed his work.

[3] Julian of Laodicea, who flourished around the year 497. He was the author of a work entitled *Episkepsis astronomikê* 'Survey of Astronomy'. Pingree says it is more astronomical than astrological, so perhaps Rhetorius refers to another work by the same author.

pha Piscis Australis]

The Bright [Star] of Corona Borealis 15 Lib 20 North 1st magnitude, of a mixture of Venus and Mercury. [Alphecca or Alpha Coronae Borealis]

These stars in the ASC or in the MC make those born thus to be not only notable and well-to-do and renowned, but also very knowledgeable, philosophical, learned, capable, scientific, good-looking, fond of the arts, artistic, good-natured, enjoyable, [fond of] fine living, cheerful, sensible too, and intellectual, shrewd, successful, pretty much self-taught, and generally held in honor because of the excellence of their words (i.e., their minds), admirers of excellent things, eloquent, pleasing in speech, charming, harmonious in disposition, earnest, discriminating, high-minded, sometimes too promiscuous, fickle in love affairs if Mars is also rising, above the horizon, and aspects one of them in the ASC. But if the angular Mars is in aspect, they are also involved in [business or political] affairs on account of writings or [some personal] desires, especially if, with Mars so [placed] with respect to the Sun,[1] it is in the ASC.

But if [the star] is found in the IMC [and either] Venus or Mars is in the ASC or the DSC, from their oppositions they make prudent persons and God-fearing or ineffective in sexual relations or having few children or having [only] daughters. For a great difference comes about from the relation of Venus and Mars with respect to the angles.

If Saturn aspects one of these five bright stars when it is in the ASC, they make and prognosticate those who are skilled in medicine, very learned in secret books and in the mysteries.

If Jupiter aspects one of these bright stars that I just mentioned in the ASC, it will produce greater good fortune and praise and rulership and command, and in these same we shall find removal to

---
[1] This phrase is a more elaborate way of saying 'by day'.

another place. For if the star Spica is in the ASC or the MC, it makes hierophants, greatly honored priests or philosophers or prophets of some mystic rites, and especially those born in Greece. Found thus in feminine nativities, it makes priestesses and hierophants or experts in mysteries or initiations and those abstaining from certain foods, and those who are greatly helped through the agency of the gods.

But if the [star] of Corona Borealis is in the ASC or the MC, it makes honored persons, those wearing crowns, high priests, friends of kings, and strong in their bodies, and those who become renowned [and] beloved by many.

But if the [star] of Piscis Australis [is in the ASC or the MC], it makes those having few children, or having their children late, or having [only] daughters, or childless, but very eloquent and rather handsome.

Again,

The Heart of the Lion in 6 Leo 10 North 1st magnitude, of a mixture of Jupiter and Mars. [Regulus or Alpha Leonis]

Arcturus in 5 Lib 40 North 1st magnitude, of a mixture of Jupiter and Mars. [Alpha Bootis]

The Bright [Star] of Aquila in 7 Cap 40 North 1st magnitude, of a mixture of Jupiter and Mars. [Altair or Alpha Aquilae]

Antares in 16 Sco 20 North 2nd magnitude, of a mixture of Jupiter and Mars. [Alpha Scorpii]

The Dog [-star] in 21 Gem 20 South 1st magnitude, of a mixture of Jupiter and Mars. [Sirius or Alpha Canis Majoris]

These stars in the same degree as the ASC or the MC make honored generals, subjecting and administering lands and cities and nations, and frightful men and commanders and generals,[1] admin-

---

[1]Here, he uses the word *stratêlatas* instead of the more usual *stratêgous*. Both

istrators, those who are shaken up, unconquered, outspoken, contentious, effective, shrewd, manly, those likely to conquer, with much property and very wealthy, magnanimous and ambitious, fond of nice things, but not coming to an entirely good end.

Again,

The [Star] at the end of the left foot or Orion in 23 Tau 30 South 2nd magnitude,[1] of a mixture of Jupiter and Saturn. [Rigel or Beta Orionis]

The middle one of the three [stars] in the belt of Orion in 1 Gem 00 South 2nd magnitude, of a mixture of Jupiter and Saturn. [Alnilam or Epsilon Orionis]

The one on the right shoulder of Auriga in 6 Gem 30 North 2nd magnitude, of a mixture of Jupiter and Saturn. [Menkalinan or Beta Aurigae]

The one on the knee of Sagittarius in 20 Sag 40 South 2nd magnitude,[2] of a mixture of Jupiter and Saturn. [Alpha Sagittarii]

The one of the Gorgon in 3 Tau 20 North 2nd magnitude, of a mixture of Jupiter and Saturn. [Algol or Beta Persei]

The one of the Goat in 28 Tau 40 North 1st magnitude, of a mixture of Jupiter and Saturn. [Capella or Alpha Aurigae]

These [stars] in the same degree as the ASC or the MC make those having [them] thus very wealthy and too rich and owning property in various countries and cities and fond of agriculture and fond of building. Also, if the Moon aspects one of the stars I mentioned in the ASC or the MC, [they make] these [natives] good in their habits and appointed to be censors of the elders, no-

---

words mean 'commanders of armies'. I don't know which one was of superior rank.
[1] Ptolemy's Catalogue lists this star as being of the 1st magnitude.
[2] Listed as being of the 2nd or 3rd magnitude in Ptolemy's Catalogue, but only 4th magnitude today.

ble-minded, generous, long-suffering, temperate, [and] fond of their relatives; and again in particular the one in the knee of Sagittarius and the one on the right shoulder of Auriga, if they chance to be with the ASC or the MC vertically,[1] work with quadrupeds or as charioteers, or they have to do with the birth of horses or with charioteering.

Again, the one on the head of the following Twin in 0 Can 20 North 2nd magnitude, of the nature of Mars alone. [Pollux or Beta Geminorum]

If this one chances to be with the ASC or the MC in a nativity, and especially by night, it makes those fit for rule, terrible, energetic, daring, independent, irascible, self-willed, tyrants, leaders of battles, renowned and great. By day with the ASC in a nativity it will make [the natives] insolent, crude, merciless, reckless, robbers, disorderly, [and] drunkards. But if with the MC it makes very learned individuals and friends of kings or tyrants, but not destined for an altogether fine end.

Again, the one on the right claw of Scorpio in 25 Lib 50 North 2nd magnitude,[2] of the nature of Jupiter and Mercury. [North Scale or Beta Librae]

The one on the head of the leading Twin in 27 Gem 00 North 2nd magnitude, of the nature of Jupiter and Mercury. [Castor or Alpha Geminorum]

If these happen to be with the ASC or the MC, they will make scholars, very learned individuals, public speakers, fond of music and the arts, poetic, fond of nice things, shrewd, witty, inquisitive, axiomatic, religious, loving the gods, wealthy, well-known, or and those who meet with great success in the bartering of gold and silver and such like, and freer in their association with others and es-

---

[1]The Greek has *kata katheton* 'vertically'; but we should probably read *mirikôs* 'partilely'.
[2]The Greek text has 25 Lib 03, evidently having misread a *nu* '50' as a *gamma* '3'.

pecially in a diurnal nativity. For with the ASC of those who are born by night they will make those who pretend to be wise, braggarts, pretenders, dissemblers, but also very learned, having good memory, and teachers, and cleanly in their desires.

Again, the one in the leading shoulder of Orion in 27 Tau 40 South 2nd magnitude, of the nature of Mars and Mercury. [Bellatrix or Gamma Orionis]

Procyon in 2 Can 50 [South] 1st magnitude,[1] of the nature of Mars and Mercury. [Alpha Can. Min.]

The one in the right shoulder of Orion in 5 Gem 40 South 1st magnitude, of the nature of Mars and Mercury. [Rigel, Alpha Orionis]

The one common to the Horse and Andromeda in 21 Psc 30 North 2nd magnitude, of the nature of Mars and Mercury. [Alpheratz or Alpha Andromedae]

The shoulder of the Horse in 5 Psc 50 North 2nd magnitude, of the nature of Mars and Mercury. [Scheat or Beta Pegasi]

These stars again when they are in the same degree as the ASC or the MC, especially in a nocturnal nativity, will make those fitted for generalship, terrible, active persons, ingenious, sophistical, inquisitive, learned, inflexible, shrill-voiced, cheats, achievers, but at the same time easily angered and arrogant in their desires, being destroyers of the innocent and seducers of virgins, [and] perjurers. But with the ASC in a diurnal nativity they will make [the natives] daring, crude, full of regrets, liars, thieves, godless, friendless, plotters, courting applause,[2] insolent, vile murderers, forgers, wizards, homicides, sometimes not experiencing a fine end, especially, as we have said, in a diurnal nativity.

---

[1] The Greek text has *moiras treis d' a'* '3 degrees 4 [minutes] 1'. Ptolemy's position is 29 Gem 10, and adding 3°40' we get 2 Cancer 50.
[2] Robbins, *Tetrabiblos*, iii. 13, p. 357,6, translates *theatrokopous* as 'creators of disturbances in the theatre', which may be correct.

Again, the one on the right foot of the Centaur in 12 Sco 00 South 1st magnitude, of the nature of Venus and Jupiter. [Bungula or Alpha Centauri]

The End of the River in 3 Ari 50 South 1st magnitude, of the nature of Venus and Jupiter. [Theta Eridani][1] And these stars again when they are in the same degree with the ASC or the MC will make cleanly persons, enjoying life, fond of nice things, fond of music and the fine arts, god-loving, fond of giving, prudent, fond of hearing discussions, giving good counsel, high-minded in decency, prudent, decorous in love affairs or and benefitted by female perons, magnates and good persons, and rather blonde and good-looking, slender, but especially if they aspect the Moon.

Again, the tail of Leo in 28 Leo 10 North 1st magnitude, of the nature of Saturn and Venus. [Denebola or Beta Leonis]

The one in the hip of Leo in 17 Leo 50 North 1st magnitude,[2] of the nature of Saturn and Venus. [Zosma or Delta Leonis]

The one in the neck of Hydra in 3 Leo 40 South 2nd magnitude, of the nature of Saturn and Venus. [Alphard or Alpha Hydrae]

And these again with the ASC or the MC will make fortunate individuals and those acquiring property and those who are very notorious [and] passionate, but also fellators and those who speak effeminately[3], or both fond of dancing[4] and foul-mouthed about

---

[1] Not the 1st magnitude star Achernar (Alpha Eridani), which was too far south to have been seen by the classical astronomers, but presumably the 3rd magnitude star Theta Eridani, although it is 3 1/2 degrees lower in longitude than the position given above. If there was a 1st magnitude star in the given position, then it has declined drastically in magnitude, since the star nearest that position today is only of the 6th magnitude.

[2] The Greek text has 17 Leo 08, but Ptolemy has 14 Leo 10. Also, his catalogue shows the star to be of the 2nd magnitude, but I have let Rhetorius's magnitude stand.

[3] The Greek text has *malakolalous*, literally 'speaking effeminately', but it seems likely that this is a corruption of some other word describing a sexual act, perhaps a compound of *machlos* 'lewd' (said of women), or some other compound of *malakos*, literally 'soft'. *Cf.* Ptolemy, *Tetrabiblos*, ii. 3 and iii. 14. In Modern Greek *malakia* means 'masturbation'.

[4] The Greek has *philorchestas*, which could also mean 'fond of dancers', but in ei-

love affairs, but making progress with [increasing] age participating in some priestly activities, those who are revered because of some divine religious observance or self-control, and abstaining from certain foods. And they become acquainted with certain forbidden books and fond of the fine things relating to the heavens, and having eyes somewhat grey or bright, and beautiful in the eyes.

The bright [star] of the Hyades rising in the hour of birth, lying in the zodiacal circle in 16 Tau 20 [South 1st magnitude], of the nature of Mars and Venus [Aldebaran or Alpha Tauri], makes very fortunate individuals and rich ones and those who subject or administer countries and cities and nations; for just as this star and the location of the Hyades is well-known to the whole world and to all men, or and rather it is more than famous, thus the natives with the bright [star] of the Hyades rising or with the MC become the most renowned and famous and richest of all men.

And it also makes these things when it is partile [conjunct] or rises partilely with the Moon, especially since this star alone has nearly twice the power of the other stars. For when it is rising, the bright [star] Antares is setting [since] it is situated in the same degree of Scorpio, 16°20′, and both of them are in the same zodiacal circle. Thus then both around the setting parts of the world and around the rising parts and around the other climes they are extolled and are able to do great things. And the [star] Antares itself at the setting angle itself, being found in the marriage house, makes, as I foretell, great good fortune and inheritances through feminine persons; for also the wives of those who are born thus are admired by all and become very rich, but they are not long-lived, since this Antares is setting immediately, as I said before, when it is found in the marriage house.

And the bright [star] of the Hyades being with the ASC and having the power of the force of Mars and Venus makes those who are born thus very angry and hot-blooded in their desires and undis-

---

ther case the reference is to wanton or lascivious dancing.

criminating in their love affairs. For by nature the place of the Hyades rising, in fact this [place] with the ASC from 12°20' up to 16°20',[1] makes individuals passionate in their pleasures and rather distinguished and good-looking with a beautiful neck.

And in particular, certain signs and fixed stars being found partilely in the House of the God[2] and in the IMC or else with the ASC afford great aid to the natives through manifestations of the gods or through dreams. For Scorpio being found thus, and especially around 28°16', in which is the bright [star] of Ophiuchus,[3] through the manifestation or the power of Asklepiakes or Sarapiakes,[4] or through the forceful actions of the best physicians, it heals those who are born thus. And the Spike of Virgo, which is in about 0 Lib 20,[5] being found thus signifies through the manifestation of the Mother of the Gods or Kore or Aphrodite or Hygeia.

And the [star] that is found in the head of the leading Twin in 27 Gem 00,[6] as I said previously, in the House of the Gods or in the IMC or with the ASC makes aid from Hermes or Telesphoros or Apollo. And the [star] in the head of the following Twin,[7] which is in 0 Can 20, being found thus and especially in a nocturnal nativity affords aid or manifestations from Hercules or from the Dioscori. And the bright [star] of the Dog[8] in 21 Gem 20 being found in those places which I have mentioned and especially in a nocturnal nativity affords aid or manifestations from Hecate or Anubis or else from Mars itself or else from the elements or from fire or from blood or from averting evil by expiatory sacrifice. And the one in Lyra through [the action] of Apollo or Hermes; and those in the

---

[1] The Hyades actually extend from Gamma Tauri in 12 Tau 40 to Aldebaran or Alpha Tauri in 16 Tau 20.
[2] The ninth house.
[3] Probably Rasalhague or Alpha Ophiuchi is meant. If so, its correct longitude would be 28 Sco 30 rather than 28 Sco 16.
[4] Followers of Sarapis or Asklepios.
[5] Spica or Alpha Virginis.
[6] Castor or Alpha Geminorum.
[7] Pollux or Beta Geminorum.
[8] Sirius.

horns of Capricorn[1] and the Epiphoi[2] and Aix[3] being found in the places of which I have spoken previously, will make aid and manifestations from Pan or else Hermes, especially if one of the benefics aspects the aforementioned places.

And each of the planets according to its sign [and] its nature, when it is found in the aforementioned places, and especially the benefics, will make aid and manifestations in accordance with the powers of their nature; and Saturn in diurnal nativities affords the same things or else the appearances and aid of Pluto and Poseidon, and it affords treatments from antipathy of its own plants and from all [the others]. But well situated in nocturnal nativities it affords these from deceased persons or from distinguished or god-fearing persons. And Mars affords things that are like its own nature and are useful to those who are born at night, but frightful to those who are born by day and adverse and hurtful.

59. The General Configurations of the Moon.

The Moon in Scorpio or Pisces or Cancer being in the same degree with Saturn and Mars makes lepers and those afflicted with elephantiasis or it kills by poison. The Moon with Saturn and Mars in the latter degrees of the signs makes crooked and lame persons. The Moon averted from the ASC makes the natives to think adverse things for themselves. The rulers of the [preceding] New Moon and Full Moon being in the house of the Bad Daemon[4] will make banishments. The Moon full in Pisces will always take away the father before the mother. The Moon in Sagittarius always takes away the brothers. The Moon and the Sun in the 6th or 12th, with Saturn and Mars and Mercury being angular

---

[1] Giedi or Alpha Capricorni in 11 Cap 00, Nu Capricorni in 11 Cap 20, Dabih or Beta Capricorni in 11 Cap 00, and Xi Capricorni in 8 Cap 40. Of these, Giedi and Dabih are of the 3rd magnitude, while the other two are of the 6th.
[2] The Haedi or Kids of Capella (Zeta and Eta Aurigae in 25 Tau 40 and 25 Tau 50).
[3] The Goat (Capella or Alpha Aurigae in 28 Tau 40).
[4] The twelfth house.

without Jupiter and Venus, will make dog-men[1] or those who are devoured by dogs.

The Moon and Venus together will make those suffering from a frequent flux from the eyes, sometimes too it makes wanton persons and in the DSC those who cohabit with sisters or with a mother and daughter. The Moon and Mercury square or opposite or conjoined will make liars and robbers of others, but if Mars is also present, forgers or those who are fond of drugs or runners. The Moon being opposed to its own ruler [makes] fugitives, dishonored persons, wanderers, and those living abroad. The Moon making its conjunction with the Sun or its quarter or being gibbous or at full Moon or being gibbous for the second time or at its second quarter and aspected by the malefics makes injury or illness. The Moon in the IMC makes the mother ignoble or injured, and, if her ruler is cadent, a slave; but if it also applies to a malefic, she will die a violent death.

60. The Dodecatemorion.

If the Moon's dodecatemorion is trine to her, it signifies renowned persons; but if it is in opposition, the opposite of this and inglorious persons. But if the Moon's dodecatemorion falls into her opposition in a quadrupedal sign, and she is aspected by Mars, it makes those who are eaten by wild beasts. But in human signs it makes those who are killed by robbers. And if the nativity is by night, it makes active and high-born persons. And if [the aspect] is to the [star] of Saturn, the mother will be subjected or a foreigner and the [native] himself will placed in subjection. And the great nativities suffer a loss of livelihood,[2] especially by night. And if [the aspect] falls on the [star] of Mercury, [it makes] learned persons, those who have been educated. And if [the aspect is] to Jupi-

---

[1]Those who imagine themselves to be dogs. A modern example is King Otto of Bavaria (1848-1916). See above p. 44 n.1. But his horoscope does not have this particular configuration

[2]This is the reading of MS **P**, but MSS **AV** have "And it makes the great nativities to be banished."

ter, august, god-like persons. And if [it is] to Venus, friendly, cheerful, merry persons. And if [it is] to the Sun, persons of good understanding, god-like, seeking for and speaking of the gods and of things to do with the world. But if [the aspect is] into the MC with malefics, he will get the experience of prison, and he will see a change for the worse, if [the aspect is] to the square of it, it is favorable to itself;[1] but if to that where Jupiter and Venus are, good. And if Saturn's dodecatmorion falls into its own trine, [the natives will be] inglorious. And if it is favorable to the Moon and to the Sun, the nativities will be in the likeness of kings.

And similarly too in the case of all the other stars if the dodecateemorion falls thus, it signifies the same thing. If the dodecatemorion of Saturn and the dodecatemorion of Mars falls into the place of the Moon or of the Sun, [it is] not good. But if their dodecatemoria fall into their own trines, it makes moderately good things ... whether it sees benefics or malefics.[2] If it falls into the ascending sign, they will be grieved because of children, and they will be sickly. And if into the DSC, they will experience danger from crises and falls and diseases of the eye. And if into the MC, they have hindrances to their reputations;[3] but if into the IMC, they are troubled by hidden places. And the dodecatemorion of Mars makes similar things. If the dodecatemorion of Saturn falls into the place of Jupiter, he will have controversy with the ruler; but if [it falls] into that of Mars, he will be [involved in] many legal judgments; and if into that of Mercury, he will be grieved over children and brothers; and if into that of Venus, he will be grieved over a woman; and if into that of the Sun, it harms the paternal wealth or it does some evil to the father himself. If the dodecatemorion of Mars falls into the place of Venus, he will be an adulterer; but if [it falls] into that of Mercury, he will be at odds with members of his own household or with his brothers; and if

---

[1] The last two clauses are not clear.
[2] Something is missing. Perhaps we should add "or moderately bad things, depending on."
[3] *Cf.* Valens, *Anthology*, iv. 13 (ed. Pingree, 173,1)

into that of the Sun, he will have danger from fire and from a wound or his father [will have it]. If the dodecatemorion of Mercury falls into that of Jupiter, he will be entrusted with money, and he will advance [in the world] through speech or through writing, and he will be involved with someone more powerful [than himself]; but if [it falls] into that of the Moon, he will not be [fully] educated but will always be in writing and words; and if into that of Mars or into that of Mercury or into that of Venus, he will have many censures because of women, and he will consort with elderly women or with female slaves.

61. General Configurations of Injuries and Sicknesses.

Many indeed and diverse things have the ancients written on the topic of injuries and sicknesses, and I shall set forth below in turn their general and unambiguous [precepts], demonstrating the truth [of the latter] with their own examples. For it is evident that the malefics alone in the angles or and succedent or and aspecting the lights produce injuries or sicknesses. For when the malefics are oriental they will make injuries, but when occidental sicknesses.

Similarly too, the Moon separating from the malefics alone produces injuries or sicknesses. And the sixth house and its ruler being aspected by malefics only makes injuries and sicknesses. But if the ruler of the sixth house is in the ASC in a tropical sign, it makes an injury to the eyes. But if the sixth house and its ruler[1] happen to be in a water sign aspected by Saturn, it makes disorders arising from wetness or fluxes or dysentery or such like. And if [aspected] by Mars, it produces injuries and sicknesses from baths or boiling or such like.[2] If then Jupiter happens to be ruler of the sixth house, and it is aspected only by malefics, it makes those addicted to drunkenness. And if Venus happens to be thus, it makes those who

---

[1]This sentence and the text following down to the sentence beginning "And the rulers of the sixth house . . ." is similar to Dorotheus, *Pentateuch*, iv. 1, 65-74.
[2]He means from over-heated water, such as in a bath, or from accidental scalds.

are mad for women or those affected by lung disease. But if Mercury, it makes those who are deaf or speechless or hoarse or those who stammerer or lisp. But so too does it do the same thing when it is with Saturn or in the terms of Saturn. And the Sun being with it makes those afflicted with heart disease or blind persons. And the rulers of the sixth house from the ASC do the same thing when they are aspected by the malefics alone and Jupiter and Venus are not configured with them. Mars being ruler of the sixth house or of the ASC makes maimed persons without [any aspect] of Jupiter or Venus. Similarly too, the blockading[1] of the Sun and the Moon and the ASC by the malefics makes injuries and sicknesses of the eyes and the sight.

Let it not escape you, as I said before, that Gemini measures reciprocally with Capricorn and Cancer with Sagittarius because of their equal rising; but Aries also "opposes" Virgo and Libra Pisces because of their equal power.[2] For many mistakes [in interpretation] are produced by these, as I have said before, from thinking them to be averted from each other. For the homozone [signs] do not prohibit something of the configurations.[3] And Dorotheus sets the Lot of Injury, taking by day from Saturn to Mars and the result from the ASC, but by night the reverse. And it is necessary to take note of those lying with the Lot or those aspecting the Lot or the place.[4] But and the triplicity ruler of the IMC aspected by the

---

[1]This configuration seems to be an extended case of *besieging*. Cf. Vettius Valens, *Anthology*, vii. 3 (ed. Pingree, 256,7), where in one of the examples a similar term is used to describe the situation of Venus in Scorpio with Saturn in Leo and Mars in Aquarius.
[2]In modern terminology the first set of pairs is called *contra-antiscions* and the latter set *antiscions*. Firmicus Maternus, *Mathesis*, ii. 29, explains the antiscions and says that Dorotheus (in *Pentateuch*, Book 4), Ptolemy, and Antiochus followed the same system. Unfortunately, the fragmentary and interpolated Arabic text edited by Pingree says nothing about antiscions. And our best witness to Antiochus is Rhetorius himself. The other classical authorities, such as Manilius, (and apparently Ptolemy), and Paul of Alexandria, follow the older system, which was based on a fixed zodiac with the equinoxes and solstices in the 15th degree of the cardinal signs.
[3]The exact meaning of this sentence is unclear to me.
[4]Or perhaps we should read "the Lot or its ruler."

malefics or badly situated without [any aspect] to Jupiter and Venus makes injury and sickness.

The malefics alone succedent to the luminaries injures the eyes or they make dim sight. The Moon loosening its bond from the Sun or at its full and impeded by Mars or Saturn injures the eyes. The Moon chancing to be in the injurious degrees of the signs and aspected by the malefics makes injuries or sicknesses especially affecting the eyes. And the injurious degrees of the signs are these: 18, 27, and 28 Leo; 19 and 25 Scorpio; 1, 7, 8, 18, and 19 Sagittarius; 6, 7, 8, and 10 Taurus; 9-15 Cancer; 18 and 19 Aquarius; and 26-29 Capricorn. The Moon leaving off[1] and impeded in these degrees injures the eyes, but when full it produces dim sight. And Mars indeed makes the injuries and the sicknesses from a blow or from iron or fire or a stroke or a fall, but Saturn makes the cause [arise] from a cataract or from cold or opacity of the lens or a flux or dim sight. And in particular indeed in Cancer, Capricorn, Scorpio, and Pisces, impeded by the location, they also make sicknesses[2] involving eating sores, lichens or scaly patches[3] or scrofula or elephantiasis or fistulas or cancers or something else of this sort. Sagittarius and Gemini signify [injuries] through falls and epileptic or paralytic seizures.

And when the [star] of Jupiter is oriental and aspecting the ones causing the injuries or the sicknesses, it customarily makes the injuries to be hidden and the sicknesses to be mitigated. And with the [star] of Mercury it causes the mitigations [to be done] by physicians. And the [star] of Venus aspecting those making the cause through pronouncements of the gods and oracles makes the injuries [to appear] attractive and pleasing, and causes the sicknesses to be curable through divine healing.[4]

[1]Waning.
[2]Reading *pathê* instead of *empathê*. *Cf.* Ptolemy, *Tetrabiblos*, iii. 12 (328,23 ed. Robbins).
[3]The text has *leprôn* 'leprosies' but this is too specific. Some sort of rough, scaly outbreak on the skin is meant.
[4]A number of passages in the preceding portion of this chapter closely resemble

Valens says that it is necessary to look at the [planets] aspecting the Lot of Fortune and its ruler; and if malefics alone aspect them, they give injury or sickness by that bodily part in the sign in which the Lot of Fortune or its ruler happened to be, according to its own nature and according to the bodily part it rules, as Valens set forth in the second chapter of the first book.[1] And if both of them chance to be in Saturnian signs, or if they are aspected by Saturn, they make injury through fluxes and excessive cold; by Mars, those through cuts or burns or similar things according to that bodily part which the sign signifies wherein the lot or its ruler chances to be.

And if the Ascending Node chances to be in the House of Injury or Saturn or Mars chance to be there, he will fall from a high place or into a deep well or he will have an injury in his bones; and frequently too he is injured while a prisoner. But if Jupiter and Venus chance to be there and Saturn and Mars are no longer in aspect, they are uninjured. And if the Descending Node chances to be there, it makes suffering in youth; but if Jupiter and Venus chance to be there, they will have hidden sickness; and if Saturn and Mars chance to be there, he will be uninjured in his body, but it will injure his feet.

But there are some main points about injuries but produced with configurations of the stars, e.g. the full Moon in the sixth house moving towards Mars bodily or by opposition makes club-footed persons or those who are lame or wooden-footed;[2] Saturn setting [or] in the ASC or in the twelfth makes sickness affecting the fingers. Mars being static harms the feet, but when setting the eyesight. Mars in its acronychal rising[3] makes ecstatics and those suffering from fistulas. The Moon from waning moving toward Saturn after the loosing of the bond, without [aspect to] Jupiter or Ve-

---

statements in *Tetrabiblos*, iii. 12. However, Rhetorius does not attribute them to Ptolemy. It is possible that both Ptolemy and Rhetorius's source (Antiochus ?) derived their material from a still older source.
[1]Actually, in Book 2, Chapter 37.
[2]Presumably, those fitted with artificial feet.
[3]That is, rising as the Sun sets.

nus, makes lepers,[1] mutilated persons,[2] and those suffering from fluxes. Mars in Leo, without Jupiter or Venus, [makes] makes injuries or sicknesses of the eyes or of the stomach or the spleen or the sides. Mars in Virgo, without Jupiter and Venus, makes those suffering from pain in the bowels, [and] those spitting blood. Mars in Libra, without Venus and Jupiter, makes injury or sickness of the groin. Mars in Scorpio, without Jupiter and Venus, especially in the ASC, gives the injury or the sickness in the genitals or the inner organs or the extremities. Mars elongated from the Sun by 82 degrees to the east or the west makes injury to the body or damage to the eyes. And Saturn posited in the aforementioned signs denotes the same.

But since the ancients said the rest of the chapters with configurations are not simple, these they have not subjoined. Mars and Saturn in the sixth or the twelfth make hidden sicknesses and cause the ulcer of cancer. Saturn and Mars and Venus and the Moon in Pisces or Scorpio or Cancer make leprosies or dull-white leprosies or lichens. Venus [and Saturn][3] in the ASC make retention of urine or strangury. The ASC and the Moon aspected by malefics make the nativities sickly and feeble. The Moon and Mars setting harm the eyes or make prisoners. Saturn in the twelfth or in the sixth in a water sign injures the spermatic organs or the feet or makes a chronic ulcer.

Many therefore have indicated that the destructive [stars] aspecting the lights by presence or by opposition or square or in the succeeding degrees or signs harm the sight or the eyes without the aspect of the good [stars], and especially if the Moon has little light and Saturn is in aspect by night and [when it is] full [and] Mars [aspects it] by day; and again when the malefics are angular [and] the lights are succedent; and the [star] of Saturn causing the injury, as was set forth before, makes the injuries through a flux

---
[1]Or perhaps we should read *kolikous* 'sufferers from colic' instead of *kelephous* 'lepers?'. *Cf.* Ptolemy, *Tetrabiblos*, iii. 12 (326, 22 ed. Robbins).
[2]Especially those suffering from advanced leprosy with the loss of fingers and toes.
[3]Adds Cumont, since Venus alone is not malefic.

and chilling and an influx; but the [star] of Mars from a thrust or a blow or fire or iron or a hot flux; but configured with Mercury and aspecting the Sun or the Moon, in wrestling or gymnastic schools or from the attacks of evil-doers.

62. Degrees Harmful to the Eyes.[1]

The Mane of Leo from 27°36' to 28°.[2]

The Sting of Scorpio[3] 1° Sagittarius of the nature of Venus and Mars.

The Forehead of Scorpio[4] from 9°06' to 10° of the nature of Mars and Saturn.

The Arrow of Sagittarius[5] 7°56'.

The Pleiades of Taurus[6] from 5°36' to 7°08'.

The Nebula of Cancer[7] from 10° to 15°.

---

[1] Aside from some errors in the text, the longitudes of the stars are 3°26' greater than those in Ptolemy's Catalogue of Stars (in *Syntaxis* vii & viii). This corresponds to the year 481. Cumont suggests that Rhetorius may have taken this chapter from Julian of Laodicea. Ptolemy gives a shorter list of star clusters causing blindness in *Tetrabiblos*, iii. 12: the cluster in Cancer, the Pleiades, the Arrow Point of Sagittarius, the Sting of Scorpio, the parts of Leo around the Coma Berenices, and the Pitcher of Aquarius.

[2] The stars 7 and 15 Comae Berenices, which are in a cloudy area above the Lion's Tail. Their Ptolemaic longitudes +3°26' are 27°46' and 28°16'. The Mane is on the other end of the Lion around the star Gamma Leonis in 5°36'. It is uncertain how the Mane became confused with the Tuft above the end of the Lion's Tail.

[3] Shaula or Lambda Scorpii in 0°56' Sagittarius. Just outside the Milky Way, but it is near several clusters and cloudy areas.

[4] Delta, Pi, and Beta Scorpii in 9°06', 9°06', and 9°56' Scorpio. Delta and Pi are within the Milky Way, and there are a number of small stars in the vicinity.

[5] Gamma Sagittarii in 7°56' Sagittarius. It is in the Milky Way and near a cloudy area in the sky. Also, an arrow point is an obvious hazard to the eye.

[6] The stars 19, 23, and 27 Tauri and III 170 Tauri from 5°36' to 7°06' Taurus. The whole asterism is cloudy in appearance due to the many small stars.

[7] Praesepe or Epsilon Cancri (an open cluster of stars, now usually called M44) in 13°46' Cancer. The old astrologers usually specified a range encompassing this star (actually a cluster), probably consisting of Eta, Theta, Gamma, and Delta Cancri ranging from 11°06' to 14°46'.

The Eye of Sagittarius[1] 16°36'.

The Pitcher of Aquarius[2] from 18°16' to 19°.

The Spine of Capricorn[3] from 26°46' to 29°00'.

63. Those Who Are Bald.

Properly, and as to the greatest extent, the Leonians and Virgoans and Scorpionians and Sagittarians become bald or bald in front. And specially, those who have the Lot of Fortune or of the Daemon or their rulers in Aries become bald or bald in front; and similarly too in Sagittarius and in Leo and Capricorn and Scorpio and Cancer; for the Capricornians especially become bald in front.

64. Those with Gout.

Those who have the Lot of Fortune or of the Daemon or their rulers in Sagittarius or in Capricorn or in Aquarius or in Pisces become gouty or rheumatic, especially when Saturn is in aspect to them. But if the Lot of Fortune chances to be in another sign or its ruler aspected by Saturn, it makes those having rheumatism[4] in the feet and the hands, especially in Gemini or Cancer. But look in the first book of Valens for what parts of the body the seven stars rule, and whichever of them is found to be ruler of the [Lot] of Fortune or of the Daemon and aspected by malefics, it gives injury and sickness in that part which it rules. But if the two lots and their rul-

---

[1] Nu^1 and Nu^2 Sagittarii in 18°36' Sagittarius. Ptolemy characterized this star as "nebulous." And in fact there are several stars close together nearby.

[2] Said to be in the flow of water from the Pitcher in Ptolemy's Catalogue. There are two stars, in 18°16' and 18°26'. The first of these is Lambda Aquarii; the identity of the other is uncertain. The flow of water suggested *cataracts* in the eyes.

[3] Epsilon and Kappa Capricorni in 26°46' and 28°26' Capricorn. These are dim stars in a dim constellation, and perhaps the fact that the Greek word for backbone *akantha* also means 'thorn' or 'sticker' suggested a hazard to the eyes.

[4] This doubtless includes gout, arthritis, and any other condition causing the same symptoms.

ers chance to be in hunchbacked signs,[1] they make hunchbacks. And Saturn in Leo harms the father with gout or distress from fluxes, or it makes him to die violently.

65. Madmen and Epileptics.

If the Moon and Saturn are in the ASC, and Mercury is setting, angular,[2] it makes madmen and deranged persons in the absence of aspects from the good [stars]. If Mars is setting, and Saturn and Mercury are in the ASC without Jupiter and Venus, it makes madmen and deranged persons. If the Sun and the Moon are in the ASC and Saturn is setting without Jupiter and Venus, it makes those who are raving mad and madmen. If Saturn and Mercury are in the ASC and Jupiter is setting, it makes dull-witted and senseless persons and those with little or no understanding. If Venus is blockaded by Saturn and Mars in a single sign,[3] and squared by the Moon and Mercury, it makes those inspired by a god and those who prophesy and those possessed by a divine frenzy.[4]

The Moon in the ASC and Saturn in the MC and Mercury setting makes frenzied and deranged persons. The Moon and Mars and Mercury chancing to be angular without Jupiter and Venus makes robbers, thieves, [and] burglars; but if Saturn, being in the IMC, aspects them, it makes grave-robbers. If Mars and Mercury chance to be found in the DSC aspected by the Moon by opposition or square, it makes robbers, murderers who are crucified or thrown down from a precipice.[5] Mars and Mercury chancing to be angular and in the same degrees, without the aspect of the good [stars], make cheats, slanderers, forgers, [and] perjurers; but if Saturn and the Moon are in aspect, they make dirty persons, enchant-

---

[1] Valens, *Anthology*, i. 1, mentions only Capricorn.
[2] That is, in the 7th house.
[3] In this restricted case, *blockaded* is equivalent to *besieged*.
[4] Rhetorius seems to describe three stages of divine possession: (1) simple inspiration; (2) those who speak in God's name; and (3) those who lose their wits and act irrationally.
[5] A form of punishment among the Romans.

ers, [and] those who call up the dead; the full Moon separating bodily from Saturn makes those struck by apoplexy or madmen, and sometimes too, blind persons.

[The Moon] waning and separating bodily from Mars makes the same. If Mars is in the ASC, and Jupiter in the same degrees is setting, while the other [stars] are averted, it makes those inspired by a god. If Saturn disposes of[1] the Moon opposing her, the native will be inspired by a god [and] epileptic; if the rulers of the triplicity of the light of the sect[2] chance to be opposed and aspected by malefics, it will make epileptics, especially when the ASC or its ruler are aspected by Saturn or Mars. When Mercury is averted from the ASC and the Moon, it always makes epileptics;[3] and if it is aspected by a malefic, it makes those afflicted by demons.[4] The Moon having bonding when she is full makes those taken over by a god, possessed by a god, [or] inspired; and if Mars is in aspect, it makes those afflicted by demons or madmen.

If the ruler of the Lot of Fortune or the Lot of the Daemon chances to be in the 9th or the 3rd, opposed by the malefics, it will make those making utterances or raving or making prophecies. The Moon being in her new or full phase and aspected by Saturn without [any aspect from] Jupiter or Venus makes those afflicted by demons; and [also] if the full Moon is aspected by Mars alone, especially in Sagittarius or in Pisces. [And if the Moon is with the malefics alone, the diseases are incurable; but][5] Jupiter in aspect

---

[1]The Greek text has *diepê* 'manages', which is usually used to signify the state of being the hour ruler (see Paul of Alexandria, *Introduction*, Chapt. 21) and is ordinarily intransitive. The text appears to be corrupt.

[2]The Light of the Time, i.e. the Sun for a diurnal chart or the Moon for a nocturnal chart.

[3]Beginning here, the text is similar to Ptolemy, *Tetrabiblos*, iii. 14 (the latter half of Section 169, and Section 170), sometimes word for word, but the resemblances seem to me to indicate a common source rather than a paraphrasing of Ptolemy by Rhetorius. In particular, note the references to the rulers of the triplicity and to the Light of the Time.

[4]*Cf.* Venus in the 9th house (Chapt. 57).

[5]There is a lacuna in the Greek text, but I have supplied the sense of the missing words from *Tetrabiblos*, iii. 14.

gives cures by medical treatment or dietetics or drugs; and Venus,[1] through oracles and the aid of the gods.

Mars or Saturn in the IMC [makes] those afflicted by demons and frightened by phantom images;[2] and if Venus is impeded, it makes those inspired by a god or those making utterances. Saturn or Mars situated with the [Lot of the] Daemon, or opposing it, without [any aspect of] Jupiter or Venus will make raving mad persons and ecstatics; and understand the same thing too in the case of New Moons or Full Moons. The ruler of the Lot of the Daemon being opposed to it makes those who give poor advice, those with contrary opinions, braggarts, insolent persons.

66. Lechers and Drunkards and Homosexuals.

Venus in the domicile of Mercury, with Mercury badly situated, makes pederasts. The Lot of Marriage in the domicile of Mercury, with Mercury angular in a masculine [sign], makes the same thing. Mars and Mercury occupying each other's domiciles or squaring or opposing each other will make pederasts. Venus in Capricorn or Pisces or Scorpio or Taurus aspected by Saturn or Mars makes lechers, especially [if she is] under the sunbeams. Venus in the domicile of Saturn or Mars [and] aspected by them makes lechers. Venus and Mercury and Mars aspecting each other will make lechers. Venus and the Moon in the DSC will make women lechers, and men effeminate, and more so if they are aspected by Saturn or Mars.

The Sun and the Moon in trine to each other makes men very bold and especially [does so in the case of] women. Venus under

---

[1] The Greek text has *Selênê* 'the Moon', but Venus is plainly called for. *Cf.* the very similar text in *Tetrabiblos*, iii. 14.
[2] Cumont thinks this should read *phoibazomenous* 'inspired' instead of *phoberizomenous* 'frightened', but I disagree. *Cf.* Vettius Valens, *Anthology*, ii. 37,51 "and when Saturn is found in the IMC, phantom images of the gods and of the dead appear." Cumont explains: "The malefic planets in the IMC produce necromancers because the dead were placed there, from which the worst art of the magicians taught how to elicit their shades."

the earth in masculine signs makes women of ill repute, and, if she is stationary, effeminate [men]. Mars aspecting Venus partilely by trine, square, or opposition in cardinal signs and receiving or aspecting each other's dodecatemorions, will make drunkards, effeminates, unsteady persons;[1] and if Saturn is in aspect, it makes catamites [or] lechers, especially if in feminine signs. Venus in the 6th makes pederasts; Venus in the 9th is the worst [position] for marriage for men, but good for women. Mars in the 9th is bad. The Moon in the ASC and Venus in a quadrupedal sign will make women sodomites,[2] and men lickers and reprehensible persons.

67. Houses and Degrees Producing Lechers and Homosexuals.

The ASC in the 13th, 14th, 22nd, 24th, 27th, 28th, [or] 30th degrees of Aries makes homosexuals and lechers. The ASC in Taurus in the degrees of the Hyades, from 12 to 17 [degrees], the ASC in Leo from the 25th to the 30th, the ASC in the 11th [or] 12th of Capricorn; in these degrees it is necessary to take careful note of the ASC and the DSC and Venus and the Moon and the Lot of Fortune and the Lot of Marriage and [the Lot] of Desire. And the effeminizing places are the last degrees of Aries, Leo, [and] Sagittarius. Those therefore who have their ASC in these degrees become effeminate or catamitical in their habits.

68. Decans Producing Lechers.

Venus in these. Venus chancing to be in the first decan of Aries makes lechers and eaters of unlawful meats and unlawful marriages and those who practice unmentionable vices and lickers and reprehensible persons[3] and passionate ones and sodomites and

---

[1]Perhaps, 'bisexuals'.
[2]The Greek text has *aselgopygous* lit. 'lecherous-butts', an expressive but otherwise unattested word.
[3]The Greek text has *psogistas* lit. 'fault-finders' from *psogos* 'blame'. But here it must refer to some sexual activity and is apparently a slang term synonymous

rapers[1] of women; but when it is made fortunate, not so depraved. Venus in the second decan of Gemini, out of sect and cadent [makes] sodomites, lewd, shameful persons, joining together in a fickle manner; adulterous and mad for sexual pleasures. Venus in the first decan of Leo badly situated makes amorous persons, marrying badly, practicing unmentionable vice; or else [the native] will get [gifts] from women who practice unmentionable vice and [are] promiscuous.[2] Venus in the third decan of Leo, badly situated, makes adulterers, rapers of women; but they will also suffer loss and misfortune through women.

Venus in the first decan of Libra makes lechers and shameful persons, mad in their desires. Venus in the first decan of Scorpio, badly situated and cadent, makes those who are harmed by those who act shamefully, and those fleeing because of women.[3] Venus in the third decan of Sagittarius, badly situated, makes those who act shamefully, those suffering misfortune through women, and [traveling] into deserted places or sailing the sea on account of women, and [the native] will be shameful.[4] Venus in the first decan of Capricorn, badly situated, makes lechers, shameful persons, and those practicing unnatural acts, lickers or reprehensible persons.[5] Venus in the second decan of Capricorn impeded makes adulterers, those who are reprehended, or else those in a foreign country because of a woman or with a woman, and those waiting for such a person on the sea. Venus in the third decan of Aquarius, impeded, makes promiscuous, dirty persons. Venus in the third decan of Pis-

---

with the word that precedes it (from its shape, the Greek letter *psi* was sometimes used to refer to the vulva). The same phrase also occurs below (Venus in the first decan of Capricorn).

[1] The Greek word *harpagas* means 'robbers', 'snatchers', 'grabbers', etc.; but in this context it probably means 'rapists'.

[2] The last clause is from MS **P** (to which Cumont hesitantly added the word 'gifts'); MS **A** has the shorter phrase 'or those getting wanton women'; and MS **G** omits the clause entirely.

[3] This is the reading of MS **A**; MSS **GP** have 'harm [from] women acting shamefully'.

[4] The last phrase is omitted by MS **A**.

[5] Cumont translates the last phrase, which also occurs above (Venus in Aries), as 'fellators or catamites'.

ces, impedited, makes promiscuous persons, adulterers, mad for sexual intercourse.

69. The Sun.

The Sun in the third decan of Aries and in the first, second, or third decan of Libra and in the first decan of Scorpio and in the first or third decan of Pisces makes lechers and effeminates.

70. The Moon.

The Moon in the third decan of Aries makes effeminates and lechers and passionate persons, and [it does the same in] the third decan of Leo and the third decan of Capricorn and the third decan of Libra and the third decan of Aquarius and the first decan of Pisces.

71. Saturn.

Saturn in the third decan of Aries and in the first and third decan of Libra and in the first and third decan of Capricorn makes lechers.

72. Jupiter.

Jupiter in the third decan of Aries and in the first and third decan of Libra and in the first and third decan of Capricorn makes lechers.

73. Mars.

Mars in the third decan of Aries and in the first and third decan of Libra signifies the same things.

74. Mercury.

Mercury in the first decan of Libra and in the first decan of Capricorn signifies the same things.

75. The Ascendant.

The ASC in the third decan of Aries and in the first and third decan of Libra and in the first decan of Capricorn makes lechers and those living in luxury.

The Lot of Fortune and the Lot of the Daemon and their rulers having fallen into a lecherous sign make effeminates and lechers.

76. Lecherous Signs.

The lecherous signs are Aries, Taurus, Leo, Capricorn in part, and Pisces; and Libra because the [constellation of the] Goat rises with it.[1]

77. General Configurations of Those Suffering a Violent Death.

The Lot of the Anaereta [is taken] from the ruler of the ascending sign up to the Moon, and the result [is cast] from the ASC, but by night the other way around. the Moon aspecting the Lot of the Anaereta makes those dying violently, worse if the Moon is found in the mutilated signs; when the ruler of the preceding new Moon or full Moon is averted from its own domicile and is aspected by malefics; the preceding new Moon or full Moon is only aspected by malefics; if the ruler of the ASC or the Lot of Fortune is found being aspected by malefics; if the first ruler of the triplicity of the IC angle falls badly and is aspected by malefics without [any aspect from] Jupiter and Venus. The Lot of Death [is taken] from the Moon to the eigth house from the ASC by day and by night; and wherever the Lot falls out, look at the [planets] aspecting; for if only a malefic aspects the lot, it makes those dying violently.

Otherwise according to Critodemus.[2] The ruler of the terms of

---

[1] See the note to Chapter 68 above.
[2] Some of these excerpts from Critodemus are also found in the delineations for the eighth house in Chapter 57 above.

the DSC angle being a malefic and under the Sun beams being found in the degrees of the Sun[1] signifies death from treachery and ambush; but when it is not under the Sun beams, it makes those dying violently and those who are killed in the presence of others.[2] The ruler of the terms of the DSC being a malefic and stationary or retrograde kills by injuries or poison or wounds. The ruler of the terms of the DSC being a malefic and being in human signs and being aspected by malefics makes death to be from men, and in the moist signs by water, and in bestial [signs] from wild beasts or [by a fall] from a height.

The Moon being joined by Saturn and Mars in one sign, angular or succedent, makes those dying violently. Saturn being the ruler of the eighth house and aspecting it without [any aspect of] the benefics, kills by water; but if Saturn chances to be in moist signs, in rivers or in seas; and on the dry land or in the mountains or in a deserted place. And Mercury being 24 degrees distant[3] from the Sun makes those dying violently, and Venus being 28 degrees[4] distant makes the same thing. And the Sun ruling the sign of the eighth house and standing in the houses of another [planet], with the Sun and the eighth house [both] impeded, makes death [by a fall] from a high place. And if Mars is the ruler of the sign of the eighth house and the house is impeded without [any aspect of] Jupiter and Venus, it makes death by armed robbers or wild beasts or enemies; and when Mars is aspected by the Sun, it kills by [action of] the community or the people or kings, being crucified[5] or being beheaded or fighting with wild beasts.[1]

---

[1] Note that the reference is to the terms according to Critodemus, which included the Sun as one of the planetary rulers. Cf. the table in Pingree's ed. of *The Yavanajâtaka of Sphujidhvaja* (Cambridge, Mass.: Harvard Univ. Press, 1978), vol. 2., pp. 212-213. Thus, either Rhetorius or his source (Antiochus?) had knowledge of Critodemus's system of terms.
[2] Literally 'openly', i.e. not privately, but where the deed was visible to others.
[3] That is, at its maximum elongation (actually, 28 degrees).
[4] Or should we read 48 degrees—the maximum elongation of Venus?
[5] Cumont points out that crucifixion was abolished by Constantine the Great in the fourth century. Therefore Rhetorius has preserved this text unchanged, even though it was no longer appropriate for his own epoch.

If Venus rules the sign of the eight house and both it and the eight house are impedited without [any aspect of] Jupiter, it kills by [the agency] of a woman or much wine or poison. Mercury ruling the sign of the eighth house and both it and the eighth house impedited, it kills by [the agency] of slaves or scribes. Jupiter ruling the sign of the eighth house and impedited along with the house kills by [the agency] of kings or leaders. The ruler of the eight house not aspecting it but impedited and standing in the sign of another [planet] makes the aforementioned things [to occur] in a foreign place; and if it aspects the eighth house while it is in its own domicile or triplicity or exaltation, [the native] will suffer these things in his own country.

With the eighth house and the ruler of its sign badly situated, if the benefics aspect the eighth house or its ruler, it makes the same [kinds of] deaths but not public. And also look at the third and the seventh and the fortieth day of the Moon; for the fortieth moving to a malefic makes those dying violently. So then it is necessary, as we said before, also to look for the new Moons that are eclipses. If the Ascending Node is found in the eighth house and Mars and Saturn and Mercury are in aspect, it makes those dying violently; for they are either beheaded or they are crucified. And if the Sun is also in aspect with them, they injure the sight or the feet. And if it chances to be only benefics that are aspecting the eighth house without [any aspects] of Saturn or Mars, they will make a peaceful death. If the Ascending Node chances to be in the 8th house and Jupiter and Venus and Mars chance to be there, it makes those dying a violent death or those who are beheaded.

There are also other things that make a violent death but not such simple configurations but [rather] configurations of many stars. For example, the Moon full in the midheaven, with Mars and

---

[1]Pingree, op. cit., points out that "the use of the term *thêriomachein* 'to fight with wild beasts' proves that the text [from Critodemus] must have been written after the beginning of the second century B.C. and, if it is Egyptian [in origin], after the Roman occupation of that country in 30 B.C." Since Pliny mentions Critodemus, he must have flourished prior to 77 A.D. Hence, if he lived in Egypt he probably flourished between 30 B.C. and 77 A.D.

the Sun opposing from the IC, with Jupiter and Venus being averted, makes those dying violently and being burned alive. Since therefore these things are produced by different configurations, it is not necessary that we lead the way to list them because I have set forth once from the outset the simple and insuperable things of the nativity partly to guide in making the selection from the different authorities; for I have left the rest to the authorities.

The ruler of the Lot of Fortune and the ruler of the eighth house being in opposition to each other make those dying violently. Saturn in the ASC and Mars in the DSC in opposition make hunters,[1] those who fight with wild beasts,[2] or those who are eaten by dogs. Saturn in the IC with Mars in the MC by night make those who are crucified and devoured by birds.[3] If the ruler of the terms of the planetary hour is in the house of the Bad Daemon,[4] it makes the native to be eaten by wild beasts. And if Mars and Saturn happen to be in Leo or in Cancer, they either make short-lived persons or those who die violently. The ruler of the ASC and that of the Moon opposing each other make those who die abroad. And if they are also aspected by malefics, they kill [the native] violently. The ruler of the Lot of Fortune under the Sun beams, at least without [any aspect] of Jupiter or Venus, makes those dying a bad death according to the nature of the sign. Saturn, Mercury, and Mars lying on [the place] of the Moon on the fortieth [day][5] make those dying violently. The full Moon dominated by Mars in the mutilated signs without [any aspect] of Jupiter or Venus makes those dying violently. the malefics prepollent to the lights without [any aspect of] Jupiter or Venus, make those dying violently. The Moon in the 4th in a domicile of Mars, without [any aspect] of Jupiter [or] Venus

---

[1] As Cumont notes in *L'Égypte des astrologues*, p. 62, "The hunters who pursued a dangerous quarry were themselves often victims of its ferocity."
[2] In the arena. A modern, but less dangerous, example would be bull-fighters.
[3] The bodies of those who were crucified were left exposed on the cross where birds (and dogs) could tear at the flesh. Afterwards, the remains were removed and thrown onto the city dump.
[4] The twelfth house.
[5] That is, the place of the Moon on the fortieth day after birth, i.e. what we would call the 39th day.

makes those dying violently. Mercury in opposition to the full Moon and aspected by malefics makes those dying violently.

78. General Configurations of Those Who Are Exiled.

The Lot of the House of Afflictions[1] [is taken] by day from Saturn to Mars and an equal amount [is cast] from the ASC, but by night the reverse. When this lot is only aspected by malefics, it makes the nativities perilous and dangerous. Full Moons aspected only by malefics with the Sun without [any aspect] of Jupiter or Venus signifies exiles; but even worse if their rulers are aspected by malefics or they happen to be averted from them. The rulers of the full Moons being in the house of the Bad Daemon or being impeded make exiles. The Moon departing and separating from Mars only says the nativity is not a good one; and similarly too when it is full and separating from Saturn; and sometimes too it makes raving madmen or apoplectics. The Moon separating from a malefic and moving toward a malefic signifies exile. The Moon and the ASC besieged by malefics make exile. Look next at the triplicity rulers of the light of the sect; for being badly posited and aspected by malefics or under the Sun beams, they make exile.

Similarly too, the ruler of the nativity being badly posited and aspected by malefics makes the nativities [to be] exiles. And yet, the Lot of Fortune and the Lot of the Daemon and their rulers badly posited and under the Sun beams and aspected by malefics and also with the 11th [house] of the Lot of Fortune are indicative of exile. Saturn and Mars sextile to the sun and the Moon make the nativities afflicted. The Sun and the full Moon aspected by malefics make the nativities afflicted. And yet the ASC or the Moon being aspected by malefics make the nativities sickly. And the rulers of the full Moon being averted from the places [of the Sun and Moon] or being opposed to their places are indicative of

---
[1]Literally, the 'House of Causing'; Firmicus, *Mathesis*, vi. 32.40, calls it the 'House of Afflictions and Illnesses'.

contrarieties and difficulties in attainment [of desires]. The full Moons and their rulers posited in the 12th or the 8th make exile, but also if they are out of sect and aspected by malefics. The Sun not beholding the Lot of Fortune or its ruler either [by being in] equal-rising [signs] or those of equal power or by homozone makes exile. The malefics alone aspecting the ASC or the MC make exile; and all the more if the in sect or the term-rulers of the Sun and the Moon are badly posited and have fallen under the Sun beams, they will make the parents or those rearing them to be of low degree.

79. The Phases of the Moon.

The Moon has 11 phases: conjunction; then 15 degrees distant from the Sun, rising; third, 45 degrees distant, crescent; fourth, 90 degrees distant from the Sun, [first] half^1; fifth, 91 to 135 degrees distant from the Sun, and it is called *gibbous*; sixth, 180 degrees distant from the Sun, full Moon; seventh, 45 degrees^2 distant from the full Moon, {i.e. up to 225 [degrees from the Sun], it makes its second gibbous [phase]; eighth, 270 degrees distant from the Sun, second half^3; ninth, 315 degrees distant, second crescent; tenth, from 345 to} 360 degrees distant from the Sun, setting; and eleventh, the dark [of the Moon]. It is necessary to investigate the rulers of these phases and their houses from the ASC; for the house of the phase signifies the birth and the first age, and the ruler of the phase the second age. If then the sign of the phase or the ruler of the sign chances to be in an evil house and it is beheld by malefics, it makes the nativities low-born and degraded; but if the phase happens to be angular, and its ruler is aspected by benefics, [the natives] will be well-born and renowned; and if the house chances

---

^{1}We would say 'first quarter' referring to the time in the lunar month, but the Greeks said 'first half' referring to the Moon's appearance at that time.

^{2}The text has 165. From this point on to the end the Greek text is confused and has a sizable lacuna. I have supplied the text in braces and also rearranged the text of the tenth and the eleventh phases. *Cf.* Vettius Valens, *Anthology*, ii. 36, which is very similar to Rhetorius.

^{3}We would say 'third quarter' or 'last quarter'.

to be in effective signs, but the ruler is poorly placed and aspected by malefics, being born free or well-reared, they will be have their situation reversed and become needy and subject [to others].

And if the ruler is found in effective signs and the house is poorly placed, they will be distressed in the first times [of life] because of their subject positions and later they will be deemed worthy of freedom and advancement, and especially if they are aspected by benefics. And if both the house and its ruler are poorly placed but they are aspected by benefics, after the times [dominated by] the malefics, being freed from subjection or from captivity, they will come into good conditions. But if the house is aspected by malefics and its ruler by benefics, being born second, they will be reared free or as a substitute and they will be capable of begetting children. And if the house is aspected by benefics and the ruler of the house by malefics, being born free, they will be thrust into servitude. Or they will commit themselves to subjection for want of sustenance or because of loss of security or employment. The conjunctions and first halves[1] of the Moon aspected by Saturn are indicative of exile; the full Moons and the second halves[2] aspected by Mars will make famous exiles—once in the fixed signs, more frequently in the bicorporeal, and in the tropical [signs] publicly or famously. And when they are angular, they fall from the greatest good fortune; and when they are succedent, they endure other things from others; and when they are cadent, they are driven into flight and insults and tortures and excesses and violent deaths.

80. The Ascending Node and the Descending Node.

If the Ascending Node is with Jupiter or the Moon or Venus or the Sun, it makes exiles; and with the Sun it injures the father; but with the Moon, it either makes the mother disreputable or it says that she is wanton, especially if it is angular. The Ascending Node

---

[1] Or 'quarters' as we would say.
[2] The 'third' or 'last quarters', as we would say.

with Saturn and Mars does the same thing, but in particular if they are angular. The Ascending Node is good with the benefics, while the Descending Node is good with the malefics. The triplicity rulers of the Lights, the first and the second, chancing to be inharmonious in their relation to each other or being opposed to each other and not being aspected by the Sun by day or the Moon by night, make captives or those in servitude or fugitives because of the evils that happen to them in their native land. The Moon and Saturn chancing to be in one sign always make exiles, but returning after 36 years if indeed they chance to be in a good house. If the ruler of the Lot of Fortune is found in the 7th or in the IC, they show banishment; and if it is in the 8th, they give acquisitions but not lasting; the malefics alone predominating over the lights by square or sextile make great dangers, and sometimes also violent death.

81. General Configurations of Those Enjoying Good Fortune.

The [planets that are] doryphories of the Lights make fortunate nativities when they are of the sect, and those of the benefics encompassing them, and the triplicity rulers of the Light of the Sect[1], and with the Lots of Fortune and of the Daemon being situated with their rulers by phase and by house and aspected by benefics; but indeed the 11th of the Lot of Fortune and its ruler also being well situated and aspected by benefics; similarly too, the rulers of the terms and the rulers of the signs of the lights and of the ASC being well situated by phase and by house. And [you should] also examine the third and the seventh and the fortieth [day] of the Moon[2]

---

[1]That is, the Light of the Time.
[2]*Cf.* Vettius Valens, *Anthology*, i. 15, "The 3rd, 7th, and 40th [Day] of the Moon," and the citations from Critodemus in Rhetorius, Chapters 77 and 117. *Cf.* also Firmicus, *Mathesis*, iii. 14.10, for the third day; and iv. 1.7, for the first, third, seventh, and eleventh (Cumont notes that we should read *quadragesimus* (sc. XL, not XI) 'fortieth' rather than *undecimus* 'eleventh'). *Cf.* also Hephaestio, *Apotelesmatics*, ii. 24.10-11 (from Dorotheus, *Pentateuch* i. 12.1), who mentions the third day.

[to see] if it is aspected by benefics; but also[1] the bright degrees of the stars and the degrees that chanced to rise at the same time with the fixed stars of the first and second magnitude according to their uses. And [you should] also examine the rulers of the nativities and their rulers, how they are situated by phase and by house, and by which [planets] they are aspected. For if all these configurations have fallen out well, they make great and remarkable persons and [those enjoying] successes. But if they chance to be inharmonious in the ASC, but they are harmoniously related to the Lot of Fortune, even thus they produce successes. And [you should] also examine the Ascending Node [to see its] relation to the benefics and to the Moon and the Sun.

And beware lest there chance to be existing in the nativity any one of the configurations mentioned in the chapter on exile. And it will make [the native's] success precarious and not lasting; for to be fortunate down to [the time of] death is for most people rare and undependable. And in addition to all the previously mentioned considerations, it is also necessary to investigate both the latitudes and the phases of the stars and the applications and the separations of the Moon by longitude and latitude, and whether the Moon will move from its least motion into a greater motion; for this is also a configuration indicative of success along with the rest of the configurations [that we have mentioned]. And beware too of the configurations [mentioned] in the chapter about violent death, for many persons who enjoyed success at its heighest have had a violent death. And Valens says in his 9th book[2] that of the substance in the nativity in this of the nativity well situated, if the Lot of Fortune chances to be in Cancer or Leo or Libra or Aquarius aspected by the benefics in effective signs, it makes the nativities commanding and royal and those of general officers in the army.

---

[1] Deleting *ou mên* before *alla kai*; or you could read *ou monon alla kai* 'not only [that] but also'.
[2] *Anthology* ix. 2 (Pingree's ed. p. 320,10)

82. Action and Pursuits.

Since the topic of action and pursuits is a necessary one, I have diligently pursued [the means] to describe it, making the selection from different ancient [authorities] for the inerrancy of knowledge. Therefore, concerning [the subject of] this chapter, I also commend the saying of Anubio [which goes] thus:

> In action, I first look for bodily injury; for from that
> Goes neither a splendid skill nor a lucky one...
>
> and that it is necessary to search out first of all the
> appropriate topic of injury, since how and of what
> kind the athlete's gout is generated or the shoemaker's
> hand-gout[1] or the clothes-mender's blindness.

We, then, looking out for the topic of injury, entered into the type of action in this way: the givers, then, of actions are Mercury, Venus, and Mars; the effective houses are the ascendant, the midheaven, the IC, and the [houses] succedent to these, but also indeed the sixth house, and the Lot of Fortune, and the application of the Moon, and the [star] making its morning appearance or its evening rising seven days before or seven days after. If, then, Mercury or Venus or Mars chances to be averted from the midheaven and the ascendant, they make such persons to be impractical, especially if the ruler of the midheaven also chances to be in an alien sign; for it also gives action when it is in the midheaven. But Anubio also says that it is necessary to look at the Moon, from the new Moon or the full Moon,[2] [to see] toward which [star] it is moving and to declare the action according to [the nature of] that one.

For example, if it applies to Venus from the new Moon or the full Moon, it gives good fortune from women; and if to Jupiter, it will make [the native to be] prosperous and decent; and if to Mars, it makes this one to be a military man; and if to Mercury, a secre-

---
[1]Probably either carpal tunnel syndrome or arthritis.
[2]Presumably, this means to look at the syzygy that preceded the native's birth and inspect the Moon's applications at that time.

tary¹ or an orator or a learned person; but if to Saturn, it makes a manager and an administrator and a household-manager. And it is necessary to pay close attention to the configurations in connection with the topic of action. And if on the one hand the [star] granting action chances to be in its own domicile, that one grants the characteristic action that it has obtained by its appearance; but if it chances to be in an alien sign, it also takes along the characteristic action of the [star] receiving it. For example, if the [star] granting action chances to be in one of the domiciles of Jupiter, it will make the actions illustrious and generous and very delightful and having a splendid appearance; and if in one of the domiciles of Saturn, dirty and laborious and ignominious; and if [in one] of Mars's, through weapons or fire or iron or iron-working or public affairs²; and if in one of the domiciles of Venus, womanly activities or artistic ones or those having to do with weaving or painters or modelers or perfumers or garland makers or dyers or dealers in purple and such like; and if Jupiter also gives the Lot of Action in one of the domiciles of Venus, these persons will be honored for the sake of priests or wizards or hierophants; and if in the domiciles of Mercury, it makes the actions to be from teaching or knowledge or speech-writing or calculations or speaking or writing or business or it makes those who gain their livelihood from weighing and measuring; and if in the domicile of the Sun, it gives those crafts in the market-place or in public or it gives some craft involving fire or iron³; but if in the domicile of the Moon, it grants crafts that are self-learned or self-taught.

And these things, then, are from the topical consideration; but of the signs,⁴ in which those [stars] granting the action may be, the particular characteristics that are comprehended by the form for the variation of the action, as Ptolemy teaches. For the signs of hu-

---

¹A person in charge of documents of some sort, not simply a copyist.
²Or perhaps 'prison affairs', which seems more in keeping with the nature of Mars.
³So **P**, but **AB** have 'in Leo self-taught and self-learned, and if by night, it gives these public crafts in the market-place, [involving the use] of either fire or iron'.
⁴What follows is close to *Tetrabiblos* iv.4 (Sect. 181 ff.).

man form having received the causing of action, he works in all the scientific arts and in those useful for humans; and the quadrupedal [signs], in [work with] metals and commerce and construction; and the equinoctial [signs],[1] in translations and exchanges and in geometry[2] and priestly matters; and the earth and watery [signs], in things in water or involved with water and in herbs and shipbuilding, and also in [something to do with] burials and fishing.[3]

Similarly, when the Moon holds the house of action moving away from the conjunction [with the Sun] and [joining] with Mercury in Taurus or Capricorn or Cancer, it makes soothsayers or sacrificers or practitioners of lekanomancy[4]; and in Sagittarius and Pisces, necromancers and those who rouse up demons; and in Virgo and Scorpio, magi, astronomers,[5] those who give [prophetic] utterances, prognosticators; and in Aries and Leo and Libra, those who are inspired [by a divinity], dream-interpreters, exorcists; and the greatness of the actions will be judged from the power of the ruling stars. For when they are rising or angular, they make the actions of the first rank[6]; but when setting or declining from the primary angles.[7] And when aspected by the benefics, they will make the actions to be great and much praised and profitable and infallible and gracious; but [when aspected] by the malefics, humble and inglorious and not gaining wealth and dangerous.

---

[1]*Tetrabiblos* 'solstitial and equinoctial'.
[2]*Tetrabiblos* 'measuring and agriculture'.
[3]*Tetrabiblos* 'pickling [fish] or fishing'. Robbins translates 'pickling or salting' and notes that the word 'pickling' also means 'embalming'.
[4]Literally, 'dish-diviners', i.e. soothsayers who looked at liquids in the bottom of dishes. Thus they might see flickering images reflected in the liquid or perhaps they interpreted the patterns of sediments in the dish as do the modern tea-leaf readers or coffee-cup readers. Cumont, *L'Égypte des astrologues*, p. 161, notes an example of this practice in the Book of Genesis, 44, 5 & 15. The practice is not dissimilar to the modern Rorschach tests used by some psychiatrists.
[5]*Tetrabiblos* 'astrologers'.
[6]The text has *katholikas*, literally, 'universal' but in the sense of 'universally recognized as superior'. The *Tetrabiblos* has *authentikas* 'principal' or 'authoritative', which amounts to the same thing.
[7]Reading *progônôs* 'first angles' instead of *progonôs* 'firstborn'. The *Tetrabiblos* has *kentrôn* 'angles'.

When Saturn is in opposition, colds and colors and increase and actions[1]; when Mars [is in opposition], foolhardiness and scandal.

83. The Three Stars That Signify Actions.

The [star] then will be judged by you to be the one taking the rulership of action in accordance with the method we have previously stated—we shall take the maker of action from the individual quality of Mercury and Venus and Mars and from that of the signs in which they may be found to be moving.

For, if the [star] of Mercury has charge of acting, it makes secretaries, businessmen, bankers, soothsayers, physicians and astrologers, sacrificers, lawyers, orators,[2] and in short those who are involved with or work with writings and giving and receiving[3]; and if the [star] of Saturn is aspecting it, business managers of other persons or interpreters of dreams or making their abode in sacred places for the purpose of prophecies, inspirations, or instructions. And the [star] of Jupiter, lawmakers, orators, sophists, having their abode with great persons. And the [star] of Mars, being present with it, makes sacrificers, surgeons, or those who bear arms, or who have trades working with fire or iron. And if the [star] of Mercury chances to be in the Evil Daemon,[4] it makes evil-doers, perverse persons, those fond of lawsuits. And if Saturn and Mars are in aspect with it, and they are well posited, they will make sacrificers and astrologers or singers of mythic tales. And if Jupiter is in strong aspect to them, he will be knowledgeable about the things just mentioned and a personal friend of magnates and kings.

Mars bestowing the actions and testifying or in the ASC makes stone-cutters or carpenters or stone-masons. And if the Sun is also in aspect with it, it makes coppersmiths or priests who make sacri-

---

[1]This whole phrase is corrupt as is the corresponding phrase in the *Tetrabiblos*, which has 'colds and mixtures of colors'.
[2]Omitted by Ptolemy, *Tetrabiblos* iv. 4.
[3]That is, 'buying and selling' or acting as a broker or factor.
[4]The twelfth house.

fices or dyers or [work] with fire and iron. And if Venus is in strong aspect to Mars, it gives trades involving fire or iron or anvils, especially in diurnal nativities. And Mars and the Moon and Venus being together make armed robbers and door-breakers.[1]

The [star] of Venus bestowing the actions makes perfume merchants or wine merchants or florists, or dealers in colors or dyes or spices, or druggists, weavers, painters, dyers, clothes-dealers, and those things having to do with women's dress. And if the [star] of Saturn is in aspect with it, sellers of things for enjoyment and adornment; and sorcerers and poisoners, or sometimes they govern public places, or sacred ones when Saturn is well posited. And if the [star] of Jupiter is in aspect, it makes a musician or a reciter of stories, someone in charge of sacred things or someone in charge of women. And the [star] of Mars being together with it, with the Sun configured with them, makes those whose work is with fire, [viz.] cooks, metal-casters, stokers, metallurgists; but [if] not configured with the Sun, those who work with iron—shipbuilders, carpenters, farmers, quarry-men, stone-carvers, stone-masons,[2] wood-splitters. And if the [star] of Saturn aspects it, it makes sailors, pumpers,[3] tunnelers,[4] keepers of wild beasts, cooks, bath attendants, bath workers.[5] And if Jupiter aspects Venus and Mars, it will make those who are more powerful, soldiers, tax collectors, inn-keepers, sacrificers.

Mars and Mercury bestowing the actions make sculptors or [those having] some trade involving fire or iron or again armorers, prosecutors, adulterous persons, makers of sacred monuments,

---

[1] Burglars who break open doors to gain entry.
[2] This and the two preceding occupations refer to those who use iron tools to split or carve stone. Sculptors would also be included and perhaps those who cut and polish jewels.
[3] Presumably sailors who manned the pumps in the holds of ships.
[4] Those who dig or maintain underground watercourses—probably sewers, but perhaps also fresh water conduits.
[5] The word *perichytas* translated as 'bath attendants' probably refers to the worker who poured water over the bather, while the word *balaneas* translated as 'bath workers' is perhaps a more general term for a workman in the public baths.

modellers, physicians, surgeons, evil-doers, forgers. And if the [star] of Saturn aspects them, [they make], burglars, cattle rustlers, armed robbers. And if the [star] of Jupiter aspects them, [it makes] those fond of fighting, men of action, fearsome persons, meddlesome, and those who manage the affairs of others.

When Mars and Saturn and the Sun chance to be in effective houses, especially when they are in the ASC or the MC, they make sailors [and] seafarers. And Mercury in the 3rd and Mars in the 9th make masters of the hounds.[1] Mars and Mercury in the domiciles or terms of Venus make physicians. Mars and Mercury in the ASC or in the MC make those fond of weapons, bold or heavily-armed soldiers. Saturn being in the house of actions, when it chances to be out of sect and in an alien domicile in the MC, it makes these trades involving water, i.e. pumpers, gardeners or those who fish; and it bestows seaside actions, and it makes those who work hard with toil and labor. Saturn and Mars and the Moon in the ASC or in the MC makes philosophers, orators or astrologers. When Cancer or Scorpio or Pisces is rising [and] Jupiter and Saturn in the IC, they make herb-gatherers or exhibitors of wild beasts. Saturn in the ASC and Mars in the DSC make masters of the hounds or those who fight with wild beasts or those who are devoured by dogs. Saturn and the Moon in the DSC in watery signs make sailors or seafarers. Saturn in the MC [and] Mars in the DSC make those who hate Greeks of another tribe.

Venus and Mars ruling the house, taking the rulership of actions, make dyers, perfumers, metal-casters, goldsmiths, engravers, silversmiths, armed dancers, druggists, physicians. And if the [star] of Saturn is aspecting them, they make [keepers][2] of sacred animals, sc. hunters, embalmers of men, mourners, inspired persons[3] [in places] where mystery and wailings and bloodshed make their abode. And if the [star] of Jupiter aspects them, they make re-

---
[1] That is, those who lead a pack of dogs in the hunt.
[2] Cumont supplies this word from Ptolemy, *Tetrabiblos* iv. 4.
[3] Those who claim to be inspired by divinity and hence able to utter prophecies.

ligious persons, augurs,[1] those who manage the affairs of women, matchmakers[2] or pimps. And if the Sun aspects them, it makes rope dancers [and] conjurers. And if Saturn and the Sun aspect them, they make architects or potters.

Mars and Venus chancing to be in partile conjunction, if their dodecatemories also chance to be in square to them or in trine or opposition, they make adulterers, drunkards, [and] cheats. Mars and Venus in the IC make rope-dancers or those inspired by a god. Mars and Venus in the 3rd or in the 9th make physicians.

Mercury and Venus bestowing action make the actions to be from music and musical instruments and singing, either poems or dancing and rhythm, and especially, whenever the places are interchanged, they then denote theatre workers, actors, slave dealers, musical instrument makers, guitarists, tragedians,[3] weavers, modelers, painters. And if the [star] of Saturn is aspecting them, it makes those selling women's finery. And if the [star] of Jupiter is aspecting them, they make lawyers, those in charge of counting-houses, teachers of children, leaders of the people.

If Mercury and Venus are in the ASC and Jupiter is in the DSC, they make musicians or declaimers or athletes. And if Mercury and Saturn and Venus chanced to be in the house of action, they make physicians or enchanters[4] or herb-gatherers. And if Jupiter is aspecting them, they will have good fortune from these [actions]. Mercury and Venus chancing to be in the effective houses and aspected by Jupiter make ivory-workers, painters, or goldsmiths, or adorners. Mercury with Venus in the domiciles of Venus makes flute-players or guitarists. Venus with Mercury in the domiciles of Mercury makes painters or embroiderers or carvers or statue-makers.

---

[1] Those who determine omens from the flight and cries of birds.
[2] Marriage arrangers.
[3] Or perhaps we should take the word in its later sense—'singers'.
[4] Those who cast spells by singing.

In addition to all this, examine the influences of the applications and separations of the Moon and the influences of the signs and the *paranatellonta*, and the influences of the decans of the applications and separations of the Moon. And the Lot of Action is taken by day from Mercury to Mars, and by night the reverse, and the interval [cast] from the ASC. And examine the sign in which the lot is found, and in what house the ruler of the sign is posited, and thus declare [your interpretation of] the actions.

84. Trades.

After having looked at the trades and pursuits from the stars bestowing actions, I mean in fact Mars, Venus, and Mercury, and the applications and separations of the Moon, and besides that the term-rulers of the ASC and of the two lights and their sign rulers and the Lot of Fortune, it is necessary for me to lead the way by arranging the trades and pursuits according to the activity of the stars.

Jupiter and Mercury with Mars or in the terms of Mars make athletes and those fond of wrestling. Besides, it is necessary to look at the relaxation and exertion of the configurations and of the stars and of their phases. For if Saturn is configured with them, it no longer makes athletes and famous persons, but rather those who are serious about the arts. And if the [star] of Mercury is aspecting an angular Venus by square or its terms being received by other [stars], being matutine [and] oriental, being in their own domiciles or triplicities or in those of others, they make declaimers or guitarists or dancers or those who sing and dance in a chorus or something similar to those.

85. Orators and Teachers.

If the [star] of Mercury is in strong aspect to Jupiter, being posited in a good house and its terms received by others, and not being under the Sunbeams but angular and succedent, they make sophists, secretaries, or teachers.

86. Astrologers or Diviners.

If Mercury chances to be in a good house, and especially in a domicile of Saturn, not under the Sunbeams and aspected by Jupiter and Saturn and Mars, it makes astrologers, diviners, or priests. And if Saturn chances to be in the ASC in a domicile of Mercury, or if Mercury is in the ASC, it makes infallible astrologers.[1]

87. Bath Workers.

If Saturn is aspecting the Moon and the Moon's dodecatemory is in the terms of Saturn, makes bath workers and bath attendants. But if they chance to be in cadent [houses] or in the IC angle, it makes marble polishers.

88. Removers of Corpses.

Saturn in partile [conjunction] with Mars and Mercury, [all of them] aspecting each other's dodecatemories, without any aspect from the benefics, make grave-diggers or removers of corpses or grave-robbers.

89. Architects and Potters.

Saturn in partile [conjunction] with Mars in Aries or Taurus or Leo or being in square to Mars and being aspected by Mars[2] without any aspect of the benefics, makes roofers[3] or those who walk on walls or architects or potters or lamp makers. But if Venus is in aspect, it makes rope-dancers.

---

[1] Here and in the chapter title, Rheorius uses the word *mathêmatikos* 'mathematician' to signify 'astrologer'.
[2] Mars? The name of the planet is missing in the text.
[3] Literally, 'shingle placers'.

90. Drunkards and Lewd Persons and Sorcerers.

Mars partile Venus ... by square or opposition aspecting each other, the dodecatemories without any strong aspect of the others, make drunkards, armed robbers, adulterers, [and] exiles. And if Saturn is in aspect, it makes lewd persons, lecherers, especially in feminine signs.

91. Carpenters and Tanners and Stone-masons and Gem-engravers.

If Saturn and Venus and Mars are aspecting each other in masculine signs, especially in Aries and Leo and Sagittarius, they make carpenters and tanners and those who cut leather into thongs. And if Mercury is also in aspect, stone-masons, or quarrymen, or stone polishers. And if Jupiter and the Moon are in aspect, they make gem-engravers or marble workers.

92. Masters of the Hounds and Falconers and Bird-feeders and Painters.

If Mercury is not under the Sunbeams and is partile the Moon, and they are aspecting each other's dodecatemories, and Mars and Saturn chance to be in opposition to each other in the angles, [they make] masters of the hounds and hunters. And if Mercury and the Moon chance to be in the winged signs, I mean in Virgo and in Sagittarius and in the first degrees of Pisces because of Pegasus,[1] they make falconers or bird-feeders. And if the Moon and Mars are also in aspect in the terms of Mercury, they make painters.

93. Sailors and Steersmen.

Saturn in the MC in a watery sign, with Mars and the Sun also in the MC or in aspect by square or opposition, makes sailors or

---
[1] The longitudes of some stars of the constellation Pegasus, the Winged Horse, fell in the sign Pisces.

steersmen or ship captains, especially if the ASC is also in a wet sign in the terms of Saturn and [also] the Lot of Fortune or its ruler.

94. Tailors.

Mars and Venus together or in square in each other's terms make tailors, linen-weavers, [and] dealers in linen cloth.

95. Mechanics and Jugglers.

Mercury and Mars and Venus and the Moon angular or aspecting each other by from an angle, make mechanics,[1] but when they are in cadent houses, jugglers.

96. Mimes [And Other Trades].

Mercury and Venus in their falls in their own terms or in those of each other, make mimes or politicians,[2] especially in Capricorn because of Pithecus.[3]

Mars and Mercury in the IMC make rope-walkers and conjurers.

The Moon in the DSC and applying to Saturn in watery signs or northerly descending, makes seamen.

Venus in the domicile of the Sun or in its own domicile with

---

[1] That is, those who work with mechanical devices.
[2] The exact sense of *politikous* 'politicians' here is uncertain. Elsewhere, it usually refers to a public official of some kind, but this seems inappropriate here, unless we take it in the sense of 'public' and suppose that it refers to those who perform in public off-stage. However, Vettius Valens, *Anthology*, ii. 17 (p. 72,14) has the phrase *hypokritas mimôn* 'actors of mimes', so perhaps we should read *hypokritas <mimôn>* here instead of *politikous*.
[3] Pithecus or the Ape was a constellation of the Barbaric Sphere, i.e. a non-Greek constellation. Cumont notes that in another place Rhetorius calls it Cynocephalus or the Baboon. *Cf.* Franz Boll, *Sphaera*, p. 295, where the constellation of the Ape is assigned to Capricorn. See also the 'Index of Constellation and Star Names' at the end of Appendix 1 below.

Mercury, especially when angular, make reed-pipe players or guitarists or musicians.

Venus in a domicile of Mercury with Mercury, angular or succedent, not under the Sunbeams, make painters or statue-makers or damask-weavers.

If the Sun and the Moon chance to be in succedent houses when Mercury and Venus are angular, they make charioteers, especially in Gemini and Taurus.

The Moon in Taurus with Mercury and the Sun, increasing in light, makes fowlers and falconers.

And if the ASC chances to be in Cancer or Scorpio or Pisces, with Jupiter and Saturn in the IC, and also bestowing the actions, it makes herb-gatherers [and] exhibitors of wild beasts.

Mars and Mercury angular in Leo, without Jupiter and Venus and the Sun, make bold persons, characteristically those who are thinking about shedding blood for nothing, or cheats, perjurers, sacrilegious persons, forgers, [and] treacherous persons.

If Saturn and Mercury are in a domicile of Saturn and the Moon chances to be in Taurus, they make a wise orator or a mathematician, very refined and learned, [but] it causes rheumatism in the feet or in the ankles as befits his occupation, but high-minded and pleasant.

Mars and Venus being together or in square or opposition in their climes make physicians or philosophers.[1]

97. Parents.

Examine the things relating to the father from the Sun and Saturn and the Lot of the Father and from the [sign] opposite the Lot

---

[1] From the word 'learned' in the preceding paragraph to the end of this chapter, MS **G** reads 'if Venus or Saturn or Mars are in opposition, it makes a stammerer or a rheumatic, especially in the northern climes when Saturn is in the north'.

of the Father, and the things of the mother from the Moon and Venus and the Lot of the Mother, and out of sect by day from the Sun and Venus, but by night from Saturn and the Moon and the Lots. Examine also their rulers and the triplicity rulers and the rulers of the terms, for from these factors the [things relating to] the parents will be known. And from the Lights and from Saturn and Venus and their rulers, examine those things relating to the parents, e.g. illnesses and dangers and low birth and trade and property and similar things.

And Mars signifies the family of the father, the ruler of its triplicity the father's livelihood. If then Mars has a good position, but the ruler of its triplicity has a bad position, say that the parents are well born but less fortunate and undistinguished[1] in spirit; and if Mars chances to be in the terms of a malefic, say that the father is either a slave or a low-born person; and if that malefic is in strong aspect, it will make sickness or injury for the father. And if the Sun chances to be in a bad house, but the ruler of its triplicity is in a good house and phase, say that the father will go from low-born [beginnings] into an improved livelihood; and the first ruler of the Sun's triplicity signifies the first livelihood of the father, and the second ruler the second livelihood.

Consider the same configurations of the Moon for the mother. If the Moon chances to be in the terms of a benefic in cadent houses or close to the ecliptic, especially in its South Node and aspected by malefics, while well born it makes them to be subjected to servile conditions for the sake of children, and they have a shameful livelihood; the Moon in the North Node injures the mother or makes her low-born. And if the Moon chances to be opposite a malefic and her Lot is cadent, say that the mother is a slave; and if the Moon is applying to one of the malefics, it makes the mother to die violently.

---

[1]The text has the otherwise unattested word *adiartous* 'unseparated', but Cumont suggests *adiakritous* 'undistinguished', and I suggest *adiaphorous* 'undistinguished'.

When the Sun and the ruler of its triplicity are situated badly and in the signs of other [planets], they make the father to die violently; and if they are also aspected by the malefics, they destroy the patrimony. And if [both] the Sun and the ruler of its triplicity chance to be in a bad house and aspected by malefics in a diurnal nativity, it makes the natives to be hated and rejected by their fathers. Look also at the ruler of the Lot of the Father in which house it chances to be and what its phase is and by which [planets] it is aspected, from these declare the livelihood of the father. And if the ruler of the Lot chances to be in the second or the sixth or the eighth or the twelfth [house], say that the father's estate is worthless. Take note also of the sign opposite to the Lot of the Father, and if you find the ruler of the Lot of the Father in the Lot of the Father or with the Lot, say that that person will be adopted.

Look also at the dodecatemories of the Sun and the Moon, where they fall [in the chart], and by what [planets] they are aspected, for these signify the circumstances of the parents adequately. Therefore they also look at[1] the aspecting [planets] and the passing and receiving of the stars according to Valens in the fourth book[2] and the distributions of the Lot of Fortune and the Lot of the Daemon, according to Valens.[3]

98. Parents Who Are Foreigners.

When the Sun and the Moon chance to be in tropical signs, they make the parents to be foreigners or of another race. And if the ASC also chances to be in a tropical sign, then especially say that the parents are foreigners, and even more so if the malefics are aspecting them. Similarly too, when the Lights are disjunct from each other, they make the parents to be foreigners or of another race. The Sun setting <i.e., opposite> the ASC,[4] makes separation

---

[1] Reading *skopoûsi 'they look at' rather than *diekbalon . . . kai Skorpion*.
[2] Vettius Valens, *Anthology* iv. 17.
[3] Vettius Valens, *Anthology* iv. 25.
[4] Something is missing after 'setting'; Pingree, in his edition of Dorotheus, p. 330,

of the parents. And the same thing when the Moon is in the full Moon phase. And if the ruler of the twelfth house chances to be with the Sun, say that the father is a slave or is crippled; and if it is with the Moon, say that the mother is a slave or a cripple.[1]

99. Patricides and Matricides, and Enemies of Their Parents, and Outcasts.[2]

These have the Sun in the terms of Mars by day, but by night in the terms of Saturn; with Saturn and Mars aspecting jointly by square or opposition, without Jupiter or Venus; [this configuration] makes father-killers or parricides; but if you find the Moon [there], it makes mother-killers. But those therefore who have the Lot of one of the parents in the 12th or the ruler of the Lot [there], become enemies of the parents. The Sun angular opposing Mars makes the parents enemies of their children.

If Jupiter predominates over Saturn, the parents are not harmonious with the children; and if Saturn predominates over Jupiter, the parents are harmonious with their children; if they are in opposition, they become seditious with respect to their parents; and if they are in trine, friends. Look also for the doryphories[3] of the Lights—in the case of the Sun, the morning [stars], but in the case of the Moon, the evening [stars], but also the blockading of the lights; and if they appear as doryphories to the Lights, the parents will no longer have good fortune, especially if Mars is succedent to the Sun, and Saturn to the Moon.

---

supplies *diametros* 'opposite', and I have added 'i.e.'.
[1]Here ends the edition of Rhetorius's text from **MS** 2425 in CCAG 8.4, p. 220.
[2]Here I have translated the Greek text that is edited in CCAG 2, p. 187, 15-29.
[3]Accepting Kroll's emendation *doryphorias* 'doryphories' for *dysphorias* 'difficulties'.

100. The Longevity of the Parents.[1]

Always, when investigating the [life-]times of the parents, cast the years of the child from the Lot of Parents, and look at the [planets] aspecting according to their determination or according to their passage, and from this say the years [of life] of the father or of the mother. Also, investigate the motions of the Sun and the Moon towards the malefics or the benefics according to the tables and the rising-times [given by] Valens. Also, investigate the periods and the returns of the Sun and the Moon with regard to the returns and the periods of the malefics and the benefics, and after [that] of the succedents and of the periods and of the returns of the signs towards Leo, Scorpio, and Virgo according to Valens; and you should not forget that Aries is opposed[2] to Virgo, and Libra to Pisces, and Gemini to Capricorn, and Cancer to Sagittarius.

101. The Parents from New Moons and Full Moons.[3]

The benefics beholding the preceding syzygy[4] indicate good things for the natives, but the opposite is a sign of exposing[5] and of the parents low birth; but this is done also if they have the application of the Moon. And being free, they are brought into slavery; when the conjunction of the benefics is seen, and the benefics are predominated over by the malefics, And also if the Moon herself, separating from the benefics moves towards the malefics, it makes subjection and slavery instead of freedom, as I have proven. The conjunction and its ruler signify the paternal livelihood, and the Moon and its ruler, the mother's livelihood; for many times it happens at the same time that the father is free, but the mother is a

---

[1] Here I have translated the Greek text that is edited in CCAG 2, p. 187,30-188,10. See also pp. 212-213, where a similar but shorter text is attributed to Rhetorius.
[2] Actually, these pairs of signs are those that see and hear each other, rather than signs that are mutually opposed.
[3] Here I have translated the Greek text edited in CCAG 2, 188,10-25.
[4] That is, the one immediately preceding the native's birth.
[5] That is, of discarding new born children.

slave, although from syzygy alone the separation of these results. If a malefic aspects the ruler of the Sun, the father and his estate are bad; and if [it aspects the ruler] of the Moon, the evil is for the mother. And I have found with Antigonos that either the new Moon or the full Moon signifies the mother, but their rulers signify the father.

102. Which of the Parents Dies First.[1]

Look at the Lots of the Parents, for to which of them [one] of the malefics casts a ray first by determination or by passage; that one will die first. See which of the two Lights is in the IMC angle in the domicile of another [planet] or in its triplicity, and that one will die first. Always the full Moon in Pisces kills the father first. Look at the rulers of the Lots of the Parents, which of them falls in the hemisphere below the earth, that one will die first; but if both [the rulers] are in one sign, find which one of them is afflicted or is under the Sun beams, that one will die first; and if [they are] in one sign and in the same degree, take note of the ruler of the terms of that degree, and if it is in a masculine sign, the father will die first, but if in a feminine one, the mother.

It will be necessary then to observe also the malefics that are aspecting one of the rulers of the Lots, in order that you may know which one is safer. Investigate how the Sun and Saturn are situated, and Venus and the Moon, and which of them is the more afflicted, and from the one that is most afflicted you will know the one that will die first. And if all of them are afflicted, there will be bereavement. The malefics opposed to the Lights show the parents to be short-lived. If the Sun and Saturn are in the same degree, they will kill the father first and the first brothers, but they also make inheritances. The Sun in the degree of Saturn in the whole sign with malefics shows dead bodies and injuries, it destroys the offspring and the father quickly. But if Saturn is in the same degree with the

---

[1]Here I have translated the Greek text edited in CCAG 2, p. 188,26- *Cf.* Firmicus, *Mathesis*, vii. 9.

Moon, it kills the mother first, and if Mars is also in aspect, it makes the death [to be] either from a misfortune in childbirth or from [some] hidden illnesses.

When the Moon is void of course, it kills the father first. The Sun in the 8th degree of a sign kills the father first. Mars by day on the conception Sun, the native does not know his father, but by night it makes [him] bereaved. And Saturn also makes these things on the Sun, but on the Moon alternately. And if Jupiter and Venus, it makes the father to be well-born and long-lived. Mars or Saturn in the IMC, the 4th, kills the father first. Saturn in the domicile of the Sun makes the father to die violently or to be troubled by wet things. Saturn in the domicile of the Moon destroys the mother's estate and makes bodily illnesses and chills. Mars in the domicile of the Sun kills the father quickly or does it in a foreign country, and it also injures the sight of the native. Mars in the domicile of the Moon makes bodily dangers and a quick death for the mother; and it also destroys the maternal estate, and it injures the native in the stomach, and it either makes a quick death or a violent death.

103. The Number of Children Born Previously.[1]

And if the ruler of the triplicity of the ASC chances to be in the ASC, say that these are first-born [children]; but if it chances to be in the MC, the fourth or the first, then it comes to pass in multiple births; and if in the DSC, say that the native is the first or the seventh. And look to see that a malefic is not in the same angle with the ruler of the triplicity or aspecting it by square or opposition, for that makes the death of brothers; and if it is a cadent house, it either gives the death of brothers or it causes them to live abroad. If the triplicity ruler of the ASC chances to be in the hemisphere above the earth, count from it to the ASC, for however many signs there are, say that there are that many brothers; and if it encounters a bicorporeal sign, count the sign twice. And if the triplicity ruler of the ASC chances to be in the hemisphere below the earth, count

---

[1] This chapter is edited by Pingree, in his edition of Dorotheus, pp. 333-334.

from the ASC as far as the ruler of the triplicity. And if the benefics are in aspect, say that the brothers are viable; but if the malefics are in aspect, they cause their death.

If there is no star from the MC down to the ASC, he will not have an elder brother. And if with such a configuration anyone chances to have an elder brother, he will always [live to] see his death. And if there is a malefic between the MC and the ASC, it signifies the death of those born before. And if the triplicity ruler is found from the ASC down to the IMC and a benefic is there or is in aspect, he will have brothers born afterwards. But if it is a malefic, he will not have any or they will be killed.[1]

104. Brothers, Their Friendship, and How Many There Are.[2]

I consider it burdensome and hard to make out [how] to declare the significator of brothers, for I am not entirely able, either due to the unbelievability and intemperance of the women, or mostly because of not having looked at some of those [natives] who had 13 or 14 brothers or even more. And similarly too, I decline to take the significator of children and wives to declare their number, because of those women who have been married many times, seven or eight [even], and have had 15 or 16 children. Therefore, it is necessary to avow something safe and merely to say that there will be many husbands or many marriages or many children. But since the ancients attempted to declare the number of these, I too shall at-

---

[1]This chapter, which is similar to Dorotheus, *Pentateuch* i. 17.1-11, is translated into Latin in *The Book of Hermes*, Chapt. 30.

[2]Edited in CCAG 2, p. 189, 27-34. The Byzantine epitomator of Rhetorius recast the text into this form: "It is hard to make out and hardly possible to declare the significator of brothers. For history records that Hecuba bore 19 children. And we here in Byzantium have seen a mother of 24 children. And some men take many wives, and one woman [may take] many husbands. Therefore, it is necessary to be safer by declaring that there will be many marriages or many brothers or many children and such like [statements]. And yet the ancients did not hesitate to do as much as they could and [declare] the number of the brothers; wherefore, we too are attempting to declare as much as we can."

tempt to set forth [my own opinions] as well as I can, while resisting any previous judgment with respect to those matters.

105. The Friendship of Brothers.[1]

If the ruler of the Lot of Friendship aspects the Lot of Brothers, say that the brothers are friends. If Jupiter and Venus and Mercury [as] significators chance to be in [good] houses and good phases, and are in feminine signs, they give feminine siblings, but in masculine [signs], males and long-lived ones. But if they chance to be in bad houses, they give short-lived ones or inimical ones or those who are injured, and especially if they also chance to be in bad phases. And if Saturn and Mars and the Moon chance to be in the domiciles of other [stars], they destroy the brothers, but if any one of these stars has its own domicile, it makes those who are not without wounds, but who are [also] mentally depressed, or they will be persons who are of no use to others. For [from] the effects of the bad [stars], they have become bad.[2]

106. The Third Sign from the ASC.[3]

If the third sign from the ASC chances to be bicorporeal, or if its ruler is in a bicorporeal sign or one of two natures, it makes mixed brothers,[4] i.e. from different parents. And investigate too the third sign from the ASC [to see] that it is not a sterile sign; and the sterile signs are these: Gemini, Leo, Virgo, Capricorn, and Sagittarius.[5]

---

[1]This chapter is edited by Pingree in his edition of Dorotheus, pp. 335-336.
[2]This chapter contains significations similar to those in Dorotheus, *Pentateuch* i. 20.2, 21.3, and 21.5-7.
[3]This chapter is edited by Pingree in his edition of Dorotheus, p. 336.
[4]We would call them "half-brothers."
[5]This chapter is similar to Dorotheus, *Pentateuch* i. 21.9.

107. Elder and Younger Brothers.[1]

And reckon the ages of the brothers in this fashion. Saturn signifies the elder ones; the Sun and Mars and Jupiter the middle ones; and Mercury the younger ones. And the Moon signifies the elder sisters, and Venus the younger ones. If the first and second triplicity rulers of Mars are badly placed, they make few brothers, especially if they chance to be in bad phases. And if the first triplicity ruler is in a good house and the second is in a bad house, it signifies that the brothers are exposed.[2]

108. How Many Brothers.[3]

For the sake of an example,[4] let Saturn, the Sun and the Moon be in Taurus in the midheaven sign, the ASC in Leo, Jupiter in Aquarius, and Mars in Gemini. Then the triplicity rulers of Mars, those signifying the brothers, are Saturn and Mercury. I take the number [of signs from them] to the ASC, since Mercury and Saturn chance to be in the hemisphere above the earth.[5] For if they were in the one below the earth, I [would have] counted from the ASC to the triplicity rulers of Mars. And so I find 4 signs from the MC to the ASC, 3 single[-bodied] and one double-bodied. Say [then] that he has that number of brothers, viz. 5.[6] And he says it is necessary to judge the rulers of the Lots and their houses and the terms. For if they chance to be oriental and in their own domiciles and they are in sect, they give those [natives] who are likely to survive and who are lucky in life. And as for what sort of brothers he

---
[1] This chapter is edited by Pingree in his edition of Dorotheus, p. 336.
[2] *Cf.* Dorotheus, *Pentateuch* i. 21.10,12-13.
[3] This chapter is edited by Pingree in his edition of Dorotheus, pp. 336-337. It is a simplified version of Dorotheus, *Pentateuch*, i. 21.
[4] This example is taken from Dorotheus, *Pentateuch* i.21, and refers to the horoscope of a man who was born around noon on 2 or 3 May 29 A.D. according to Pingree (ed. Dorotheus, pp. IX-X; the chart is on p. 180).
[5] Here the position of Mercury is not given, but it is mentioned in the last line of this paragraph.
[6] Three single-bodied signs and one double-bodies sign makes five bodies. Note that he counts both ends of the interval MC to ASC.

will have, look thus at [the configurations] of the aforementioned nativity. Since the Lot of Brothers[1] and the triplicity rulers of Mars chanced to be in Taurus, a feminine sign, there is a feminine sibling, and since Saturn chanced to be there, she will die; with Saturn the Sun and Mercury [there], they will kill another brother before him.

If the ASC and the Moon chance to be in Pisces or Scorpio or Cancer, they make the mother to be long-lived;[2] however, the Moon alone in Scorpio, because of its fall—especially when it is around three degrees—will make some children to be exposed. And if the Lot of Brothers chances to be in those signs, it gives, many brothers; but if the Lot chances to be in a sterile sign (that is, in Leo or Gemini or Sagittarius or Capricorn), it will make a scarcity of brothers, but in the rest [of the signs] a moderate number. And if the benefics aspect the Lot, they bestow life, but if the malefics aspect it, they bestow death.[3]

109. Application and Separation.[4]

Application and separation are made by degrees,[5] from one of which the Moon makes the rulership of the nativity, but it is going to move forward to those degrees to which it applies; and [when] it moves away from them, it makes a separation. And if the ruler of the degrees of the Moon chances to be present with it, and is found to be the closest to the Moon in the same terms, it will have the situation of separation. And if this does not chance to be the configuration, but [it is rather] an application, if it is going to unite with

---

[1] The Lot of Brothers = Jupiter - Saturn + Asc; in this case 315 - 45 + 246 = 45 or Taurus.
[2] Dorotheus, *Pentateuch*, i. 18 says that with the Moon in those signs, "his mother will bear many children."
[3] *Cf.* Dorotheus, *Pentateuch* i. 18, 19, 21.
[4] This chapter is edited by Heilen (*Cf.* Preface to the Fourth Edition). The simple definitions of application and separation were given in the earlier Chapters 35 and 37. Here we have a more elaborate discussion with special reference to the applications and separations of the Moon.
[5] Reading *moiras* 'degrees' instead of *moikas* 'lengths'.

one of the stars, or if either the Moon appears to be joined together with it in the same degree, or again by aspect, it will be necessary to look just where it is going to go, the terms or the Moon; to seek out the things of the star—the one to which it has cast its ray—and if it chances to be thus, it has the configuration. But [if] the application is not chancing to be into those terms which the Moon is departing from, [but rather] to be found in those same terms of the star that is casting the ray—the application will not be dominant.

And the same situation also [exists] in the separations. When the Moon makes a separation from one of the stars; indeed from being together with it, the Moon has separated from those degrees; and having separated from those degrees, the separation will be the ruler. But if it has separated from those degrees, the Moon does not happen to meet with those terms of the star from which it has been found to have been separated, the separation is said to be powerless.

If indeed at whatever time the middle phase with the Sun is made, either by application or separation, they will be ineffective. Indeed the more powerful applications and separations are when they are the degrees of those casting rays, of the separating stars closer to those degrees of the Moon, and the rays of the same are stronger, indeed they touch lightly in their same degrees. For as again in the combinations, more powerful are the stars having the application and the separation in the same degrees, so according to the degree and according to the star it appears more powerful in the application or separation. So then he said first that from the Moon being close to those degrees, it makes [her] the Ruler of the Nativity. If the ruler of the degrees encounters the Moon in the same sign or degrees or is aspecting her, and the Moon approaches, it comes together with it partilely, but being away from there it has made a separation.

110. An Example.[1]

Let the Moon be in Virgo, the 24th degree of Virgo, the Sun in the 20th degree of Pisces, Mercury in the 18th degree of Pisces, Saturn in the 26th degree of Scorpio, Jupiter in the 3rd degree of Taurus, Mars in the 19th degree of Taurus, Venus in the 27th degree of Aquarius.[2] The terms of Virgo, which is the sign of the Moon, [are these:] the first 7 are those of Mercury, then Venus 10, Jupiter 4, and 7 of Mars, in which the Moon is, then 2 of Saturn. And the Moon is sextile Saturn, trine Jupiter and Mars; opposite the Sun and Mercury; and inconjunct Venus. I look for one that will be necessary to make the application or the separation.

Mars being ruler of the terms of the Moon has no relevance; then the application to Saturn is said to be by a sextile ray, being near to the sixty [degrees]. And it is from its terms[3] that the Moon is going to depart a degree towards it.[4] And it must be called a separation from Mercury and Venus and Jupiter, from whose terms she has [already] separated. For Jupiter's trine being longer than the trine <aspect> of 120 degrees, Mercury is closer to 180 degrees, and Venus is inconjunct. Then the separation must be judged to be from Mercury, since she separated from its opposition. Besides, then to show the closer separation, being one of 6 degrees, I took Mercury,[5] but since the interception of the Sun happened by opposition, this separation will not be dominant.

But the Moon does not become very closely configured when she chances to be in the last degrees of the signs. For if she runs into the terms in the sign, she will make an application by means of it, and [yet] the application will be ineffective for the stars. Just as

---

[1] This chapter is edited by Heilen.
[2] MS 2425 has Venus in 27 Gemini, as Pingree reported in his edition of Dorotheus, p. XII. However, in his edition of Rhetorius, he has now put it in 27 Aquarius, since the text says that Venus is inconjunct the Moon (and Venus in Gemini would be impossible with the Sun in Pisces).
[3] Mars's terms.
[4] Actually, 2 degrees (from 24 Virgo to 26 Scorpio).
[5] But the separation from the trine to Mars would have been the closest separation.

again, chancing to be in the first degrees of the signs, she does not make a separation. And in that same way, with the stars being a three-degree distance from the Moon, they make a *kollêsis*; and, if they have the situation of application or separation, they do become effective. And it is [something] by all means to be known.

[Note. In his edition of Dorotheus, p. xii, Pingree gives the planetary positions of what he calls the "example horoscope" that it contains, along with his own computation of positions for 24 February 601.

Planet	Text	Pingree
Saturn	Scorpio 26	Scorpio 14
Jupiter	Taurus 3	Taurus 6
Mars	Taurus 19	Taurus 21
Sun	Pisces 20	Pisces 9
Venus	Gemini 27	Aquarius 2
Mercury	Pisces 17	Aquarius 17
Moon	Virgo 24	Libra 0

Pingree concludes from this that Rhetorius must have written after 601. But in my opinion Pingree is mistaken! These positions are not from an example horoscope! They are merely arbitrary positions chosen to illustrate the topic of applications and separations that was discussed in Chapter 109. This is immediately obvious because there is no mention of an ASC, nor are any facts given about the life of a specific person. Astrologers use horoscopes to illustrate the principles of delineation in an example chart. This cannot be done if there is no ascendant and no facts about the person whose horoscope it is. So this is not an example horoscope! And the other evidence in Rhetorius's Compendium indicates that he wrote a few years after 500 A.D., not a century later as Pingree will have it.]

111. Bonding.[1]

Bonding is [said] of the Moon when, appearing with the Sun, it <does not> depart from it [by more than] the degrees of its daily passage; and it dissolves the bonding when it goes away from it by those same degrees. But, when it is closer than that to the degree of the Sun, it is powerful.

112. Void of Course.[2]

Void of course is [said] of the Moon when it is about [to apply] to no [star]—neither by sign, nor by degree, nor by *kollêsis,* nor by aspect, nor when it is going to make an application within 30 degrees. When indeed the stars are first having connections with regard to the Sun, either by conjunction or by an aspect to it, or by making a setting by application, it is also said to be void of course. And it is more [significant] if both of the stars come together partilely by motion. For the separations give judgment on the things that have preceded and have been preserved; and the applications give judgment on the things that are going to be and those that are hoped for.

113. The Nativity of a Grammarian.

This man[3] was born at Thebes, a poor grammarian for 32 years; but, from age 33, having married, he began to rise at Ath-

---

[1] This chapter is edited by Heilen. The sample definition of the term *bonding* was given earlier in Chapter 38.

[2] Edited by Heilen. The simple definition of the term void of course was given earlier in Chapter 39. The present chapter begins like Porphyry, Chapter 23, but continues at greater length: "Void of course is said whenever the Moon applies to nothing, neither zodiacally nor by degree, nor by aspect, nor by bonding, nor within 30 degrees of the nearest application or conjunction that it makes; and such nativities are undistinguished and without advancement."

[3] According to Neugebauer and Van Hoesen, *Greek Astrology* (Philadelphia: The American Philosophical Society, 1959), pp. 140-141, the subject of this chapter was identified in 1923 by A. Delatte and P. Stroobant as Pamprepius, a poet who took part in the revolt staged by Illus and Leontius. Actually, Pamprepius was a pagan scholar who rose to a high position under Illus and Leontius when they re-

ens,[1] and then fleeing into Byzantium, he attached himself to a great man, and representing himself as a wizard or priest, he became a quaestor, then a consul,[2] then a patrician, and after this, as a traitor, he was killed in a military fortress[3] at age 44 and 1/6. And he was also lewd. The Sun in Libra 5°08'; the Moon in Taurus 8°04'; Saturn in Taurus 25°; Jupiter in Libra 23°08'; Mars in Capricorn 26°08'; Venus in Scorpio 26°; Mercury in Libra 23°; the ASC in Aquarius 23°30'; the MC in Sagittarius 5°03'; the [preceding] full Moon in Aries 2°42'; [the Lot of] Fortune in Virgo 26°34'; [the Lot of the] Daemon in Cancer 20°34'; the Exaltation of the Nativity in Virgo; the Lot of Destruction in Aquarius.[4]

Investigating the foregoing nativity, I found the Moon and Saturn and Venus and Mars by degree to have been cadent,[5] but by sign the Moon and Saturn and Venus angular, and the Sun and

---

belled again the Isaurian emperor Zeno (426-491), but who perished when the revolt failed. His birthplace according to the historians was Panoplis (the modern Akhmîm 26N35 31E48) in the Thebaid. He was born on 29 September 440 and died about November 484.

[1] He studied under the philosopher Proclus (412-485) at the University of Athens and was then appointed Professor of Grammar (literature and philology). Bury says "he established himself in the favour of Illus by the public recitation of a poem," but in 478, while Illus was out of town, his enemies banished him, and he fled to Pergamum. (See J. B. Bury, *History of the Later Roman Empire* (New York: Dover Publ., 1958. 2 vols.), vol. 1, pp. 398-399, for a fuller account of Pamprepius and the rebellion of Illus and Leontius.

[2] This appears to be a mistake. Illus was consul in 478, but I do not find Pamprepius's name in the list of consuls.

[3] The fortress of Cherris in the Isaurian mountains (in south central Turkey).

[4] The planetary positions were obviously calculated from Ptolemy's *Handy Tables* for about 4 PM LAT (= 3:50 PM LMT) Alexandria Time. The position of the Sun is exact to the minute of arc, the lunar position is only 4 minutes of arc different, and most of the others are correct to the stated degree. The position of Venus is given in the printed text as 26°, but this is evidently a simple scribal error for 20°06' (having been written in Greek letters κϛ (26) for κ' ϛ' (20 6), which is very close to the calculated position of 20°15'. Neugebauer's comment (*Greek Horoscopes*, p. 141) that the position of Venus (26°) must be based on non-Ptolemaic tables, etc., is therefore wrong! The stated position of the previous full Moon is also in exact agreement with the *Handy Tables*—viz. Aries 2°42'. The discrepancy between the Ptolemaic longitudes and actual tropical longitudes is of course mainly due to the erroneous value of the precession adopted by Ptolemy.

[5] The chart is considered two ways: by Alchabitius house division, which Rhetorius calls "by degree," and by the Sign-House division, which he calls "by

Mercury and Jupiter by sign to have been cadent, but by degree the Sun chanced to be in the succedent of the DSC. I see then Saturn being ruler of the ASC and first ruler of the triplicity of the ASC and of the Light [of the Time], signifying the first age, in the cadent of the IC angle and retrograde and aspected by Mars with an equal-sided trine,[1] but also Venus, ruler of it and of the Moon posited in opposition to her. How could he not have had a troublesome first age, but indeed also flights made in many places because of the Moon's being opposed by its own sign ruler. For he[2] says:

Behold the Moon is in the domicile of some star;
And if you find that one lurking in opposition,
He will also indeed be a fugitive, obscure and a wanderer.

And these things [occurred] in his first age down to his 25th or 30th year, i.e. down to the rising of Taurus or of the Moon's or of Saturn's time period; but after these rises the second ruler of the triplicity, i.e. Mercury with Jupiter, [ruled] from the 32nd year. For the years of the period of Mercury are 20 and of Jupiter 12, which make 32 years, after which his fortunes began to look up, since Mercury also chanced to be the ruler of the Lot of Fortune. So, partly by the passage of time and partly by fortune, he advanced because of Mercury's being ruler of the Lot and of his second age and its being in partile conjunction with Jupiter and also making its evening rising. Hence, with the passage of years and in conformity with his fortune, he advanced.

---

sign." The house positions are not the same. In the Alchabitius system the chart has no angular planets, but in the Sign-House system the Moon, Venus, and Saturn are all angular.

[1]Neugebauer and Van Hoesen, *Greek Horoscopes*, p. 141, translate this clause as "injured by Mars because of the equilateral triangle. But the Greek text has *isoskelê*, which should be translated as 'equal-sided trine'. The term 'equal-sided' is superfluous, since nothing more is meant than a trine aspect. And apparently Rhetorius considered that a sinister trine aspect from the malefic Mars would "injure" Saturn.

[2]No name is given in the text. Cumont supplied 'Dorotheus', but this passage is not recognized by Pingree as being one of the fragments of Dorotheus. However the surviving text of Dorotheus is incomplete. At any rate, Rhetorius is attributing the poem to an earlier writer.

114. Why He Was a Grammarian.

See that the Lot of Fortune has fallen into a Mercurial sign; similarly too, that Mercury, the ruler of the lot, is in a sign of human form and in the same triplicity partilely with Jupiter and in the face of Jupiter and in the terms of Mercury, and Venus, and these points embellish the maxims, especially because of the partile conjunction of Mercury and Jupiter. And by this fortune he became a quaestor.

115. Why He Was a Traitor.

See Mercury prevailing over Mars by square. For one of the wise men says: and if now there is a four-sided figure[1] and Mercury holds the upper part, and the worst [planet] Mars dwells at the humblest place, dangerously it denotes villains or those wanting to be robbers and to make losses for others, migrating from one [place] to another, and [changing allegiance] from one man to another man; at another time we also find the rest: they will fall upon traitors with their own mischief, and they will strip them bare of [their] property.

> If Mercury is strong, being in the upper part of the square,
> And Mars holds the humble house of friendship,
> Dangerously it decrees villains or those wanting to be
> Robbers or plunderers of other peoples' property,
> Changing alliances from one man to another,
> We find . . . and [as] traitors will fall upon the rest
> With their own mischief, and they will strip [them] bare of property[2]

---

[1] That is, a square aspect. The Greeks originally conceived of the aspects as being the sides of polygons inscribed within the circle.

[2] The Greek text of these verses is wretchedly depraved. Cumont and Bidez attempted to correct it, but not with entire success. The translation is therefore uncertain. Similar passages are found in Dorotheus, Anubio, and Julius Firmicus Maternus. Dorotheus, *Pentateuch* 2. 15 has '...the native will be inferior, feeble, illegally seizing the property of the people....he will be exasperated with his relatives....spiteful, greedy for properties, and....the pursuit of wealth' (Pingree's translation). The prose paraphrase of Anubio (ed. Pingree) seems fairly close: 'But if Mercury prevails over Mars, it produces dangerous persons, robbers of

116. His Lechery.

See that the ruler of the ASC and the Lot of Fortune and the Lot of the Daemon have [all] fallen into lecherous signs. But of course the opposition of Saturn to Venus in the domicile of Mars and [the position of] Saturn in the domicile of Venus was also causing his lechery.

117. The Rising of His Fortune.

His fortune was [due] to rise from his 32nd year, as I said before, because of the period of Mercury and Jupiter; and his fortune was to rise again in his 35th year because of the rising of Scorpio. And in his 36th year he fled to Byzantium, in so far as Taurus and the Moon and Saturn rose. The rising time of Taurus was 25, the period of the Moon 25, the period of Saturn 57; altogether they make 107 times; a third [of which] is 35;40 times; and Taurus as a cadent signified living abroad; and Saturn and the Moon as being cadent, signified his flight. And from age 38 1/3 his luck revived, for it was [the time of] the rising of Virgo and Libra—Virgo, as having received the Lot of Fortune, and Libra, as having received the Sun and Jupiter and Mercury [which was] the ruler of the Lot of Fortune. At this time, he became quaestor, consul, [and] a patrician. And in his 41st year he traveled into his own country with a large armed guard and much arrogance, for Jupiter was rising and also Mercury; the period of Mercury 76 years, and the period of

---

others' property; for these persons go from one person to another, so that, inflicting some evil on them, they betray them and strip them of their possessions.' Firmicus, *Mathesis* vi.11. 'But if Mercury is elevated, and, possessing the right side, aspects by square Mars posited in a lower place, that configuration will make evil, malign, and malicious persons, always armed with a very bad and pestiferous greediness of mind, exercising all the actions of deceit – greedy persons and those who feed upon the things of others with an avaricious greediness of mind, and who cross over from one man to another, always seeking with eager thought one on whom they inflict the wound of a pestiferous sting, so that, captured by their own nefarious machinations, and made destitute by crafty deceits, to the advantage of those whom an injurious dishonesty arms, having been stripped bare by malign deceits, they suffer from the loss of the entire substance of their own personal wealth.'

Jupiter 12; altogether it makes 88 times; the half [of which is] 44; and since they chanced to be in their own triplicities, he made his travel into his own country. And it was also the seventh day of the Moon, moving towards Venus. Finally, at the age of 44 years and two months the native was killed as a result of these causes.

[118.] The Nativity of a Child Who Died Early.

This was the child of a king,[1] and it died at [the age of] 5 and 1/6 months in Byzantium. [It was born in] the year of Diocletian 179 on April 25 at the 7th hour of the day.[2] The Sun in Taurus 3, the Moon in Capricorn 23, Saturn in Aquarius 26, Jupiter in Virgo 17, Mars in Aries 1, Venus in Aries 15, Mercury in Taurus 26, the ASC in Leo 26, the MC in Taurus 17, the North Node in Aquarius 24, [the preceding] Full Moon at the 6th hour of the night in Libra 24°36', [the Lot of] Fortune in Taurus 16, [the Lot of the] Daemon in Sagittarius 6, [and the] Exaltation [of the nativity] in Leo 11.[3]

Demonstration of the reason [for the child's short life]: the rulers of the triplicity of the ASC and those of the Light of the Time declined, being in opposition to each other and aspected by Mars.[4]

---

[1] A child of the Byzantine Emperor Leo I (401-474) and Empress Aelia Verina.
[2] This date corresponds to 25 April 463, and the time to about 1 PM LAT (= 12:56 PM LMT). It is discussed by Neugebauer & Van Hoesen, *Greek Horoscopes*, pp. 141-142.
[3] The longitudes in this nativity were calculated with Ptolemy's *Handy Tables* (or with Theon's edition of them). The resulting positions are: Sun 2°57' Taurus, Moon 21°58', Mercury 25°52' Taurus, Venus 14°27' Aries, Mars 0°27', Jupiter 16°55' Virgo, Saturn 25°54' Aquarius, North Node 23°43'. The Ptolemaic longitudes were too small by a nominal 2°28' in 463 due to Ptolemy's precessional error. (*Cf.* the note to the planetary positions in Chapt. 113 above.)
[4] This statement is only partially true. The triplicity rulers of the ASC are the Sun, Jupiter, and Saturn; those of the Light of the Time (in this chart, the Sun) are Venus, the Moon, and Mars. If Rhetorius was viewing the chart as a Sign-House chart, then all the triplicity rulers of the Sun are cadent (Venus and Mars in the 9th, and the Moon in the 6th), but none of the triplicity rulers of the ASC are cadent–in fact, two of them are angular and the other is succedent. Nor are any of the planets in opposition to any of the others. If aspects are reckoned on a whole-sign basis as was the ancient custom, then Mars is sextile Saturn and square the Moon. Cumont thinks the Greek text has been truncated. It is possible that it is also defective.

Appendix I.
Translator's Preface.

Teucer of Babylon[1] wrote a treatise on the natures of the 12 signs of the zodiac and another on the natures of the planets (see Appendix II below). His material seems to have been the principal source of such information for later astrologers. Another source for information on the signs and planets was Ptolemy's *Tetrabiblos*. Rhetorius evidently mingled information from Teucer with information from Ptolemy, so the version of Teucer that he compiled is interpolated.

Teucer of Babylon apparently lived before Vettius Valens (last half of the 2nd century A.D.), since that author's *Anthology* contains some of the same material, although Valens does not mention Teucer by name. This probably means that Teucer's material appeared in the work of some other author that Valens used as a source. The first mention of Teucer by name in works that have come down to us is by Porphyry in his *Introduction to the Tetrabiblos*. (written about 295 A.D.).

The whole question of the contents of Teucer's work and its relationship to that of the other Greek (and Arabic) astrologers is discussed in detail by Franz Boll, *Sphaera* (Leipzig: B.G. Teubner, 1903; Hildesheim: Georg Olms, 1967. repr. in facs.) Boll also discusses the non-standard constellations that are mentioned in Teucer's account of the 12 signs of the zodiac. I have relied upon his discussion for the notes given below. And I have added an index of all of the constellations mentioned by Teucer. The names of the non-standard ones are italicized.

Modern readers should be aware that the longitudes of the bright stars in the text are, except for errors of transcription, those

---

[1] Wilhelm Gundel suggested that "Babylon" was not the ancient Mesopotamian city, but rather a Roman military fortress of the same name that is now a part of the city of Cairo, Egypt. This seems reasonable, since the material contained in Teucer's treatises is essentially Greek and Egyptian in content, rather than Babylonian.

of Ptolemy's Catalogue of Stars with 3 degrees and 40 minutes added to them, which would be the precession from Ptolemy's Catalogue epoch of 137 A.D. to 504 A.D., which is either the year in which Rhetorius wrote or the year in which some author wrote whom Rhetorius used as a source. Also, whoever compiled the list of stars says mistakenly that they *rise* with the degrees given. This is not true! They rise with other degrees depending upon the latitude of the place. The longitudes given are simply catalogue longitudes. Furthermore, since 1500 years have passed since the time of this compilation, the stars are now more than 22 degrees advanced in longitude from the positions shown in the text.

The position of the non-standard constellations can only roughly be located on the celestial sphere, and it is not known what stars are included in them. There must once have been a description of those constellations and perhaps even a catalogue of the positions of their stars, but unfortunately those have not come down to us.

The descriptions of the characteristics of the zodiacal signs themselves rely to some extent upon the characteristics of the animals or humans that they represent.

But now, here is a translation of the compilation made by Rhetorius.[1]

---

[1] I have translated the Greek text edited by Franz Boll in CCAG 7, pp, 194-213, for the signs of the zodiac, and pp. 213-224 for the Planets.

The Twelve Signs from Teucer of Babylon.

The zodiacal circle moves obliquely and is divided into 12 sections called signs, and the first section is the sign Aries.

[Aries.]

The sign Aries is masculine, tropical, vernal, days and nights are equal, harmful, quadrupedal, living on dry land, royal, barren, easily changed, irascible, bright-burning, MC of the cosmos, increasing, eloquent, licentious, fiery, mutilated, fleshy, weak-eyed, servile, half-voiced, unruly, commanding, looking towards the southeast.

It has 30 degrees, and the degree 60 minutes, and the minute 60 seconds, and so on. [It is the] domicile of Mars, the exaltation of the Sun around the 19th degree, the fall of Saturn around the 21st degree; the triplicity by day of the Sun, by night of Jupiter, common [to both] Saturn, the detriment of Venus. And it has 3 decans, and the following [stars] rise with the first decan: Athena and the Tail of Cetus, and the third of Triangulum, and the Cynocephalus bearing the lamp and the Head of Ailouros of the *dodecaoros*[1]; with the 2nd decan there rise Andromeda and the Middle of Cetus and Gorgon and the Sword of Perseus, and half of Triangulum, and the middle of Ailouros of the *dodecaoros*[2]; with the 3rd decanate there rise Cassiopeia sitting on her throne, Perseus head downwards, the Head of Cetus, and the rearmost part of Triangulum, and the Tail of Ailouros of the *dodecaoros*.

---

[1] The word *dodekaoros* means literally 'twelve hours'; but it refers to the Babylonian 'double hours' and by extension becomes a synonym for the "barbaric" constellations.

[2] *Ailouros* or "The Tomcat" is a constellation that is mentioned in the list of "non-standard" constellations called the *dodecaoros*. See Franz Boll, *Sphaera* (Leipzig: B.G. Teubner, 1903), pp. 295 ff. The others, which are mentioned under the succeeding signs are: The Dog, The Snake, The Beetle, The Donkey, The Lion, The Billy Goat, The Bull, The Falcon, The Baboon, and The Crocodile. These are perhaps Egyptian constellations. Here, and in what follows, I have used Boll's discussions of the constellations.

And besides this, the first decan bears the influence of Mars, the second of the Sun, the third of Venus.

And in this [sign] the bright star, the End of the River, rises in 3 degrees and 50 minutes, latitude south, of the 1st magnitude, of the nature of Jupiter and Venus.[1]

And it has terms of the five planets: from the 1st degree to the 6th Jupiter, and from th 7th to the 12th Venus, and from the 13th to the 20th Mercury, and from the 21st to the 25th Mars, and from the 26th to the 30th Saturn.

And there are climes subject to the sign: Persia, according to Ptolemy Britain, Galatia, Germany, Palestine, Idumea, [and] Judea.

And of [the parts of] the body, it rules the head, and the face, and all the conditions and misfortunes relating to the head, that is headaches, weak sight,[2] apoplexy, deafness, blindness, leprosy, scurvy, falling out of the hair, baldness, unconsciousness, wounds, and they are accustomed to experience those things affecting the hearing and the teeth.

And it also rules the letters *alpha* and *nu*.[3]

---

[1]This star is unidentified. Its longitude in Ptolemy's Catalogue of Stars is 0 Aries 10 and latitude 53S30. Adding 3 degrees and 40 minutes to its longitude, we have 3 Aries 50, which agrees with the text; but the text has lost the numeral for 50 from the latitude. Today, there is no bright star there, so the position given may have been an error in Ptolemy's Catalogue, or else the star has unaccountably dimmed. Also, here, the author uses the word *epanatellei* 'rises', but in most cases hereafter he uses *paranatellei* "rises alongside" inappropriately in both cases, for throughout this text, he merely gives the *catalogue longitudes* of the stars increased by a constant 3 degrees and 40 minutes (where not altered by errors). However, these are not the *paranatellonta* positions, i.e. the ASC longitudes with which the stars rise in some particular latitude, but simply Ptolemy's catalogue positions reduced to the epoch of the writer.

[2]The exact signification of the word *episkiasmos* 'overshadowing' is uncertain. Since it is used here in the plural, it may mean sudden obscurations of the vision.

[3]These letters are simply the 1st and the 13th letters of the Greek alphabet. Those assigned to the next sign, Taurus, are the 2nd and the 14th letters, etc. Thus, the assignments are based strictly on the sequence of the letters in the Greek alphabet, which fortunately contained 24 letters.

And it is the side and the voice. There arises from the 1st degree to the 3rd the boundary of the sign, from the 3rd to the 7th the head, from the 8th to the 10th the neck, from the 11th to the 13th the chest, from the 14th to the 18th the waist, from the 19th to the 21st the hips, from the 22nd to the 24th the back, from the 25th to the 27th the tail, and from the 28th to the 30 the feet.

And when it is rising or containing the Moon, it denotes [those who have] a flushed face, [are] long-nosed, black-eyed, with a bald forehead, dignified, slim, shapely, skinny-legged, with a pleasant voice, [and are] magnanimous. And those in the 1st decan are energetic, ruling. To abandon or to flee from his native land, and, passing through much land and sea, and admired abroad, to turn about for a time, and having injured many things; and his father will not have an easy death, and his inheritance will be dissipated, and he will cast out his brothers, and the secret places of his body will fall away. Those in the 2nd decan will be rich, and beset by sorrows and losses and the recovery of possessions. Those in the 3rd [decan] [will have] many toils, being involved in dangers or imprisonments. And due to hatreds [it makes] them leaving[1] their own [country] in youth and returning late and being separated [from it] again. For the most part, they have no children.

[Taurus.]

The second sign is Taurus, feminine, nocturnal, northern, slanting, semi-voiced, fixed, vernal, half-finished, quadrupedal, mutilated, sterile, unchangeable, terrestrial, wealth-bringing [house] of the cosmos, lewd, terminal, earthy, domicile of Venus, exaltation of the Moon around the 3rd degree, fall of none, rising from the rearmost parts, setting right-side up, of which the larger part is situated in the invisible [part] of the Cosmos, looking towards the south. It has 30 degrees, etc., as was previously said about Aries; triplicity by day of Venus, and by night of the Moon, common Mars, detriment of Mars. It has 3 decans; and in the first decan

---

[1] *Misesi d' autous eâsai.*

there rises the sword-bearing Orion, and half of the Pleiades, and the remaining half of the Dead Woman, and the head of the Dog of the *dodecaoros*. In the 2nd decan there arises the Baboon holding the bare statue, and the Sceptre, and the remaining other half of the Dead Woman, and the middle of the Dog of the *dodecaoros*. In the 3rd decan there arises the Cavalryman, and Auriga, and the Chariot, and the Goat raised up by Auriga; and the 1st decan bears the face of Mercury, the 2nd of the Moon, and the 3rd of Saturn; and there arises in this [decan] the bright star of the Gorgon in 3 degrees and 20 minutes, north [latitude], 2nd magnitude, of the nature of Jupiter and Saturn.[1] Again, there arises in this [decan] all of the Pleiades, from the 6th to the 8th degree; and these degrees are harmful to the eyes. Again there arises the bright star of the Hyades in 16 degrees and 20 minutes, south [latitude], 1st magnitude, of the nature of Mars and Venus.[2] Again there arises the bright star in the pointed foot of Orion in 23 degrees, south [latitude], 1st magnitude, of the nature of Jupiter and Saturn.[3] Again there arises the bright star in the leading shoulder of Orion in 27 degrees and 40 minutes, south [latitude], 2nd magnitude, of the nature of Mars and Mercury.[4] Again, there arises the bright star of Capella, which is also the name of the star itself, in 28 degrees and 40 minutes, north [latitude], 1st magnitude, of the nature of Jupiter and Saturn.[5]

And it has terms of the 5 planets: from the 1st degree to the 8th, Venus; from the 9th to the 14th, Mercury; from the 15th to the 22nd, Jupiter; from the 23rd to the 27th, Saturn; and from 28 to 30, Mars.

And there are these climes subject [to it]: Babylon, Parthia, Media, Persia, the Cyclades Islands, Cyprus, Asia Minor.

And of the [parts] of the body, it rules: the sinews [of the neck],

---

[1] Algol or β Persei.
[2] Aldebaran or α Tauri.
[3] Rigel or β Orionis. Its longitude should be 23 degrees and 30 minutes.
[4] Bellatrix or γ Orionis.
[5] Capella or α Aurigae.

the neck, the gullet, swelling of the glands of the neck, suffocation and the nostrils, injury and disease of the eyes.

And it rules the letters *beta* and *xi*.

There arises from degrees 1 to 3, the head; from 4 to 7, the horns; from 8 to 10, the neck; from 11 to 13, the chest; from 14 to 18, the waist, from19 to 21, the hips; from 22 to 24, the hinder parts; from 25 to 27, the tail; and from 28 to 30, the hooves.

And it denotes those who will be fuller[1] in color, with a large mouth, sharp-haired, and heavy-spirited and those who have been turned out of houses. And of these, those in the 1st decan are involved in many dangers, extravagant, childless, having few brothers. And those in the 2nd decan, uneducated, laborers, wretched persons, losing their inheritance, and having brothers. And those in the 3rd decan, dignified, good-looking, wealthy, renowned, living splendidly, but afterwards becoming involved in anxieties and penalties.

[Gemini.]

The third sign is Gemini, masculine, diurnal, voiced, slanting, bicorporeal, semi-sterile, the twelfth house of the Cosmos, sinewy, of human form, looking to the southwest, domicile of Mercury, exaltation of the Ascending Node around 15 degrees, fall of the Descending Node around 15 degrees, detriment of Jupiter, triplicity by day of Saturn, by night of Mercury, common Jupiter. It has 3 decans, and in the first decan there arises Auriga, and the Chariot, and the Wheel underneath the Chariot, and the half of the anterior parts of the Dog, and the head of the Snake of the *dodecaoros*. In the 2nd decan there arises Lyra, and Hercules, and the Snake on a tree, being pursued by Hercules, and the middle of the Snake of the *dodecaoros*. In the 3rd decan there arises Apollo and Lyra and the Dog and the Dolphin and the anterior parts of the Ursa Minor and the hinder parts of the Snake of the *dodecaoros*.

---

[1]Reading *pleioterous* 'fuller' with MSS **TV** rather than *leioterous* 'smoother'.

And the 1st decan bears the face of Jupiter; and the second, of Mars; and the 3rd, of the Sun.

And there arises in it a bright star, the middle one of the three in the Belt of Orion, in the 1st degree, south [latitude], 2nd magnitude, of the nature of Jupiter and Saturn. Again, there arises a bright star, the one in the right shoulder of Orion, in the 5 degrees and 40 minutes, south [latitude], 1st magnitude, of the nature of Mars and Mercury. Again there arises a bright star, the one in the right shoulder of Auriga, in 6 degrees and 30 minutes, 2nd magnitude, of the nature of Jupiter and Saturn. Again, there arises a bright star, the one of Canis [Major], in 21 degrees and 40 minutes, 1st magnitude, of the nature of Jupiter and Mars. Furthermore, there arises the one in the head of the leading one of the Twins [Gemini], in 27 degrees, 2nd magnitude, of the nature of Jupiter and Mercury.[1]

And it has terms of the 5 planets: Mercury 6, Jupiter 6, Venus 5, Mars 7, Saturn 6.

And there are these climes subject [to it]: Cappadocia; [and] according to Ptolemy, Hyrcania, Armenia, Matiana, Cyrenaica, Marmorica, Lower Egypt.

And of the parts of the body, it rules the shoulders and the hands.

And it rules the letters *gamma* and *omicron*.

And there rise from the 1st to the 2nd degree the hair of Apollo, from the 3rd to the 5th [his] head, from the 6th to the 9th the neck, from the 10th to the 12th the shoulders, from the 13th to the 17th the belly, from the 18th to the 20th the thighs, from the 21st to the 23rd the middle[2] lower legs, from the 24th to the 25th the feet, and from the 26th to the 30th the last northern [parts] that are adjacent to Cancer.

---

[1] Alnilam or ε Orionis, Betelgeuze or α Orionis, Menkalinan or β Aurigae, Sirius or α Canis Majoris, Castor or α Geminorum.
[2] This word should probably be omitted.

And it denotes swarthy persons, with heavy beards, meeting eyebrows, with bald foreheads, swift in their walk, versed in business, wealthy. And of these, those in the 1st decan are honored and managers of important affairs and they will receive their paternal inheritance; they will be both gymnasts and miserable, executing vain and foolish [performances], very experienced, inventive.[1] And those in the 2nd decan, very dangerous, adulterous, at odds with their parents, hating scoundrels, sensible, foolhardy, wealthy. And in the 3rd decan, liable to conquer, honored, and governing their fatherland.

[Cancer.]

The fourth sign is Cancer, tropical, summery, straight, voiceless, feminine, nocturnal, changeable, digging,[2] rough-skinned, lewd, watery, ASC of the Cosmos, of good manifestations, common, prolific, amphibious, domicile of the Moon, exaltation of Jupiter around 18 degrees, fall of Mars around 28 degrees, detriment of Saturn, triplicity by day of Venus, by night of Mars, common the Moon. It has three decans. And in the 1st decan there arises the hinder parts of Ursa Minor, and the Satyr touching the club, and Musa playing the lyre, and one of the Graces, and the head of the Beetle of the *dodecaoros*. And in the second decan there arises half of the Manger and the [North] Asellus, and the middle of the Graces, and half of the Beetle of the *dodecaoros*. And in the 3rd decan there arises the third of the Graces, and the other [the South] Asellus, and the other half of the Manger, and the end of the Beetle of the *dodecaoros*.

And the 1st decan bears the face of Venus, and the 2nd of Mercury, and the 3rd of the Moon.

And there arises in this a bright star that is in the head of the leading one of the Twins [Gemini] [in 0 degrees and] 20 minutes,

---

[1] The Greek text seems a bit shaky. Perhaps what is meant is that this decan denotes clever and hard-working but unsuccessful gymnasts.
[2] The crab characteristically burrows into the sand.

north [latitude], 2nd magnitude, of the nature of Mars alone.¹ And there also arises the Nebula² from 9 degrees to 15 degrees; these degrees happen to be harmful to the eyes.

And it has terms of the five planets: Mars 7, Venus 6, Mercury 6, Jupiter 7, Saturn 4.

And there are these climes subject [to it]: Armenia; according to Ptolemy, Numidia, Charcedon, Africa, Bithynia, Phrygia, Colchis.

And of [the parts of] the body, it rules the chest and the stomach, the breasts, the heart, the spleen, the hidden places, obscurely because of the Nebula, white [or] lichen-like [or] leprous [patches on the skin], apoplexy and dropsy, hunch-back, moles.

And [it rules] the letters *delta* and *pi*.

And there rises from the 1st to the third degree the top, from the 4th to the 7th the head, from the 8th to the 10th the belly, from the 11th to the 13th the feet, from the 14th to the 19th the end parts, from the 20th to the 24th the back, from the 25th to the 27th the left claw, from the 28th to the 30th the right or southern [claw].

And it denotes dark-complexioned [persons], small-necked, chesty, bow-legged or moving sideways in their walk,³ well-formed, the extravagances of others. And of these, those who are born in the first decan will be prosperous and beneficent to many and he will gain the friendship of many. And those in the 2nd decan are petty-minded, chronically ill, successful, living abroad, suffering injury to the eyes, skillful. And in the 3rd [decan], generally subordinated to someone and becoming dangerous; but also those having few brothers and who are estranged from their family, fond of the sea, but also foolhardy for the sake of profit, blest with children, but also having bodily injuries.

---

¹Pollux or β Geminorum.
²Praesepe or M44 in the constellation Cancer.
³Again, characteristics of the crab.

[Leo.]

The fifth sign is Leo, masculine, diurnal, voiced, straight, fixed, ruling, commanding, hot, summery, fiery, irritable, immovable, irascible, indomitable, ascending, political, public, sterile, quadrupedal, mutilated, lewd, succedent of the Cosmos, having only one offspring, commanding, looking towards the east, domicile of the Sun, exaltation and fall of none, detriment of Saturn, triplicity by day of the Sun, but by night of Jupiter, common Saturn. It has 3 decans. And in the first decan there arises the Dogface[1] shooting an arrow, and the half of the Ship, and the head of Hydra, and the head of the Donkey of the *dodecaoros*. And in the 2nd decan there arises the other half of the Ship, and a God having extended his hands upwards, and the back of Hydra, and Crater, and the Cymbal, and the Phrygian Flutes, and the middle of the Donkey of the *dodecaoros*. In the 3rd decan there arises Auriga holding the wheel, and the little Boy following him, and the middle of Hydra, and the hinder parts of the Donkey of the *dodecaoros*.

And the 1st decan bears the face of Saturn, the 2nd of Jupiter, and the 3rd of Mars.

And there arises in this [sign] a bright star, the one in the neck of Hydra, in 3 degrees and 40 minutes, south [latitude], 2nd magnitude, of the nature of Saturn and Venus.[2] Again there arises a bright star, the one in the heart of Leo, which is called Regulus, in 6 degrees and 12 minutes, 1st magnitude, of the nature of Mars and Jupiter.[3] Again there arises a bright star, the one in its tail, in 28 degrees and 12 minutes, 1st magnitude, of the nature of Saturn and Venus.[4]

---

[1] Perhaps the Egyptian god Anubis, who is represented as having the head of a jackal.
[2] Alphard or α Hydrae.
[3] Regulus or α Leonis, whose longitude should be 6 degrees and 10 minutes rather than 6 degrees and 12 minutes.
[4] Denebola or β Leonis, whose longitude should be 27 degrees and 10 minutes rather than 28 degrees and 12 minutes.

And it has terms of the 5 planets: Jupiter 6, Venus 5, Saturn 7, Mercury 6, Mars 6.

And there are these climes subject [to it]: Asia, Italy, Galatia, Apulia, Phoenicia, Chaldea, Orchenia.

And [of the parts] of the body, it rules: the sinews, the bones, the hips, the heart, the eyesight, manliness.

And [it rules] the letters *epsilon* and *rho*.

And there rises from the 1st degree to the 3rd the head, from the 4th to the 7th the neck, from the 8th to the 11th the back, from the 12th to the 14th the waist, from the 15th to the 19th the hips, from the 20th to the 22nd the tail, from the 23rd to the 25th the knee-bends, from the 26th to the 28th the point around the knee-bends coming outside a part of the tail, from the 29th to the 30th the soles and nails of the hinder feet.

And it denotes pale complexioned persons, maimed, very sharp-eyed, big-mouthed, with thin-set teeth, a fine neck, short-nosed, broad-chested, flat-bellied, slim below, and fine-boned, deep-voiced, hard, reared. And of these, those [who are born] in the 1st decan [are] fond of their brothers, mountaineers, toilsome. And according to the 2nd, [they are] regal, bold, high-minded, ruling, short-lived, losing their inheritance. And according to the 3rd, [they are] dirty, grim-looking, chilling, wealthy, commanding, on foreign service, showing kindness to many, but also mistreating many, casting off brothers, and putting them to death improperly.

[Virgo.]

The sixth sign is Virgo, compound, straight, feminine, nocturnal, summery, winged, three-faced, rational, descending, voiced, earthy, changeable, mystical, subservient, bicorporeal, of human form, sterile, looking towards the southwest, cadent of the Cosmos, domicile of Mercury and exaltation of Mercury around 15 degrees, fall of Venus around 27 degrees, detriment of Jupiter, triplicity by day of Venus and by night of the Moon, common Mercury. It has three decans; and in the first decan there arises a goddess seated upon a throne and holding a child, whom some say is the goddess Isis in the atrium nursing Horus. Also rising alongside is the Spike [of Virgo], and the middle of Hydra, and the head of Corvus, and the head of the Lion of the *dodecaoros*. And in the 2nd decan there arises Mousa playing the lyre, and the middle of Corvus, and the tail of Hydra, and the half of Boötes...of the Bull-head, and the half of Arotron, and the half of the Lion of the *dodecaoros*. And in the third decan there arises the other half of Boötes, and the other half of Arotron, and the tail of Corvus, and the Spike, and the tail of the Lion of the *dodecaoros*.

And the 1st decan bears the face of the Sun, and the 2nd of Venus, and the 3rd of Mercury.

And Virgo does not have any bright stars arising [in it], I mean of the 1st or 2nd magnitude.

And there arises only the one in the end of the southern or left wing,[1] and third magnitude, of the nature of Mercury and Mars, north [latitude]. And again in the right wing the so-called Vindemiatrix,[2] in 15 degrees and 36 minutes, north [latitude], 3rd magnitude, of the nature of Saturn and Mercury.

And it has the terms of the 5 planets: from 1 to 7 degrees Mercury, Venus 10, Jupiter 4, Mars 7, Saturn 2.

And these climes are subject [to it]: Greece, Ionia, Achaia, Mesopotamia, Babylonia, Middle Ethiopia, Assyria, Crete.

And [of the parts] of the body, it rules: the belly, and all the entrails, and the hidden [parts].

And [it rules] the letters *zeta* and *sigma*.

---

[1]Zavijava or β Virginis. Its longitude should be 2 degrees and 40 minutes.
[2]Vindemiatrix or ε Virginis, its longitude should be 15 degrees and 50 minutes.

And there rises from the 1st degree to the 3rd the head, and from the 4th to the 6th the nose, from the 7th to the 10th the neck, from the 11th to the 13th the arms, from the 14th to the 18th the fingers, from the 19th to the 21st Spica, from the 22nd to the 23rd the shins, from the 24th to the 27th the [parts] towards the north, and the remainder towards the south.

And it denotes those with a good complexion, shapely, easy to deal with, cheerful, kindly, accused of [actions] with children, and mostly as lovers of boys. In the 1st decan [they are] long-lived, hard-working, progressing with the aid of magnates, but often harmed by their love of boys. In the 2nd [decan, they are] wise, lewd, and losing [things] in their youth, but more fortunate in their old age, successful, susceptible to illness. And in the 3rd [decan, they are] humble in life, those taking a subordinate position, and enduring much along with his just deserts.

[Libra.]

The seventh sign is Libra, masculine, equinoctial, straight, diurnal, voiced, tropical, of human form, ascending, just, airy, changeable, autumnal, IC of the Cosmos, common, political, waxing and waining, domicile of Venus, exaltation of Saturn around 21 degrees, fall of the Sun around 19 degrees, detriment of Mars, triplicity by day of Staurn, and by night of Mercury, common Jupiter. It has three decans; and there arises in the first decan the Unseen, and Mousa playing the lyre, and the Ferryman, and part of the Acherousia Harbour, and part of the Skaphos, and the head of the Goat of the *dodecaoros*. And in the 2nd decan there arises Auriga, and the Boy, and the anterior parts of the Centaur, and the middle of Skaphos, and the middle of the Acherousia Harbour, and the Fountain, and Agora, and the middle of the Goat of the *dodecaoros*. And in the 3rd decan there arises the hinder parts of the Centaur, and the end of Skaphos, and the end of the Acherousia Harbour, and Ariadne upright having her left hand on her head, and the Crown of Ariadne, and two heads in the sky, and the so-called Ballistas, and Adonis, whom they call Uranus, and the end of the Goat of the *dodecaoros*.

And Libra comes about from the Claws of Scorpio; and it also has the power of a bicorporeal [sign] because of the balance-pans of the scales.

And the 1st decan bears the face of the Moon, the 2nd of Saturn, and the 3rd of Jupiter.

And there arises in this [decan] a bright star, the one in the Spike,[1] in [no degrees and] 20 minutes, north [latitude], 1st magnitude, of the nature of Venus and Mercury. Again there arises a bright star in Boötes, the one [called] Arcturus,[2] in 5 degrees and 40 minutes, north [latitude], 1st magnitude, of the nature of Mars and Jupiter. Again there arises a bright star, the one in the northern Crown, in 15 degrees and 20 minutes,[3] north [latitude], 2nd magnitude, of the nature of Venus and Mercury. Again there arises the bright star in the claw of Scorpio, in 25 degrees and 50 minutes,[4] north [latitude], 2nd magnitude, of the nature of Jupiter and Mercury.

And it has the terms of the 5 planets: Saturn 6, Mercury 8, Jupiter 7, Venus 7, Mars 2.

And these climes are subject [to it]: Libya, Cyrene, Bactriana, Caspia,[5] Serica,[6] Thebais, Sakis,[7] Troglodytica.

And [of the parts] of the body, it rules: the hips, buttocks, groins, belly, colon, the hinder parts, the bladder. And it is lewd

---

[1] Spica or α Virginis.
[2] Arcturus or α Bootis, but its longitude should be 0 degrees and 40 minutes.
[3] Alphecca or α Coronae Borealis, but its longitude should be 18 degrees and 20 minutes. Perhaps the longitude of β Coronae Borealis was inadvertently copied.
[4] Zubeneschamali or β Librae.
[5] Ptolemy has Casperia.
[6] China, or its western part.
[7] As Robbins points out, probably a blunder for Oasis, which Ptolemy (*Tetrabiblos* ii. 3) includes between Thebais and Troglodytica.

and prolific like the Goat.

And [it rules] the letters *eta* and *tau*.

And there rise from the 1st degree to the 4th, the beginning of this [sign], from the 5th to the 6th the opening within and the cord (?), from the 7th to the 10th the [parts] next to the head, from the 12th to the 13th the head itself, from the 14th to the 17th the neck, chest, and abdomen, from the 18th to the 20th the belly, from the 21st to the 22nd the things, from the 23rd to the 24th the shoulders, from the 25th to the 27th the feet, and the remainder the [parts] towards the south.

And it denotes temperate persons, black-eyed, with beautiful hair, patient, [and] just. And of these, those in the 1st decan [are] virtuous, manly, fond of their friends, wandering about. And in the second [decan, they are] handsome, wise, commanding, renowned, fond of women, on foreign service, just, well-known, [and] having few brothers. And in the 3rd [decan, they are] handsome, but extravagant and fickle, [and] not harmless.

[Scorpio.]

The eighth sign is Scorpio, feminine, nocturnal, straight, fixed, autumnal, voiceless, watery, prolific, causing destruction, descending, curved, rough-skinned, leprous,[1] immovable, irascible, piercing, cunning, a sculptor, fifth house of the Cosmos, domicile of Mars, exaltation of none, fall of the Moon around 3 degrees, detriment of Venus, triplicity by day of Venus, and by night of Mars, common the Moon. It has three decans. And in the 1st decan there arises Hygiea and the hinder parts of the Centaur, and the leading parts of the Bull of the *dodecaoros*. And in the second decan there arises Asclepius, and the middle of the Centaur, and the middle of the Bull of the *dodecaoros*. And in the 3rd decan there

---

[1] *leprôdes*, *alphôdes* 'leprous, leprous'. The first of these words means 'scaly', 'rough', or 'leprous'; the second is a rare word that just means 'leprous' and especially the condition of leprosy that is visible as a white patch on the face.

arises the leading parts of the Centaur touching the Hare, and the leading parts of the Dog, and Ophiucus, and the hinder parts of the Bull of the *dodecaoros*.

And the first decan bears the face of Mars, and the 2nd of the Sun, and the 3rd of Venus.

And there arises in it a bright star, the one on the right foot of the Centaur,[1] in 12 degrees, north [latitude], 1st magnitude, of the nature of Venus and Jupiter. Again there arises a bright star, the so-called Antares,[2] in 16 degrees and 20 minutes, south [latitude], 2nd magnitude, of the nature of Mars and Jupiter.

And it has the terms of the 5 planets: Mars 7, Venus 4, Mercury 8, Jupiter 5, Saturn 6.

And these climes are subject [to it]: Italy, Matagonits, Mauretania, Getulia, Syria, Commagene, [and] Cappadocia.

And [of the parts] of the body, it rules: the pudenda, and the bladder, and the groins, and the seat. And it makes, because of the sting, dimness of vision, weakness of sight, [kidney] stones, strangury, tumors, tumors in the throat, the practice of unspeakable vice, sexual promiscuity, fistulas, cancer, hemorrhage.

And it rules the letters *theta* and *upsilon*.

And there rises from the 1st degree to the 3rd the claws, from the 4th to the 7th the head, from the 8th to the 10th the neck, from the 11th to the 13 the chest, from the 14th to the 16th the abdomen, from the 17th to the 21st the back, from the 22nd to the 24th the sting, from the 25th to the 27th the middle, from the 28th to the 30th the end of the sting.

And it denotes dark-complexioned, dark-eyed persons, austere,

---

[1] Alpha Centauri, whose latitude is south not north. And I have adopted the reading of 12 degrees (which agrees with Ptolemy) given by MS **R** in place of 11 degrees given by MSS **TV** and adopted by Boll.

[2] Antares or α Scorpii.

kinky-haired, weak-voiced, courageous, swift and disdainful. And in the 1st decan [they are] unjust,[1] wandering about, exposed to many dangers, manly, [and] moderate in his life. And in the 2nd [decan, they are] hard-working, sensible, stubbornly opinionated, living abroad, involved in great [matters], childless, and injuring the body. And in the 3rd [decan, they are] crooked, cunning, suffering, raging often and doing wrong to many, abandoning his relatives, living a hard life, [and] short-lived.

[Sagittarius.]

The ninth sign is Sagittarius, masculine, bicorporeal, ruling, of human and animal form, sinewy, two-faced, terrestrial, quadrupedal, weak-eyed, half-voiced; and it is called two-faced because it has behind the head another part of the face of the face bearing a diadem, on which account it is also called ruling; straight, autumnal, fiery, semi-sterile, good, cadent of the Cosmos and the house of slaves, domicile of Jupiter, exaltation of the Descending Node around 15 degrees, fall of the Ascending Node around 15 degrees, detriment of Mercury, triplicity by day of the Sun, and by night of Jupiter, common Saturn. It has three decans; and in the first decan there arises a god posited upside down, and he is called Talas, and a Raven is touching his head, and a Dog is turned away, and the head of Hercules of the *dodecaoros*. And with the second decan, there rises Cepheus extending his right hand to Lupus, and the head of Lupus, and the half of Argos, and the leading parts of Delphinus, and the middle of the Falcon of the *dodecaoros*. and in the 3rd decan there arises the remaining parts of Delphinus, and Pelagos, and the half of Ursa Major, and the tail of the Falcon of the *dodecaoros*.

And the 1st decan bears the face of Mercury, and the 2nd of the Moon, and the 3rd of Saturn.

And there arises in this a bright star, the one in the knee of Sagit-

---

[1]Reading *adikous* 'unjust' rather than *adikôs* 'unjustly'.

tarius,[1] in 20 degrees, north [latitude], 2nd magnitude, of the nature of Jupiter and Saturn. Again there arises a bright star, the one in Lyra, the so-called Lyric,[2] in 21 degrees, north [latitude], 1st magnitude, of the nature of Venus and Mercury.

And it has the terms of the 5 planets: Jupiter 12, Venus 5, Mercury 4, Saturn 5, Mars 4.

And these climes are subject [to it]: Cilicia, Tyre,[3] Celtica, Spain, [and] Arabia Felix.

And [of the parts] of the body, it rules: the thighs, [and] the groins. And it often makes superfluous limbs [and] those having birth-marks, bald or weak-sighted persons, epileptics or having pain in the eyes, or those being maimed by a barb or by a fall from a height because of Talas,[4] or danger from quadrupeds, or the loss of limbs, or injury by wild beasts because of Cepheus.

And it rules the letters *iota* and *phi*.

And there rises from the 1st degree to the 3rd the head, from the 4th to the 7th the bow, from the 8th to the 10th the bow-string, from the 11th to the 14th the hands, from the 15th to the 19th the neck and shoulders, from the 20th to the 22nd the back, from the 23rd to the 25th up to the middle the point, from the 26th to the 28th the feet, from the 29th to the 30th the hooves.

And it denotes those of moderate coloration, a nicely-shaped mouth, nice eyes, and also shapely in form, swift and reckless and invincible, petty-minded and generally unstable. And in the 1st decan [they are] destroyers of their own kindred, inclined to eating alone and deficient,[5] very laborious, living in foreign places, or

---

[1] Alpha Sagittarii, but its longitude should be 20 degrees 40 minutes, and it is in south latitude, not north.
[2] Vega or α Lyrae.
[3] Ptolemy has Tyrrhenia instead of Tyre.
[4] Talas is described above as being the constellational figure of "a god upside down"; hence, like unto a person falling head over heels.
[5] Or perhaps we should read *ellipous* 'greasy' rather than *ellipeis* 'deficient'.

ending their lives there. And in the 2nd [decan, they are] braggarts, involved in many business affairs and acquisitions and losses, losing their paternal inheritance, living abroad in many places and generally unsettled, [and] suffering grief because of his children and wives. And those who are born in the 3rd decan [are] notable, held in honor in foreign lands, promiscuous in their sexual relations, and fickle.

[Capricorn.]

The tenth sign is Capricorn, feminine, nocturnal, tropical, slanting, wintery, living on both sea and land, rough-skinned, leprous, causing destruction, barren, descending, chilled, half-voiced, lewd, making riddles, of double form, very wet, agricultural, half-finished, hunchbacked, lame, brutal,[1] mutilated, scaly, DSC of the Cosmos, domicile of Saturn, exaltation of Mars around 28 degrees, fall of Jupiter around 15 degrees, detriment of the Moon, triplicity by day of Venus, and by night of the Moon, common Mars. It has three decans; and in the first decan there rises the other half of Argo and of Ursa Major and Nereis and Lyra and the head of the Big Fish and the anterior part of the Baboon of the *dodecaoros*. In the 2nd decan there arise Eileitheia seated upon a throne, and half of the Wheel, and the Vine, and half of the Big Fish, and the Censer, and the middle of the Big Fish, and the middle of the Ominous One of the *dodecaoros*. And in the third decan there arises the other half of the Wheel, and the tail of the Big Fish, and the Censer, and the Headless Daemon holding his own head, and the hinder parts of the Ominous One of the *dodecaoros*.

And the 1st decan bears the face of Jupiter, the 2nd of Mars, the 3rd of the Sun.

And there arises in this a bright star, the one in Aquila,[2] in 7 degrees and 40 minutes, north [latitude], 1st magnitude, of the nature

---

[1] Perhaps, merely 'animal' (i.e., not human), rather than 'brutal'.
[2] Altair or α Aquilae.

of Mars and Jupiter.

And it has the terms of the 5 planets: Mercury 7, Jupiter 7, Venus 8, Saturn 4, Mars 4.

And these climes are subject [to it]: Syria, India, Ariana, Gedrosia, Thrace, [and] Macedonia.

And [of the parts] of the body it rules the knees and the sinews. And it makes dim sight and maiming because of the spiny backbone, and madness and distress from humors and fluxes. And it is also lewd and productive of shameful actions.

And it rules the letters *kappa* and *chi*.

And there rises from the 1st degree to the 3rd the horns, from the 4th to the 7th the nose, from the 8th to the 10th the neck, from the 11th to the 13th the abdomen, from the 14th to the 19th the back, from the 20th to the 21st the thighs, from the 22nd to the 24th the tail, from the 25th to the 27th the [parts] towards the north, [and] the rest the hooves.

And it denotes a small face, slender ankles, fond of women, liars, conceited, servile, religious, loving his friends, dependable, those receiving aid, so that they lack nothing, eloquent, fool-hardy. And in the 1st decan long-lived, charming, aquatic, and honored in foreign countries, but also sickly, and involved in many losses. In the 2nd decan, wandering, away from home, good persons, subordinates, experiencing injuries or dangers in wet places, and living better in old age than in youth. In the 3rd decan, conclusive, wandering, renowned, loved by many and extolled in foreign countries, benefactors, favorable persons.

[Aquarius.]

The eleventh sign is Aquarius, masculine, diurnal, slanting, voiced, dew-producing, fixed, wintry, airy, very cold, descending, of human form, immovable, childless, fearful, mossy, scaly, corpse-like, hunchbacked, succedent of the Cosmos, [and] of the DSC, and eighth house [of the Cosmos] concerning death, domicile of Saturn, exaltation and fall of none, detrimiment of the Sun, triplicity by day of Saturn, and by night of Mercury, common Jupiter. It has three decans; and in the first decan there arises the river Eridanus holding a pitcher, and the head of Centaurus, and its hand, or the right hand stretched out, and the head of the Ibis of the *dodecaoros*. And in the 2nd decan there arises the middle of the Centaur, and the two Snakes having application towards each other, and the middle of the Ibis of the *dodecaoros*. And in the 3rd decan there arises the Big Bird, which is called Cygnus, . . .[1] which they call Centaur, and the Wolf biting his right hand, and the hinder parts of Pegasus, and the end of the Ibis of the *dodecaoros*.

And the first decan bears the face of Venus, the 2nd of Mercury, [and] the 3rd of the Moon.

And there arises in this a bright star that is called Piscis Austrinus, in 12 degrees, south [latitude], 1st magnitude, of the nature of Venus and Mercury.[2] Again there arises a bright star, which is called Bird, in 12 degrees and 50 minutes, north [latitude], 2nd magnitude, of the nature of Venus and Mercury.[3]

And it has the terms of the five planets: Mercury 7, Venus 6, Jupiter 7, Mars 5, Saturn 5.

And these climes are subject [to it]: Egypt, Sauromatica, Oxiana, Sogdiana, Arabia.

And [of the parts] of the body it rules: the shins, the legs, the sinews.

And it makes those suffering from dropsy, arthritics, crazy people, those who are castrated and wounded and those suffering from

---

[1] Some words are missing.
[2] Fomalhaut or α Piscis Austrini, but its longitude should be 10 degrees 40 minutes.
[3] Deneb Adige or α Cygni.

elephantiasis, jaundiced persons, black bile, disabled in a limb because of the Pitcher.

And it has the letters *lambda* and *psi*.

And there rises from the 1st degree to the 3rd, the head; from the 4th to the 7th, the neck; from the 8th to the 10th, the belly; from the 11th to the 13th, the hands; from the 14th to the 19th, the shoulders; in the 20th, the heart; from the 21st to the 22nd, the private parts; from the 23rd to the 25th, the thighs; from the 26th to the 27th, the feet; from the 28th to the 30th, the hips.

And it signifies good coloration, easy to heal, sensitive, vain-glorious, fond of cleanliness, [and] braggarts. And in the 1st decan, [they are] beneficent, but often showing ingratitude, living abroad and happily married, [and] bothered by drugs. And in the 2nd [decan, they are] cheerful, playful, guileless, having difficulties in watery places, pleasant, those who are excessively well off and renowned in arms. <And in the 3rd decan, those who are> kingly, being side by side,[1] and experiencing many dangers or wounded from waters.

[Pisces.]

The twelfth sign is Pisces, feminine, bicorporeal, nocturnal, slanting, watery, wintry, descending, voiceless, good, changeable, prolific, salacious, very wet, mutilated, scaly, variegated in color, rough-skinned, leprous, unstable, lewd, common, finned, the good cadent of the Cosmos, the House of God, domicile of Jupiter, exaltation of Venus around 27 degrees, fall of Mercury around 15 degrees, triplicity by day of Venus, and by night of Mars, common the Moon. It has 3 decans; and in the first decan there arises the anterior parts of the winged horse Pegasus, and the head of the Stag having two serpents in its nostrils, and the beginning of Linos, and

---

[1] The text has the otherwise unattested word *sympleusomenous* 'being side by side'?, and MS **V** has *anaxiois* 'to or for kings' instead of Boll's emendation *anaxious* 'kingly', so perhaps we should read 'side by side with kings' or something like that?

the tail of the Crocodile of the *dodecaoros*. And in the second decan there arises the middle of the Stag, and half of Hercules, and half of the Crocodile of the *dodecaoros*. And in the third decan there arise the hinder parts of the Stag, and the other half of Hercules, and the end of Linos, and the head of the Crocodile of the *dodecaoros*.

And the 1st decan bears the face of Saturn, the 2nd of Jupiter, the 3rd of Mars.

And there arises in this a bright star, the one in the Horse, in 5 degrees and 50 minutes, north [latitude], 2nd magnitude, of the nature of Mars and Mercury.[1] Again, there arises a bright star, the one common to the Horse and Andromeda, in 21 degrees, north [latitude], 2nd magnitude, of the nature of Mars and Mercury.[2]

And it has the terms of the five planets: Venus 12, Jupiter 4, Mercury 3, Mars 9, Saturn 2.

And these climes are subject [to it]: the Red Sea, and the Indian land, Garamantia, Lydia, Cilicia, Pamphylia.

And [of the parts] of the body it rules: the soles of the feet, and the feet, and the sinews of the feet, and the ankles.

And it makes arthritics, those suffering from gout, hunchbacks, rough-skinned or leprous or those having scurvy or scabs, lewd and also blameworthy persons, licentious, promiscuous, troubled by diseases involving humors.

And it rules the letters *mu* and *omega*.

And there rises from the 1st degree to the 3rd the head, from the 4th to the 7th up to the middle of the bond, from the 8th to the 10th the [parts] towards the south, from the 11th to the 13th the abdomen, from the 14th to the 19th the shoulders, from the 20th to the 27th the northerly [parts], from the 28th to the 30th the hooves [!].

---
[1] Scheat or β Pegasi.
[2] Alpheratz or α Andromedae, but its longitude should be 21 degrees 30 minutes.

And it denotes pale complexioned persons, with nice hair, ingenious, hard-drinkers, [and] spendthrifts. And in the 1st decan, [they are] reckless, unjust because of greed, moderate in life, curious about stories or knowledge, having many friends, skillful, esteemed, liked by women. And in the 2nd [decan, they are] gluttonous, curious, [and] those living abroad. And in the 3rd [decan, they are] devoted to enjoyment, scholarly, renowned, much-experienced, having favor among women, spendthrifts, and also impetuous and spectators of many, easily losing and acquiring [things].

[Summary.][1]

And of these signs, some are *straight* and some are *crooked*; and the *straight* ones are from Cancer to Sagittarius, and the *crooked* ones are from Capricorn to Gemini. And also, some of these are *diurnal* and some are *nocturnal*; and the *diurnal* ones are ♈ ♊ ♌ ♎ ♐ ♒; but the *nocturnal* are ♉ ♋ ♍ ♏ ♑ ♓. These trines[2] are also called *oriental* ♈ ♌ ♐; these same are both fiery and regal. And earthy are ♉ ♍ ♑, and these are northerly. And of the trines of Gemini and Libra and Aquarius; these are also called airy, [and] it happens to be *occidental*. Similarly too, the trines of ♋ ♏ and ♓, which are watery, and they are also called fertile; and these same happen to be southerly. And the squares[3] are [those] of ♈ ♋ ♎ ♑, which are also called tropical[4]; again, ♉ ♌ ♏ ♒, which are called fixed; and the bicorporeal squares ♊ ♍ ♐ ♓. And the oppositions of the tropical [signs], ♈ to ♎ and ♋ to ♑; and of the fixed [signs], ♉ to ♏, and ♌ to ♒. And the sextiles are the masculine [signs] to the masculine ones, and the feminine to the feminine. Indeed, the masculine [signs] are just as we wrote in those earlier nocturnal ones, sc. ♈ ♊ ♌ ♎ ♐ ♒; and those sextiles are called both diurnal and masculine; but [as for] ♉ and ♋ and ♍ and

---

[1] Boll says that he doubts that this section was written by Rhetorius; consequently, it may be a gloss added by a copyist.
[2] Now called *trigons* or more commonly *triplicities*.
[3] Now called *quadruplicities*.
[4] Now called *cardinal*, and subdivided into *equinoctial* a and *tropical* a.

♉ and ♑ and ♓, these again are sextile each other and are called both feminine and nocturnal. From these signs everything is known and also which star [is involved].

Index of Constellation and Star Names[1]

Acherousia	Libra	1,2,3				
Adonis (Uranus)	Libra	3				
Agora	Libra	2				
Ailouros	Aries	1,2,3				
Andromeda	Aries	2				
Apollo	Gemini	3				
Argo	Sagittarius	2	Capricorn	1		
Ariadne	Libra	3				
Ariadne's Crown	Libra	3				
Asclepius	Scorpio	2				
Asellus, North	Cancer	2				
Asellus, South	Cancer	3				
Athena	Aries	1				
Auriga	Taurus	3	Gemini	1	Leo	3
Baboon	Taurus	2	Capricorn	1		
Ballistas	Libra	3				
Beetle	Cancer	1,2,3				
Big Fish	Capricorn	1,2,3				
Boötes	Virgo	2,3				
Boy	Libra	2				
Bull	Scorpio	1,2,3				
Bull-head	Virgo	2				
Cassiopeia	Aries	3				
Cavalryman	Taurus	3				
Censer	Capricorn	2,3				
Centaur	Libra	2	Scorpio	1,2,3	Aquarius	1,2,3
Cepheus	Sagittarius	2				
Cetus	Aries	2,3				
Chariot	Taurus	3	Gemini	1		
Charioteer	Libra	2				

---

[1] I have made this Index for the convenience of the Reader. The names shown in italics are non-Greek constellation figures. The numbers following each sign refer to the decan within the sign in which the constellation appears. Note that some of the constellations appear in more than one decan and even in more than one sign.

191

Corvus	Virgo	1,2,3					
Crater	Leo	2					
Crocodile	Pisces	1,2,3					
Cygnus	Aquarius	3					
Cymbal	Leo	2					
Cynocephalus	Aries	1					
Dead Woman	Taurus	1,2					
Dog	Taurus	1,2	Gemini	1,3	Scorpio	3	
Dog (continued)	Sagittarius	1					
Dogface	Leo	1					
Dolphin	Gemini	3	Sagittarius	2,3			
Donkey	Leo	1,2,3					
Eileitheia	Capricorn	2					
Eridanus	Aquarius	1					
Falcon	Sagittarius	2,3					
Ferryman	Libra	1					
Fountain	Libra	2					
Goat	Taurus	3	Libra	1,2,3			
God	Leo	2					
Gorgon	Aries	2					
Goddess	Virgo	1					
Graces	Cancer	1,2,3					
Hare	Scorpio	3					
Headless Demon	Capricorn	3					
Hercules	Gemini	2	Sagittarius	1	Pisces	2,3	
Hydra	Leo	1,2,3	Virgo	1,2			
Hygiea	Scorpio	1					
Ibis	Aquarius	1,2,3					
Linos	Pisces	1,3					
Lion	Virgo	1,2,3					
Little Boy	Leo	3					
Lupus	Sagittarius	2					
Lyra	Gemini	2,3	Capricorn	1			
Manger	Cancer	2,3					
Musa	Cancer	1	Virgo	2	Libra	1	

Nereis	Capricorn	1		
Ominous One	Capricorn	2,3		
Orion	Taurus	1		
Ophiucus	Scorpio	3		
Pegasus	Aquarius	3	Pisces	1
Pelagos	Sagittarius	3		
Perseus	Aries	3		
Phrygian Flutes	Leo	2		
Pleiades	Taurus	1		
Plow	Virgo	2,3		
Raven	Sagittarius	1		
Satyr	Cancer	1		
Sceptre	Taurus	2		
Ship	Leo	1,2	Libra	1,2,3
Snake	Gemini	1	Gemini	2,3
Snake on a Tree	Gemini	2		
Snakes	Aquarius	2		
Spike	Virgo	3		
Stag	Pisces	1,2,3		
Sword of Perseus	Aries	2		
Triangulum	Aries	1,2,3		
Unseen	Libra	1		
Ursa Majoris	Sagittarius	3	Capricorn	1
Ursa Minor	Gemini	3	Cancer	1
Vine	Capricorn	2		
Wheel	Gemini	1	Capricorn	2,3
Wolf	Aquarius	3		

Appendix II.

The Nature and Force of the Seven Planets.[1]

The nature of Saturn is cold and dry and a shadowy image; and of the parts of the body it rules the thighs, knees, sinews, lymph, phlegm, bladder, kidneys, and the hidden injuries, those from cold and moisture, gout in the feet, [and] gout in the hands.[2] It signifies the father, the older brothers, orphanhood of children, agriculture, gloomy,[3] treacherous, dirty, slow, solitary, deceitful, black-clothed, inheritors, given to seafaring, violent. And it is also the star of Nemesis. And it is of the diurnal sect; and astringent to the taste; and among the metals, it has lead; and it shares [the rulership of] the nostrils with Venus.

It has 5 phases: rising, setting, first station,[4] second station, and the acronychal phase. First then it rises, then it stands still at the first station, then [it is in the] acronychal phase, then the second station,[5] then the setting. For when it is separated from the Sun by 10 degrees, it makes [itself to be] matutine. Similarly, when it is separated from the Sun by 120 degrees, it makes its first station; and with the Sun approaching it, it retrogrades. And when the Sun is separated from it by 120 degrees, then it begins to make its acronychal phase. Similarly, running backwards, it makes its second station. And when the Sun has separated from it by 240 degrees, then it begins to make its natural motion. And again, standing away from it by 10 degrees, it makes its evening setting. And it continues in the setting until when it is again separated by 10 degrees. And it goes through the zodiacal circle in thirty years. And in this is the theory [of its movement].

---

[1]This material is also from Teucer of Babylon. Similar but less detailed material is found in Vettius Valens's *Anthology*.
[2]Probably in most cases *arthritis* is meant, since that is more common than gout.
[3]The word *endomychous* can mean 'gloomy' or 'stay-at-home'.
[4]What we call 'static retrograde'.
[5]What we call 'static direct'.

And when this star takes the rulership of the nativity, it signifies the old, and the internally hidden, the dark, and the self-willed, and the more-silent, and deeply-depraved, and without imagination, and laborious, and more downcast until late in time. And it makes those given to seafaring, and those who are inclined to be over-careful with regard to god, and not fortunate in their children and brothers. And being effective by day in a nativity in its own domiciles or its exaltation, of the same sect, angular, or being succedent [and] oriental, it will give rulership of fields or buildings or watery property, and excellent holdings or the possessions of others or inheritance or windfalls, and subjecting and enslaving others, or benefiting from the losses of others, and from the old, or from past transactions, or assistance from elder persons. And acting in nocturnal nativities, and in the domicile of the other sect [while] angular or succedent from the angles, it is injurious, and bringing dangers from powerful and elderly persons through old and past transactions, and it brings [the native] into debts and prison and false accusations and guards and fetters and unshorn hair and banishments, and chronic misfortunes and poisonings, or fluxes and chills and nervous illnesses and lingering illnesses, or illnesses in the hidden parts [of the body].

And it is necessary for you to note that with him [being] the apparent Ruler of the Nativity, it makes these things that have been predicted; and being configured with others or mixing those things with the domiciles of others, we shall arrange the sayings about the blending in what follows.

Saturn taking the rulership of death makes [it to occur] through protracted illnesses or through tuberculosis and fluxes and fits of ague and colic and ailments of the uterus and the placing together of those things by a superfluity of liquid. Saturn in the ASC degree makes [persons who are] swarthy, misshapen, dry, sullen, scanty-bearded, hollow-eyed, troublesome, fierce, short, liars, malignant, thieves, roaming, despisers, hypocrites, secret drinkers, having cautious behavior or living alone, ecclesiastics, entirely morose.

2. The Nature of Jupiter.

Jupiter's nature is windy and fertile and hot; of the bodily parts, it rules the feet, the semen, the womb, the liver, the right-hand parts, and the teeth. And it signifies the begetting of children, offspring, associations, knowledge, the friendship of great men, the desire for wealth and abundance, prosperity or gifts, justice, authority, terms in public office, honors, presidencies, priesthood, trusts, and victories. It is of the diurnal sect, and grey in color, and sweet to the taste. And among the metals it has silver; and in common with Mercury it has [the rulership of] the ears.

And it has five phases: rising, setting, first station, second station, acronychal. First, therefore, it rises; then it stands still at its first station; then [it makes] its acronychal phase; then its second station; and then its setting. For when the Sun is elongated from it by 10 degrees, it makes its morning rising; just so, departing from that same Sun by 120 degrees, it makes its first station; and, with the Sun approaching it, it retrogrades; and when the Sun has stood away from it by 180 degrees, then it begins to make the acronychal phase; similarly, running along backwards, it makes its second station; and when the Sun has separated from it by 240 degrees, then it begins to make its natural motion; and again, overtaking it by 10 degrees, it makes its evening setting; and it continues in the setting until when it is again separated by 10 degrees. And it goes through the zodiacal circle in twelve years.

When this star has the rulership of the nativity in a diurnal geniture, and when it is [also] angular in its own domiciles or in its exaltation, or when it is in sect, it denotes magnates and those who are renowned, acceptable, dignified, good, honest, high-minded, [ruling] over cities or managing the affairs of the common people, and having the approbation among one another, either of kings or of the chief men, well spoken of because of their goodness and piety, receiving the honors of offerings or of priestly offices, those who are fond of their relatives, and beneficent in friendship, and delighting in their wife and children, unless it is in the DSC angle;

for then they are not happy in that way with their children; but if it is severely injured by destructive [stars] assailing it, conformable in his good deeds, and decreasing very much the powers of the high-minded, and begrudging progress [in life]. And similarly, it has those significations that are in accordance with it— and it makes those when configured in other [places], in those [that are] said next. And it makes white-skinned [persons], plump, with a large full beard, good in his manner, dignified, full-statured, with a broad forehead, blue or gray eyes, having hair in his nostrils, bald in front, large-headed, giving good counsel, dealing with everyone. This one dies from [some] throat ailment, pneumonia, headache, cardiac conditions, and those [conditions] that show an excess of wind.

3. The Nature of Mars.

Mars's nature is fiery and burning and drying; of [the parts of] the body, it rules the head, the seat, the private parts, the bile, the blood, the excretion of feces, and the hinder parts [of the body]. And it signifies the middle brothers and injuries and illnesses, violent, envious, warlike persons, robbers, arsonists, adulterers, banishments, captivities, seductions of women, miscarriages, cuttings and fluxes, attacks by soldiers or robbers, tricks, lies, thefts, perjuries, house-breakers,[1] grave-robbers, and actions resembling these. It is of the nocturnal sect, and red in color, and sharp in odor. And among the metals it has iron. It has joint rulership of the mouth with Mercury.

It makes seven configurations: rising, and 90 days, and its first station, and the acronychal phase, and its second station, and the second 90 days, and its setting.[2] For when the Sun is elongated

---

[1] Lit. 'those who break through walls' to gain entry to a house.
[2] The 90 days are more properly 90 degrees. These are not phases in the usual sense of the word, but points in Mars's motion with respect to the Sun. They are first mentioned by Pliny, *Natural History*, II, xii (Section 60), where he says: "The planet Mars being nearer feels the sun's rays even from its quadrature, at an angle of 90 degrees, which has given to his motion after each rising the name of 'first' or 'second ninety-degree'. (H. Rackham's translation in the Loeb Classical

from it by 10 degrees, it makes its morning rising. And the second 90 days when the Sun squares the star. And the first station when the Sun becomes trine to it and is separated from it by 120 degrees. And then the star begins to stand still, and to move backwards; and the acronychal phase is made when the Sun opposes the star and is separated from it by 180 degrees; similarly then too from the retrogradation, for when the Sun becomes in right trine of the star and is separated from it by 240 degrees it stands still in its second static position, and it makes its natural course, and it adds to its degrees. And when the Sun is becoming in dexter square to it, then it makes its second ninety days. And again as the Sun moves towards it, before [it comes to] 10 degrees it makes its evening setting. And it marches through the zodiacal circle in nearly two and a half years.

When this star has the rulership of the nativity in a nocturnal geniture, and when it is oriental in its own domiciles or in sect, it will make daring, valiant, reckless, terrible, indomitable persons, gladly being [involved in] in looting and in foreign mercenary service, conversant with danger, those who are deprived of their paternal or maternal [inheritances] and of those things they acquired from their first age, receiving an experience of wounds or cuts, especially if it afflicts the Moon, but through burning if it also afflicts the Sun, but unstable and intemperate around their wives, entwined in unworthy acts or adulteries, whence also for them the account is made unstable around their children and distressing. But if he is born by day [and] it is found acting in a house of the other sect, it will turn the aforesaid into a worse [condition], making them headstrong, godless, blasphemous, doing many wrong things, very unrestrained, not persevering in their actions, easily reversed, drawing back from nothing, those who are distressed by the common people or magnates, in these wrongs enduring more severe sufferings in the body. For it is generally necessary to notice on the one hand that the benefic stars lessen their doing good

---

Library edition). And note that the reading of MS **V** 'second ninety days' is confirmed by the passage in Pliny's NH, rather than '<and> the first' of the CCAG editor and MS **T**.

when acting out of sect, but the malefics efficaciously in their own houses in sect with injury produce both a dangerous and evil person. But in houses of the opposite sect and acting out of sect, the damages are worse; and these, if they are found in inactive signs or they have gone under the Sun beams, being found to be Rulers of the Nativities or chart rulers, they will produce these humble things and no measurable progress. Similarly, Mars changes those things in those configurations with the other [stars] in those that are next.

Mars makes blonde, blue-eyed, with small ears, good-sized, wealthy, swift, bold, having wounds in the body, important, warriors, distressed, adulterous by nature, hard drinkers; and [as] ruling death, it makes those experiencing a semi-tertian fever, sudden blows, kidney disease, erysipelas, spitting blood, hemorrhages, destructive miscarriages, and those things caused by conflagrations and excessive heat.

4. The Nature of the Sun.

The Sun's nature is hot and dry, *intellectual light*, the housekeeper spirit, the ruler; of the bodily parts, it rules the head, the organs of sense, the right eye, the ribs, and the heart. It signifies the king, the father, the ruler, the elder brother, and honor. And it is of the diurnal sect, and citron in color, and acrid in taste. And among the metals it has gold. It shares the eyes with the Moon.

It makes four configurations, which are called tropics. When it is Cancer, the Sun makes the summer tropic around the first degree, and it begins to take away from the day and add on to the night. And in Libra it makes an equinoctial autumn in the same first degree; in the same manner, it takes away from the day and adds to the night. And in the first degree of Capricorn it makes the winter tropic, and it begins to take away from the night and add to the day, until it arrives at the first degree of Aries; being present there, it equalizes the day and night again just as [it did] in Libra, making the spring tropic. It divides the circle of the year into 365 days and 6 hours. The Sun is turned also, to those if it happens and the Moon, and in the same, for the Sun makes stout, healthy persons, and the Moon makes even-tempered, plump, good-looking, beautiful, angelic, swift, truthful, travelers, in due proportion to their age.

5. The Nature of Venus.

Venus's nature is mild and wet; and it rules the sense of smell and all the hinder parts, the sexual parts, the lungs within, and pleasure. And it signifies the mother, the younger sisters, love affairs, lusts, variant sexual intercourse (for the god is male/female), priestly, wearing a crown,[1] cheerful, friendly, marriages, children, cleanly skills, music, painting, shapely, mixed complexion, dyes, parti-colored, market supervisors, measures, weights, laughter, good-natured, drinking parties, embraces, mutual pleasures.[2] And it is of the nocturnal sect. White in color, and greasy to the taste. Among the metals it has tin.[3] And it shares [the rulership] of the nostrils with Saturn.

And it makes six configurations; having begun from the [time of] the evening rising, then the western station, then the western setting, then the morning rising, then the morning station, then the morning setting. It makes the western rising when it is separated 20 degrees from the Sun[4]; and the western station when it is separated from the Sun by 42 degrees[5]; and the western setting when the Sun overtakes the star by 6 degrees; for example, let Venus be in the 10th degree of Aries and the Sun in the 4th degree of the

---

[1] High priests and some of those of the second rank habitually wore crowns or chaplets as insignia of their rank, a practice that was copied by the Christian clergy.

[2] The Greek text has *synallagas kai êdonas*, lit. 'exchanges and pleasures'.

[3] We would expect copper to be assigned to Venus. I think the assignment of tin is a mistake. Vettius Valens does not give any metal for Venus (probably a lacuna in the text.)

[4] Too great! Venus becomes visible as morning or evening star when it is separated from the Sun by about 6 degrees, as he says later in the same paragraph.

[5] Not so! Venus makes both its stations when it is about 30 degrees from the Sun. I think Teucer has confused Venus's maximum elongation from the Sun with its elongation at the stations. And its maximum elongation is 48 degrees, not 42 degrees (or 40 degrees).

same [sign], and it will make the western rising when it separates from the Sun by 5 degrees; and it makes the morning station when [the Sun] is separated from the star by 40 degrees[1]; it makes the morning setting when the star overtakes the Sun by being 2 degrees from it; and it passes through the cycle in 13 months of the year.

When this star has the rulership of the nativity in a nocturnal geniture, and when it is effective in its own domiciles or rising in sect, it will make handsome persons, witty, cleanly, illustrious, religious, loving tenderly, successful, esteemed with praise by the people, or they stand out in appearance, wearing gold (priests, or those adorned with such honors), wealthy, noted, those blamed in good [actions],[2] those who are done well for by women, and women by men; and if it operates out of sect, it lessens the benefits, for they are regarded with jealous hate at the end of their success, and it lessens limits (?), and it exchanges for the testimonies of the others; we say these things in a combined word.

Venus makes white persons, stout, heavily bearded, good in character, elegant, good-looking, short, well-provided with honor, swarthy, with small feet, fortunate, magnanimous, charming, rich, agreeable, loved by women, fond of love.

6. The Nature of Mercury.

Mercury's nature is sometimes wet and sometimes dry; of the bodily parts, it rules the hands, shoulders, the fingers, the joints, the belly, the entrails, the kidneys, the arteries and veins, the tongue. And it signifies the younger brothers, learning, speech, wisdom, calculation, geometry, astronomy, business, messages, foreknowledge, divination, combat. And it is of the common sect. Blue in color, sour in taste. And among the metals, it has brass. And it shares the mouth with Mars.

---

[1] Again, the station is made when Venus is about 30 degrees from the Sun, not 40 degrees.
[2] This does not seem appropriate. Perhaps *psogizomenous* 'blamed' is a mistake.

It makes four configurations: evening rising, evening setting, morning rising, and morning setting. It makes the evening rising when it is 3 degrees distant from the Sun. And it sets when the Sun has fallen below it by 2 degrees. And it makes the morning rising when the Sun is 3 degrees distant from it. And it sets in the evening when the star is 2 degrees from it.[1] And it goes through the cycle of the year in very nearly 11 months.[2]

Taking up the matter of rulership and the Rulership of the Nativity, the star is common, it prefers those things in the testimonies and in the blending of the domiciles, of these we shall speak next. And when it is oriental and effective, especially in its own places or conforming well with a benefic or in the body, it makes industrious persons, especially if it aspects the Moon, and also skilled, sensible persons, possessing judgment and education, well suited to all things, easily understood and also apt at teaching, and contriving . . ., successful in intellectual matters, having many friends, sociable, ingenious, living abroad, respected by many, involved in many changes in transactions, and knowledgeable about all this; but if the Ruler of the Nativity or the ruler is found to be well situated, but when the co-ruler of the ruler of the sign in which the Ruler of the Nativity is found is badly situated, part of the life will be fortunate, and part unfortunate. And take note in which particular area it is situated. For those around the ASC are indicative of the first age, and those around the MC of middle age, and those around the DSC and down to the IMC of the later age.

Mercury signifies slim, pale, well-proportioned, curly-haired, full-bearded persons, but having spots in the vision,[3] stout,[4] speak-

---

[1] All these numbers are too small. Mercury must be 10 or 11 degrees from the Sun to be visible in either the morning or evening sky. Possibly the numbers were originally written as ι β '12' or ι γ '13' and the ι was lost in each case.

[2] If Teucer means that Mercury can run through all the signs of the zodiac in 11 months, he is correct, although that does not happen very often–about 1 year out of 6.

[3] The word *opsei* can mean either 'vision' or 'eye', so it is uncertain whether Teucer means 'spots on the eye' or 'spots in the vision', i.e. *muscae volitantes* or 'floaters' as they are sometimes called today.

[4] Note that *pacheis* 'stout' is inconsistent with *ischnous* 'slim' mentioned earlier.

ing sweetly, liars, sneak-thieves, knowing writing, dice-players, pursuers in battle, imposters, talkative, tall, bankers, scribes, notaries, and death through madness and ecstasy and melancholy and epilepsy and related diseases, and those brought on by an excessive or fatal dryness.

7. The Nature of the Moon.

The Moon's nature is wet and cold; and it gets its light from the reflection of the light of the Sun; of the bodily parts, it rules the left eye, the stomach, the breasts, the sex organs. And it signifies the queen, the mistress, the mother, sight on the left, the body, comprehension, legal marriage and maintenance, elder sister, beautiful visage, goddess, good fortune. And it is of the nocturnal sect. Light green in color, and salty in taste. And among the metals, it has glass. And it shares [the rulership] of the eyes with the Sun.

It has 10 configurations that are called *phases*; and they are these: *conjunction*,[1] *coming forth*, *rising*, first *moon-shape*,[2] first *dichotomy*,[3] first *gibbous*, *full Moon*, second *gibbous*, second *dichotomy*,[4] second *moon-shape*; and some also add an 11th phase, the *approaching full*. And it runs through its cycle in 28 days 2 hours 18 minutes very nearly.[5] And the *conjunction* is when the Moon chances to be partile the Sun in the same sign; coming forth whenever the Moon has gone one degree past the Sun; rising whenever it has passed 15 degrees; first *moon-shape* when the Moon, in the following direction from the Sun, is distant by 60 degrees, placed in the sextile relationship; and the first *dichotomy* is

---

[1] We would call this phase 'new Moon'.
[2] What we would call "crescent."
[3] The Greek term is first *dichotomos*, which could be literally translated as 'first half', which is in fact the Moon's appearance at that phase. But in English we call this 'first quarter', since it is at a fourth of the lunar month. However, in Italian one can speak of *il prino quarto di luna* or *la mezzaluna*. And similarly in French.
[4] Again, we would say 'last quarter' rather than 'second half'.
[5] The numbers given do not correspond to either the sidereal period of the Moon (27 days 7 hours 43 minutes) or to the synodic period (29 days 6 hours 44 minutes); they are in fact equal to 365.25 divided by 13.

when the Moon, in the following direction from the Sun, is distant by 90 degrees, being in the square aspect. And the first *gibbous* is when the Moon, in the following direction from the Sun, is distant by 120 degrees, being in the trine aspect. And the *approaching full* is when it is from 150 degrees in the fifth sign in the following signs from the Sun, but not yet making the opposition. And the *full Moon* is when, in the following direction from the Sun, it is 180 degrees distant, being in the opposition position. Which is called 'the full Moon bonding'. And the *waning* is when the Moon passes by the degree of the solar opposition, the so-called 'declining' down to the 60th degree. And the second *gibbous* is when, from the direction behind the Sun, it is distant 120 degrees, being in the trine aspect. And the second *dichotomy*, when the Moon, from the direction behind the Sun, is distant 90 degrees, being in the square aspect. And the second *moon-shape* is when, from the direction behind the Sun, it is distant 60 degrees, being in the sextile configuration. Then properly, according to the exchange of configurations, it has the term. For the *conjunction* was called from the uniting of the Moon with the Sun and their running in the same path. And the *coming forth* was called since having passed by that same first degree it begins to appear [but] not yet to us. And the *rising* when, having passed beyond 15 degrees, it appears having taken up a line of light. And it was called *moon-shape*, when it appeared having taken a form similar to itself. For it is called the Moon because it makes a monthly rising. And the *dichotomy* was called, since its halving happens to appear like a half of its full light. And the *gibbous* was called because the view of its light appears humped on both sides. And the *approaching full* was called from the sixth sign that it appears in. And the *full Moon* [was called] because its light was made full from the beams of the Sun, appearing to it in an opposition position, having the brightness of its light wholly completed, whence also a circular figure appears similar to it when it is at *full Moon*. And *waning* was called because, having passed by the rays by opposition, from then on it has a waning and lessening of its light. And look at the Moon when it is found in one of the aforesaid places [to see] which of the stars it makes an application to or from which of the stars it makes a separation, and render it thus.

The Moon denotes those having stout legs, broad knees, heavy-set, short, nice eyes, feminine features, feminine in form, and fat.

Appendix III.

Judging an Eclipse[1]

Look at the eclipse that is being made, either of the Sun or of the Moon, to see in which sign it occurs. And look at the decan, indeed in which face it falls. And if the sign is masculine and the decan is masculine, being in a human sign, being aspected by Mars, say that there will be injury among the males, indeed [affecting] a man and a child, by war or murder. Bodily destruction of the blood. If the eclipse is in the hemisphere under the earth, the astrological signification is made in secret, or a plot in treachery. But if it chances to be in the hemisphere above the earth, the astrological significations are rendered openly. And if it is a masculine sign, but the decan is feminine, look at the ruler of the sign and the ruler of the decan [to see whether] it is aspected by benefics or by malefics. And for example if it is found to be aspected by malefics, say that that one will be wounded much. And the one that is aspected by benefics, that one will be wounded less. And consider similarly also if it is in a feminine sign according to what was said before in the case of masculine signs. And if it is found in an earth sign, the wound will be on the body of the earth according to the decan that is found.

If, for example, it is a decan of Saturn, it will damage those things by means of astringency and dryness and coldness. And if it is Jupiter, it will harm those things that are sweet to the taste and of a mild nature. And if it is Mars, those things that are sharp [to the taste] and of a hot and dry nature. And if it is the Sun, those things that are piercing to the taste. And if it is Venus, those things that are smooth [to the taste], indeed nuts and olives, and those things similar to these and of a mild nature, and those with an odor, that is

---

[1] This chapter (edited in CCAG VII, pp. 224-226) follows after the chapter on "The Nature and Force of the Seven Planets" in MS *Vaticanus graecus* 191 (written about 1300), and Boll says that he does not doubt that it is also part of Rhetorius's compilation.

to say ointments and fragrances. And if it is Mercury, those things that are sour in taste, of double form indeed wheat and barley. And if it is the Moon, those things that are salty, and by nature wet and cold. And if it is a windy sign, it makes damage in the winged creatures. And if it is in an animal signs it makes it in the wild lands for deer and wild goats. And if it is a water sign, it makes damage in fish and those things that make their sustenance in wet places.

You must look at those things about the signs only; and you must look at the faces of the seven stars thus. If Saturn is found in its own place, in the ASC or in the MC in a place portending gain, it makes damage among nobles, chamberlains, or elders or well-known elder persons; and if it is a cadent house or in its fall or if it is posited in a poor house, it makes damage among servants or chamberlains, i.e. little-known ones. And if Jupiter is in a notable house, it signifies that the damage will be among generals, commanders, or well-known military men; and if it is under the Sun beams or retrograde or in its fall, the damage will be among physicians, gold-smiths, and, in a word, among those who have their occupation with fire and iron or butchers, hunters and cooks. And if it is the Sun, it signifies damage among kings.

And if Venus is posited in a notable house, it signifies the damage will be among notable and great women and high priests; and if it is under the Sun beams or retrograde or in its fall, it signifies that it will be among lowly women or those involved in trade. And if it is Mercury, it will be good among merchants, grammarians,[1] surveyors, and those having their skill in mercurial occupations; and if it is under the Sun beams or in its fall, cheats, forgers, abusive persons, and those similar to these. And if it is the Moon, among queens and notable women. And usually the Moon's damage is common among all those previously mentioned, since it is signifying the cause of the actions.

And if Saturn aspects the degree of the eclipse, it gives saturnian illnesses and death. And if it is Mars, it gives serious wounds

---

[1] Those who work with written documents.

and squirting blood or injuries or vomiting. And when the Moon is diminished in light, it causes damage whenever it is eclipsed [at the] Ascending Node; but if it is eclipsed [at the] Descending Node, the damage is made greater.

Appendix IV.

House Division

How the Points of the Twelve Houses must be found to the exact Degree.[1]

An example of a nativity.[2] Clime 5. Years of Diocletian 145, Thoth the 10th to the 11th, the beginning of the 4th hour of the night.[3] Sun 14°19' Virgo, Moon 3°04' Pisces, Saturn 14°31' Sagittarius, Jupiter 15°41' Libra, Mars 21°06' Virgo, Venus 25°40' Leo, Mercury 3°37' Libra, ASC 25°16' Taurus, MC 3°37' Aquarius, Ascending Node 3°41' Capricorn; the [preceding] New Moon 1°26' Virgo, the Part of Fortune 6°31' Sagittarius, the Part of the Daemon 14°01' Scorpio.

We shall make the exposition of the 12 houses by degree by our demonstrating according to the natural and following method, reckoning the cardinal and cadent distances of the degrees thus.

For since the 5 degrees rising before <the aphetic places> as Ptolemy says,[4] subtracting those from the given degrees of the ASC, we shall find the beginning of the angle of the ASC to be 20°16' Taurus; to these there corresponds in the right sphere 137°42' as rising times.[5] And taking the horary times of the 20°16' Taurus according to the 5th clime 17°44'[6] and doubling them, we

---

[1]There is an earlier translation of this tract in O. Neugebauer & H. B. Van Hoesen's *Greek Horoscopes* (Philadelphia: The American Philosophical Society, 1959) pp. 138-140, with a confusing diagram on p. 139.
[2]It has not been possible to identify the Native.
[3]This date is equivalent to Friday 8 September 428 A.D. at about 9:20 P.M. LAT presumably at Constantinople.
[4]Ptolemy, *Tetrabiblos* (Robbins's ed.), iii, 10.
[5]137°42' is the right ascension + 90° of the ASC 20°16' Taurus. And the RA's of the 12th, 11th, and 10th house cusps that are subsequently calculated are also RA cusp + 90°.
[6]The Greek text has 17°42', but it should be 17°44', so I have corrected it.

have 35°28′ times[1]; and subtracting that from the 137°42′, we find 102°16′; and to that 102°16′ there corresponds in the right sphere 13°21′ Aries. And again in the same way subtracting from the 102°16′ the 35°28′, we have the remainder 66°48′. Corresponding to this again in the right sphere, we find 4°08′ Pisces.[2] Then that same degree of Pisces 4°08′ will be for us the beginning of the 11th house[3]; therefore the Moon is rather in the 10th house. And again, taking away the 35°28' from the 66°48′, the remainder is 31°20′, corresponding to which we find in the right sphere 29°07′ Capricorn; this will therefore be the beginning of the MC; and there was from the beginning of the MC 3°37′ Aquarius to come forth therefore 4°30′ and it should go forth by 5 degrees; therefore it differs by 30 minutes.[4] And this is the cause, for Ptolemy says that neither time degrees nor longitudinal degrees should go before the angle, but those of the ideal sign of the fixed [zodiac, which is used for calculating] the aspects, [i.e.] the moving longitudinal and time degrees. And we have taken the 5 moving and perceptible degrees. Then when Ptolemy says "and the right sextile to those 30 degrees," he is speaking about the perceptible degrees. For those are like the 30 degrees that are always configured accurately to each other. And those that are moving have the widest [variation].

But the houses must be set forth more accurately again. Since from 29°07′ Capricorn to 29°07′ Cancer the times of the culmination are 180 degrees of the hemisphere, of which those from 29°07′ Capricorn to 20°16′ Taurus are corresponding in horary times to 6 times 17°42′, i.e. 106°24′. Therefore, the remainder from 20°16′ Taurus to 29°07′ Cancer corresponds in times to the

---

[1]This is 1/3 of the RA arc between the MC and the ASC.
[2]This should be 4°53′ Pisces, also in the next sentence.
[3]Following this, the text has the phrase "and the 3°11′ Aquarius as the beginning of the 10th [house]", which is inappropriate, so I have deleted it.
[4]Neugebauer and Van Hoesen remark that Rhetorius is surprised that the difference is not 5°. The true reason is that making a 5° offset at the ASC slightly altered the rising time of the ASC; consequently, that altered the revised MC by a slightly different amount, so that the offset there was not exactly 5°.

remainder of the hemisphere 73°36′, of which a third of the times is 24°32′. Then subtracting the 24°32′ from the given 31°20′, there remains 6°48′, to which corresponds 6°13′ Capricorn. Therefore, the beginning of the 9th [house] will be 6°13′ Capricorn. And again from the 6°48′ subtracting 24°32′, the remaining degrees are 342°16′, to which corresponds 16°46′ Sagittarius[1]; and therefore the beginning of the 8th house will be 13°48′ Sagittarius. And again subtracting the 24°32′ from the 342°16′, the remainder is 317°44′, to which corresponds 20°16′ Scorpio, which indeed is according to the opposite to the ASC. And the opposing signs will be the beginnings of the houses under the earth, that is the 2nd, 3rd, 4th, 5th, and 6th.

One must know that if anyone wishes to delineate according to Ptolemy, it is necessary to delineate from the horary times and methods of Ptolemy and from the Lot of Fortune. And if he wishes to delineate according to the Egyptians, it is necessary to delineate from the Egyptian horary times and methods. And if he wishes to delineate from Valens, it is necessary to calculate according to the methods of Valens and the ASC and the MC, and everything will be concordant with the others; for they have both their examples and their methods for the ASC and the MC. And then he seems to hit the mark with his examples. And it is necessary with all the aspects, either good or evil, to offer prayer to God the Gracious to obtain [aid] from Him; for only He can do everything.

Translator's Comment

This is the earliest known mention of what is called the Alchabitius method of House Division. Alchabitius (Abû al-Ṣaqr al-Qabîsîd. 967) was an Arabian astrological writer, the author of *Introduction to the Art of Judgments of the Stars*,[2] in which he mentioned this type of House Division. However, we see from this

---

[1]This is a mistake. It should be 13°48′ Sagittarius.
[2]See the entry for Alchabitius in my book, *A History of Horoscopic Astrology* (Tempe, Az.: A.F.A., Inc., 1996, pp. 124-125, and 2nd ed. 2006, pp. 129-130)

tract by Rhetorius that the method was known to the Greek astrologers not later than the early 6th century.

The Alchabitius method is simply a variation of the Porphyry method of House Division, in which the zodiacal arc from the MC to the ASC is divided by 3 and each 3rd is added to the MC degree to obtain the cusps of the 11th and 12th Houses. And the zodiacal arc from the DSC to the MC is also divided by 3 and each 3rd is subtracted from the MC degree to obtain the cusps of the 9th and the 8th Houses. Then the cusps of the remaining Houses are opposite the cusps of those Houses. But instead of dividing the *zodiacal arcs*, the Alchabitius method divides the *Right Ascension arc* from the RAMC to the RAASC by 3 and adds each 3rd to the RAMC to obtain the RAXI and the RAXII, and, having obtained the RA's of the cusps, they are converted to the zodiacal longitudes of the cusps. And similarly for the *RA arc* from the RADSC to the RAMC to obtain the cusps of the 9th and 8th Houses.

When Ptolemy's *Handy Tables* became available in the 4th century, some Greek astrologer must have thought that dividing the RA arcs was more scientific than dividing the zodiacal arcs. The method later passed to the Arabs, and, from translations of their works, to the late medieval and early renaissance European astrologers. And it remained popular until Regiomontanus's tables were published in 1490, after which there was a fairly rapid transition from Alchabitius cusps to Regiomontanus cusps.

Appendix V.

The Time of Life according to all the Rulers and the Ruler of the Nativity.

If the Lot of Fortune is the aphetic place, the Sun being impedited by Saturn and Mars will be the anaeretic place. For he says, ". . . the Moon being ignored, and the place of the Sun being anaeretic," and the following. But also, in other nativities of the full Moon sort, with the Lot of Fortune not being the aphetic place, but nevertheless also then with the Sun being impedited and in a *kollêsis* with the Lot of Fortune or with any one of the malefics, it is necessary to see that the Native is not also born with a deadly climacteric, because of the Lot of Fortune being the lunar ASC and being able to be angular, and if it is in a cadent in a new Moon nativity, the same thing must no longer be noted.

Appendix VI.

Comparison of the Chapters of Antiochus's *Treasury*[1] and Rhetorius's *Compendium*.

Antiochus	Rhetorius	Antiochus	Rhetorius	Antiochus	Rhetorius
1	1	31	31	61	61
2	2	32	32	62	62
3	3	33	33	63	63
4	4	34	34	64	64
5	5	35	35	65	65
6	6	36	36	66	66
7	7	37	37	67	68
8	8	38	38	68	69-74
9	9	39	39	69	76
10	10	40	40	70	77
11	11	41	41	71	78
12	12	42	42	72	79
13	13	43	43	73	80
14	14	44	44	74	81
15	15	45	45	75	82
16	16	46	46	76	83
17	17	47	47	77	84-85
18	18	48	48	78	97
19	10	49	49	79	98
20	20	50	50	80	99
21	21	51	51	81	100
22	22	52	52	82	101
23	23	53	53	83	102
24	24	54	54	84	103
25	25	55	55	85	104
26	26	56	56	86	109
27	27	57	57	87	111
28	28	58	58	88	112
29	29	59	59	89	113-117
30	30	60	60	90	118

---

[1] The *Epitome* was edited by Pierre Boudreaux from MS *Parisinus graecus* 2425 in CCAG, VIII 3, pp. 104-111.

Bibliography

Astrologer of the Year 379
   Apotelesmata tês tôn aplanôn asterôn epochês.
   [*The Effects of the Positions of the Fixed Stars in Nativities.*]
   ed. by Franz Cumont
   CCAG V.1 (1904), pp. 194-211.

Bezza, Giuseppe
   Arcana Mundi.
   [Italian translation of astrological texts]
   Milan: Biblioteca Universale Rizzoli, 1995. 2 vols. boxed 1149 pp.

al-Bîrûnî, Abû'l-Rayḥân
   The Book of Instruction in the Elements
   of the Art of Astrology.
   the Arabic text with a translation
   by R. Ramsay Wright, M.A., LL.D.
   London: Luzac & Co., 1934. xviii,333,[7]

Bury, J. B.
   History of the Later Roman Empire.
   New York: Dover Publications, 1958. repr. 2 vols. paper

Catalogus Codicum Astrologorum Graecorum. (cited as CCAG)
   [Catalogue of Greek Astrological Manuscripts]
   various editors & publishers
   Brussels, 1898-1953. 12 vols. paper

Dorotheus Sidonius
   Carmen astrologicum.
   ed. by David Pingree
   Arabic text with an English translation
   Leipzig: B. G. Teubner, 1976. xix,444 pp.

Firmicus Maternus, Julius
   Matheseos libri viii.
   ed. W. Kroll, F. Skutsch, and K. Ziegler
   Leipzig: B. G. Teubner, 1968. 2 vols. repr.

Mathesis.
   trans. by James Herschel Holden
   Tempe, Az.: A.F.A., Inc., 2009. [forthcoming]

Holden, James Herschel
   A History of Horoscopic Astrology.
   Tempe, Az.: A.F.A., Inc., 1996. paper. xv,359 pp.
   Tempe, Az.: A.F.A., Inc., 2006. 2nd ed. rev. paper xvii,377 pp.

Hübner, Wolfgang
   Grade und Gradbezirke der Tierkreiszeichen.
   [Degrees and Degree Areas of the Signs of the Zodiac]
   Vol. I Edition of texts
   Vol. 2 Commentary
   Stuttgart & Leipzig: B. G. Teubner, 1995. 2 vols.

Hypsicles
   Die Aufgangszeiten der Gestirne.
   [The Rising-Times of the Stars]
   ed. and trans. into German by V. De Falco and M. Krause
   Göttingen: Vandenhoeck & Ruprecht, 1966.

Neugebauer, O. and H. B. Van Hoesen
   Greek Horoscopes.
   Philadelphia: The American Philosophical Society, 1959. ix,231 pp.

Paul of Alexandria
   EISAGOGIKA
   [*Introduction*]
   ed. by Emilie Boer
   Leipzig: B. G. Teubner, 1958.

Introduction to Astrology.
   trans. by James Herschel Holden
   Tempe, Az.: A.F.A., Inc., 2009. [forthcoming]

Pingree, David
   "Antiochus and Rhetorius"
   Classical Philology 72 (July 1977): 203-223.
   "From Alexandria to Baghdad to Byzantium"

International Journal of the Classical Tradition
Vol. 8, No. 1 (Summer 2001):3-37

Porphyry
   Introductio in Tetrabiblum Ptolemaei.
   ed. by Emilie Boer and Stephen Weinstock
   CCAG V.4 (1940).

Introduction to the Tetrabiblos.
   trans. by James Herschel Holden
   Tempe, Az.: A.F.A., Inc., 2009. [forthcoming]

Ptolemy, Claudius
   Tetrabiblos.
   ed. and trans. into English by F. E. Robbins, Ph.D.
   The Loeb Classical Library
   London and Cambridge, Mass., 1940.

ΑΠΟΤΕΛΕΣΜΑΤΙΚΑ.
   [Apotelesmatics]
   ed. by W. Hübner
   Stuttgart & Leipzig: B. G. Teubner, 1998. LXXV, 439 pp.

Vettius Valens
   Anthologiarum libri.
   ed. Wilhelm Kroll
   Dublin/Zürich: Weidmann, 1973. repr. of 1908 ed. XVII, 420 pp.

Anthologiarum libri novem.
   ed. by David Pingree
   Leipzig: B. G. Teubner, 1986. XXI,583 pp.

Index of Persons

Aelia Verina, Empress, 164 n.1
Antigonus, *astrologer*, 15 n.1
Antiochus, *astrologer*, ix,xi,xiii,xv,xvii,xix,15 n.2,35 n.1,47 n.1,113 n.2,126 n.1,217
Anubio, *astrologer*, 134,162 n.2
Bean, Roy, Judge, 55 n.3
Bezza, Giuseppe, *astrologer*, xvii
Bidez, Joseph, *editor*, 47 n.2,162 n.2
al-Bîrûnî, *scholar*, 13 n.3
Boer, Emilie, *scholar*, xi n.1
Boll, Franz, *scholar*, xii,17 n.3,28 n.1,3,29 n.2,144 n.3,165,166 n.1, 167 n.2,181 n.1,189 n.1,207 n.1
Bury, J. B., *historian*, 160 n.1
Cipolla, Jack, *artist*, xx
Cumont, Franz, *scholar*, ix n.2,xii,15 n.2,35 n.1,37 n.1,2,41 n.1,43 n.3,44 n.1,50 n.2,52 n.3, 53 n.3,55 n.2,58 n.1,59 n.2,61 n.1,2,63 n.2,64 n.1,65 n.1,2,3,4,5,67 n.1,2,71 n.3,4,73 n.1,2,74 n.2,79 n.4,80 n.3,82 n.3,87 n.1,88 n.1,89 n.2,90 n.2,93 n.2,93 n.3,97 n.1,99 n.2,116 n.3,117 n.1,121 n.2,126 n.5,128 n.1,132 n.2,136 n.4,144 n.3,146 n.1,161 n.2,162 n.2,164 n.4
Delatte, A., *scholar*, 159 n.3
Dorotheus, *astrologer*, x,xii,xvii,xix,5 n.1,17,18,29,50 n.3,58,112 n.1, 113,132 n.2,147 n.4,151 n.1,153 n.1,2,3,5,154 n.1,2,3,4,155 n.2,3,157 n.2,158,161 n.2,162 n.2
Egyptians ix,x,12-14,29 n.4,37,65 n.3,66 n.2,127 n.1,167 n.2,175 n.1,213
Firmicus Maternus, Julius, *astrologer*, xx,1 n.1,7 n.2,13 n.3,29 n.1,30 n.2,31 n.1,47 n.2,52 n.1,3,53 n.1,2,3,54 n.1,2,55 n.3,57 n.2,59 n.2,61 n.2,65 n.4,5,66 n.1,2,4,67 n.1,71 n.1,2,4,73 n.2,74 n.1,2,3,75 n.1,79, 82n.2,4,5,89 n.2,93 n.1,2,94 n.1,95 n.1,2,96 n.1,97 n.1,2,99 n.3,113 n.2,132 n.2,150 n.1,162 n.2
Gundel, Wilhelm, *scholar*, x n.3,165 n.1
Heilen, Stephan, *scholar*, xx
Hephaestio of Thebes, *astrologer*, 15 n.1,132 n.2
Hypsicles, *mathematician*, 30 n.3

Illus, *consul*, 160 n.1

Leo I, Emperor, ix n.2,164 n.1

Leontius, *patrician*, 160 n.1

Malalas, John, *historian*, ix n.1

Morin, Jean Baptiste, *astrologer*, 57n.3,84 n.2

Neugebauer, Otto, *scholar*, 29 n.4,31 n.1,160 n.4,161 n.1,164 n.2,211 n.1,212 n.3

Otto, King of Bavaria, 44 n.1

Pamprepius, *scholar*, 160 n.1

Paul of Alexandria, *astrologer*, x,xii,xix,17,19 n.1,20 n.3,24 n.1,55 n.2,82 n.2,83 n.1,113 n.2,120 n.1

Phnaes the Egyptian, *astrologer*, x

Pingree, David, *scholar*, ix,x n.2,xi-xii,xv,xvii-xx,5 n. 1,13 n.2,17 n.3, 29 n.1,79 n.1,111 n.3,113 n.1,2,126 n.1,127 n.1,133 n.2,147 n.4,151 n.1,153 n.1,3,154 n.1,3,4,157 n.2,158,161 n.2,162 n.2

Porphyry ix-xi,xix-xx,10 n.1,12 n.1,2,13 n.3,15 n.1,20 n.3,22 n.3,24 n.3,24 n.3,26 n.1,165,214

Proclus, *Neoplatonist*, 18 n.1,160 n.1

Ptolemy ix-xi,xix,4,7 n.2,12-13,17,18,20 n.3,23 n.1,31 n.1,32 n.1,36, 50 n.2,66 n.3,81 n.1,82 n.2,83 n.1,105 n.1,106 n.2,3,164 n.3,165-166, 168,172,174,179 n.5,7,181 n.1,183 n.3,211-214

Rhetorius, *astrologer*, *passim*

Riske, Kris Brandt, *editor*, xx

Stephanus, *astrologer*, xx

Stroobant, P., *scholar*, 159 n.3

Teucer of Babylon, *astrologer*, x,xii,xvii,9,165,167,195 n.1,201 n.5

Theon of Alexandria, *astronomer*, 164 n.3

Theophilus, *astrologer*, xx

Van Hoesen, H. B., *scholar*, 211 n.1

Vettius Valens, *astrologer*, x,xix,19 n.1,30 n.3,37 n.3,41 n.2,50 n.2,56 n.3,29 n.3,61 n.4,71 n.3,87 n.1,113 n.1,121 n.2,130 n.2,132 n.2,144 n.2,147 n.2,3,165,195 n.1,201 n.3

Weinstock, Stephen, *scholar*, xi n.1,15 n.4

Wright, R. Ramsay, *scholar*, 4 n.2

Zeno, Emperor, xix,159 n.3

www.ingramcontent.com/pod-product-compliance
Lightning Source LLC
Chambersburg PA
CBHW032249150426
43195CB00008BA/375